The material elements of writing ha[...]
dismissed by recent historicizing [...]
elements – sound, signature, letters – can transform our understanding of
literary texts. In *Anti-Mimesis from Plato to Hitchcock* Tom Cohen shows how,
in an era of representational criticism and cultural studies, the role of close
reading has been overlooked. Arguing that much recent criticism has been
caught in potentially regressive models of representation, Professor Cohen
undertakes to counter this by rethinking the "materiality" of the text itself.
Through a series of revealing new readings of the work of writers including
Plato, Bakhtin, Poe, Whitman, and Conrad, Professor Cohen exposes the
limitations of new historicism and neo-pragmatism, and demonstrates how
"the materiality of language" operates to undo the representational models
of meaning imposed by the literary canon.

Anti-Mimesis from Plato to Hitchcock

Literature, Culture, Theory

General editors

RICHARD MACKSEY, *The Johns Hopkins University*

and MICHAEL SPRINKER, *State University of New York at Stony Brook*

The Cambridge *Literature, Culture, Theory* series is dedicated to theoretical studies in the human sciences that have literature and culture as their object of enquiry. Acknowledging the contemporary expansion of cultural studies and the redefinitions of literature that this has entailed, the series includes not only original works of literary theory but also monographs and essay collections on topics and seminal figures from the long history of theoretical speculation on the arts and human communication generally. The concept of theory embraced in the series is broad, including not only the classical disciplines of poetics and rhetoric, but also those of aesthetics, psychoanalysis, semiotics, and other cognate sciences that have inflected the systematic study of literature during the past half century.

Titles published

Return to Freud: Jacques Lacan's dislocation of psychoanalysis
SAMUEL WEBER
(*translated from the German by Michael Levine*)

Wordsworth, dialogics, and the practice of criticism
DON H. BIALOSTOSKY

The subject of modernity
ANTHONY J. CASCARDI

Onomatopoetics: theory of language and literature
JOSEPH GRAHAM

Parody: ancient, modern, and post-modern
MARGARET ROSE

The poetics of personification
JAMES PAXSON

Possible worlds in literary theory
RUTH RONEN

Critical conditions: postmodernity and the question of foundations
HORACE L. FAIRLAMB

Introduction to literary hermeneutics
PETER SZONDI
(*translated from the German by Martha Woodmansee*)

Anti-mimesis from Plato to Hitchcock
TOM COHEN

Anti-Mimesis from Plato to Hitchcock

TOM COHEN

University of North Carolina at Chapel Hill

CAMBRIDGE
UNIVERSITY PRESS

Published by the Press Syndicate of the University of Cambridge
The Pitt Building, Trumpington Street, Cambridge, CB2 1RP
40 West 20th Street, New York, NY 10011-4211, USA
10 Stamford Road, Oakleigh, Melbourne 3166, Australia

First published 1994

Printed in Great Britain at the University Press, Cambridge

A catalogue record for this book is available from the British Library

Library of Congress cataloging in publication data
Cohen, Tom, 1953–
Anti-mimesis from Plato to Hitchcock / Tom Cohen
p.   cm. – (Literature, culture, theory; 10)
Includes index.
ISBN 0 521 46013 1 (hardback) – ISBN 0 521 46584 2 (paperback)
1. Language and languages – Philosophy.   2. Criticism.   I. Title.
II. Series.
P106.C593   1994   93-43559
401 – dc20   CIP

ISBN 0 521 46013 1 hardback
ISBN 0 521 46584 2 paperback

TAG

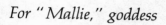

For " Mallie," goddess

"How good are the copies?"

"Almost perfect."

"Then why do you want the originals? Collector's vanity."

"Changes, Mr. Snide, can only be effected by alterations in the *original*. The only thing not prerecorded in a prerecorded universe are the prerecordings themselves. The copies can only repeat themselves word for word. *A virus is a copy.* You can pretty it up, cut it up, scramble it — it will reassemble in the same form. Without being an idealist, I am reluctant to see the originals in the hands of the Countess de Gulpa, the Countess de Vile and the pickle factory..."

William Burroughs, *Cities of the Red Night*

How might one free oneself from the cowardliness pressing upon social convictions of the present, subjugated as they are to reactive, mimetic, and regressive posturings?

Avital Ronell, *Crack Wars*

Contents

Acknowledgments

The volume owes a number of debts that are difficult to trace. Of the ones that are apparent, I am particularly grateful to J. Hillis Miller as a reader whose clarity and support have been essential to me. In diverse ways, I want to thank: James Thompson and Trudier Harris for their friendship and intelligence; Johanna Prins for the timely gift of her company and critical brilliance; Betsy Dillon and Sarah Pelmas for their insightful response to earlier versions of the Hitchcock chapter; Christopher Diffee for his help and critical acumen; and William Schouppe for his helpful comments. In a special category, I want to thank Barbara Herrnstein Smith, whose generous criticism was decisive to the final form of at least one chapter. I also thank Tom Hadju and Andy Milburn for the stimulus of their rare energies, Michael Sprinker for his support and advice, and Dan Myerson for being himself. Finally, I am grateful to Professor Joseph Flora of the UNC English Department, Professor Ruel Tyson, and the Institute for the Arts and Humanities at UNC Chapel Hill for securing for me leave for this work.

Three of the chapters have appeared whole or in part previously: chapter five in *Arizona Quarterly* (Summer, 1993 [copyright of the Arizona Board of Regents]), chapter seven in *Rereading the New: A Backward Glance at Modernism*, edited by Kevin Dettmar (Ann Arbor: University of Michigan Press, 1992), and chapter nine in *Qui Parle* (Fall, 1993), and I gratefully acknowledge permission to reprint.

The legs of sense

These are moments when something powerful − and dangerous − is happening. Figuration is about resetting the stage for possible pasts and futures. Figuration is the mode of theory when the more "normal" rhetorics of systemic critical analysis seem only to repeat and sustain our entrapment in the stories of the established disorders. Humanity is a modernist figure; and this humanity has a generic face, a universal shape.

> Donna Haraway, *Ecce Homo, Ain't (Ar'n't) I a Woman, and Inappropriate/d Others: The Human in a Post-Humanist Landscape*

To convert mimesis is to virilize it.

> Philippe Lacoue-Labarthe, *History and Mimesis*

The essays in this volume are geared toward asking a recurrent series of questions: what is the interventionist role of "reading" (indeed, of too close reading) after the era of cultural studies? How does the materiality of language re-assert itself as a transformative agent in reading canonical writings from a post-humanist perspective? How do we exceed, today, the ideologies of retro-humanism in the various forms it takes on the right and the left? How much has a mimetic bias to the traditions of interpretation constituted a conservative politics of its own, and is there, today, an anti-mimetic or anti-representational politics located in the activity of reading?

Each of these issues is located in a history. If I choose to make "materiality" or the materiality of language the touchstone from which to undertake a series of transvaluative readings (and the Nietzschean echo is unavoidable), it is nonetheless with a particularly unromanticized notion of the material in mind. What I mean does not point to a material, historical narrative which situates a textual event, but rather the manner in which the facticity of the textual event itself is thematized on the level of inscription, sound, letters, signature, and other figures; not as "formalist" elements of play divorced from the realm of experience and social change, but as active agents of transformation in the inner history of reading/writing itself.

Accordingly, these essays "return" to a scene that has been occluded during the return to history of the 80s. What the reader is asked to recall is the odd loop that the drift from high theory (post-structuralism and deconstruction) to neo-pragmatism, new historicism, and finally identity politics has entailed. While a thumb-nail sketch is here called for, it is not only a caricature, since one of the interesting phenomena of historicizing the swing from "theory" toward "practice," from the linguistic to the political, has in many ways been how that move effected the opposite of what was intended. The clichés that associate the "nihilism" of deconstructive techniques with apolitical "play," and political engagement with a return to the world have not always played as predicted. To begin with, a certain alliance between the right and elements of the left against textualism that insisted on a return to the agency of the subject (and a requisite intentionality) can be said to have produced a very different outcome than that which the left, in any event, desired. Rather than a return to history in some definitive way, there has been on the whole a regressive drift back into the neo-conservative right in the 90s. Indeed, it seems at times that the rhetoric of the political – while correctly aimed and in many ways effective (though we can as readily attribute "multi-culturalism" to demographics as to theory) – is if anything a return to the fold of that *mimetic ideology* that determines the arguments that support traditionalist humanism. A covert theologism and anti-intellectualism have not been without consequence as well, even as a "crisis in the left" has become evident. If the final swing away from high theory has been toward the balkanized field of identity politics with its diverse political agendas and attendant return to "strategic" foundationalism, it may indicate less that the renown "death of the subject" was announced too early than itself be the after-effect of that event, a parade of the undead. It is fairly easy, today, to see new historicism as itself a Reaganite phenomenon, with its reclamation of the semantic reserves of reference and its speculative mimeticism. My point in this digression is not to seize on a deviance within the movement back to representationalism, but to suggest, emblematically, a blind spot within it – what I call its mimetic ideology – that may be structural and ultimately aesthetic. It at times seems that the (re)turn into *representationalism* has involved a larger form of cultural hegemony, an aesthetic regime based on the prevalence of a certain trope, mimesis, that, when identified with "the political," displays an often suspect complicity (and even ahistoricity) of its own. My point in the following essays is to raise and rethink this question by asking if we have not missed something in dismissing as "formalist" concerns with the materiality of language as such, and whether there is not an *anti-mimetic politics* in post-humanist reading?

The very neatness, however, of the official history of recent critical development may be a bit too eudemonistic, a bit too pat. For if we have supposedly surpassed "theory" (textualism, deconstruction, post-structuralism) by returning to "practice," and have finally engaged politics and the important questions of democratic institutions, yet there seems to be a counter-narrative that haunts this story – evident in the return, nationally, to a greater conservatism rather than the opposite. Certainly, in the official narrative, there has been no "other" so universally accessible of scapegoating as the incipient formalism of close reading. It is interesting that even the official recuperation of Derrida after the "death" of deconstruction has had to pass through various purging rituals. According to one narrative, spawned by Gasche's *The Tain of the Mirror* and recently codified in a piece in *PMLA* by Jeffrey Nealon ("The Discipline of Deconstruction," *PMLA* [October, 1992]), Derrida was wrongly appropriated by "American deconstruction" (the Yale School in the first instance), and subsequently misread as other than what he really is, a "philosophical" text not about literature. If he is reappropriated by philosophy (thus purified as an origin), his text can be recuperated not only for that restricted domain but more generally for post-liberal politics. The castigation of deconstruction as apolitical and text-enclosed was not wrong, only misapplied to Derrida. The partitioned scapegoat that then becomes the "American" wing of deconstruction, with its rank textualism and incipient "nihilism," is best demonstrated by the vulnerable name of "de Man." According to this story, de Man was primarily extending the methodology of formalist new criticism, making the form of close reading he practiced or spawned all the more politically limited and dubious: by purging "deconstruction" of this American wing, in some extended sense, Derrida can be recuperated, purged, and re-admitted to the domicile.

Yet, as I said, there is something not only too pat but deeply evasive in the above narrative. Indeed, the scandal going into the 90s is not the conservatism of post-structuralism (a claim supplanting that of its "nihilism," which is only the short-hand used about those installing a different model of meaning from the perspective of those standing to be supplanted) but that of factions of the left and various anti-theory pragmatists. To begin with, the very accusation of "formalism" itself is one that has long concealed a potential repression. Why would "formalism" be so universally and routinely castigated if it did not pose, or conceal, a deeply material threat? Indeed, some impasses in theory or anti-theory today can be traced, in some ways, to a confusion that inhabits this site. However necessary as a recent moment in critical development, it may turn out that a phenomenon like the ferocious abjection of de Man – through whatever narrative devices (war-time writings, new critical links) – has more to do with the way in which his work (and *late* work in particular) undermines the broad-based *mimetic ideology* of cultural and critical thought, than any arguments of a methodological, "moral," or historical nature. It may even be, keeping the name de Man in mind here for its iconic value, that rather than turning aside from the direction pointed to in his late work – a turn toward the materiality of inscription as a means of addressing "history" in non-mimetic terms – an *acceleration* of some of its micro-textual elements might be first considered in order to break through to a different concept of *mimesis* itself. Like the late Lacan, the late de Man might be said to turn increasingly toward a concept of "the Real" beyond the meliorations of historicism, identification, or the "symbolic," only instead of hypothesizing the hoary epiphanies of "the Thing" outside of language (as we find, say, in Slavoj Zizek's ideology critique), de Man posits a facticity of *inscription* situated in the crossings and erasures of historically encrusted signifying chains (see "Hypogram and Inscription," in *Resistance to Theory* [Minneapolis: University of Minnesota Press, 1986, 51]). It may be that, in certain respects, the past decade has been regressive – a partial counter-revolution, in the name of "History" (or, worse, historicism), returning to the very *humanist model* that had been, indeed, intricately jeopardized. Such a model would have been present within the academic institutions of knowledge management – institutions persisting in a state of denial of the very practical collapse of the educational system tied to them. Perhaps this untracked drift of elements of the left toward the right is best exemplified by the ideology of (neo)pragmatism as genealogized by Cornel West in *The American Evasion of Philosophy* (1989), where the call to political activism under the ruse of American nationalism (opposed to its Euro-theoretical "other") masks a return to a theologically constructed communitarianism that operates like a panopticon of surveillance while restituting the humanist subject as its own formalist premise.

The premise that this book wants to re-open is not that a "return to 'reading'" is at hand in a simple or cyclically formalist sense – like a retreat into fetishist pleasures before the impasses of internationalism, identity politics, and formal democracy – but that a radical form of textualism remains a pivotally transformative option on the table today, one in which the politics of mimesis can, in ways, be particularly well addressed. Further, that it is a necessary option in securing a post-humanist landscape.

The concept of reading I put forward in these essays asks where a focus on a linguistic *materiality* that precedes figuration can be utilized as a pivotal moment to get beyond or out of mimetic interpretation (or to *alter* the concept of mimesis itself). Moreover, it points to a post-humanist project that is, realistically, already in place in popular culture: the transformations of technology, and, in fact, classical "literature." Here the material is not something that is to be opposed to language, rather language itself continues to be one mode in which it must be thought reflexively. Accordingly, in each of the three sections and ideological clusters I address (Dialogism, Americanism, Modernism), the categories bear a certain exemplary interpretive burden. "Dialogism" as appropriated by American Bakhtinians for a neo-conservative humanist and inter-subjective model is exposed as a misappropriation that has led to the evisceration of "Bakhtin" on the critical scene. This gives way to a more properly agonistic, apostrophic, triadic, self-cancelling, and post-humanist model that leads from "voice" to the problem of inscription, anteriority, the dead word, allegory, and memory; the Americanist ideology of the self (as represented, in part, by neo-pragmatism) is exposed as antithetical to the "classic" texts it often rests upon, or means to contain. Similarly, modernism, treated as a contemporary trope re-invented to contain its pseudo-other, the "post-modern," is evacuated by linguistic events it cannot conceptually account for in key texts. In each case, the problem of *pre*figural signifying agents – sound, signature, and letters – is mobilized to disempower a reigning ideology (a term I use, here, in a post-marxist sense as marking an inevitable and defensive meaning distortion, rather than as some sort of false consciousness).

What emerges in these essays – which the title of the second part, "Parables of exteriority" emblematizes – is that a different "politics" within alternate models of mimesis and new technologies of reading must be contemplated, and this in a way that renders the traditional opposition of the right and left increasingly secondary (as it is on the

international scene as well). Rather, we are more frequently con-
fronting an opposition *between* models of meaning or history that
return to interiorizing premises (self-privileging, exclusionary, humanist) and models which implement some form of radical exteriority
(post-humanist, social, linguistic) that close out the prior model and,
indeed, the very opposition it rests on. This is not entirely charted
terrain. Just as the rhetoric of some on the left and the right criss-cross
here (the left's endorsing of nationalism against the eviscerations of
late capitalism, for instance, also returns to the exclusionary and proto-
fascistic logic which that entails), so a turn to the prospect of a more
radical "materialism" that exceeds both and requires new categories is
also posited (of the subject, gender, agency, and reading).

It is not, perhaps, accidental that the trope of the material returns
with a certain urgency today across different projects – whether in the
analysis of ideological anamorphosis in a late Lacanian idiom by Slavoj
Zizek (see *The Sublime Object of Ideology* [New York: Verso, 1989]), or
the retheorization of the fetish as a verbal figure by William Pietz
("The Problem of the Fetish I," *Res* 9 [Spring, 1985], 1–22), or Michael
Taussig's Benjaminian allegorization of Latin American realities (*The
Nervous System* [New York: Routledge, 1992]), or Judith Butler's post-
feminist turn to the problem of "inscription" in theorizing gender.
Since inscription is perceived as external or material (it might better be
called "*ex*scription"), it occupies a similar public space as does the
social "other's word," say, of Bakhtin, which itself shades into what is
called the (material) "alien" or "dead word" of anterior language or
history. There is a corollary easily overlooked, then, between the
social word and the idea of inscription itself. I explore this in the most
public (and yet clearly inscribed) "dialogue" of Plato's, the *Protagoras*,
which is both situated as if in the agora and encrypts in this publicness
the most literal reading scene in Plato.

To ask, today, where the materiality of language functions as
cultural intervention may be, necessarily, to reconvene the traditional
form of "the reading" – only to introduce there the problem of the
prefigural in general, and its havoc-wreaking effect on the inherited
institutions of interpretation and iconography. In the following
essays, the question of the prefigural – what I call, here, the "legs" of
sense – operates actively to transform cultural icons: in the case of
Bakhtin, it delivers us from an inter-subjective model; in that of Plato,
from the way we "narrativize" his text and make him an icon of
Platonism; in the case of Whitman, it delivers us from a historically

installed domestication of the "voice." The essays here inter-lace and network in ways hardly indicated by their general ordering: the pragmatism of Protagoras returns in the question of the pragma in American neo-pragmatism; the dialogism of Bakhtin is rewritten in the essay on Whitman; while the semiotic problem of the "sea" drifts between Conrad and Melville, as does the issue of signature. Moreover, the concept of pragma as (linguistic) "thing" that emerges in relation to Protagoras and launches a critique of American neo-pragmatism, returns in the discussion of Hitchcock as a revision of Zizek's Lacanian use of "the Thing," rewriting its pretense to a kind of epiphanic (if impossible) transparency as an event of inscription.

It is not accidental, then, that the figure of legs — the material order of the body or sign as reflected in the most persistent corporeal trope — persists throughout the texts analyzed. It is present not only in Cassio's cut off leg in *Othello*, or the name of Conrad's "secret sharer" Leggatt, but in Poe's "foot d'or" and Hitchcock's "thirty-nine steps." I mean the term to be heard in the sense Derrida develops in essays like "Legs of Freud," where the figure echoes with the ramifications of feet (hence rhythm), but also the law, legitimation, legacy (hence anteriority), and reading (*legere*). The feet or legs represent a prefigural moment in which the traces of anteriority conflate the material bearers of sense precedent to any metaphorization. They are the site not only of inscription, but also disinscription or re-inscription — what Donna Haraway terms a site for charting new pasts and futures. It is not accidental that a typical prefigural trope, prosopopeia, names a site of mimetic crisis: the emergence (and emergency) of the face and speaker, allowing us to reconvene the interlocking systems that produce that virtual reality, allowing us to reinscribe it otherwise. The figure of legs also dismantles any bodily metaphor that permits a master-slave opposition between the Cartesian head (subject, meaning, cognition) and the legs (material conveyors), since it frequently happens in these texts that the legs usurp the position of the head, or become severed and independent agents of transvaluation. If legs may be understood as a corporeal analogue for the material base of language itself, that entails the brute dependence of semantic relations on what precedes mimesis and figuration; on what, in the course of marking itself, gets woven into and alters meaning-production; on what seeks and implements *a mimesis without models*. If this trope stands in opposition to the (Cartesian) head in a classic binary of low and high, signifier and signified, matter and mind, its corollaries include animals (which carry interchangeable riders), slaves or servants in the social order (in Plato), machines of transport (Whitman's ferry, cars in Hitchcock). Legs is one term for a materiality that precedes figuration, that produces "figuration" as its evasion. The reader is asked to consider the direction of these readings, in the light of a different sort of pragmatism or materiality, much as the title "Anti-Mimesis" is not meant to be heard simply as a classic rejection or opposition to mimesis (with the classic of Auerbach echoing in the background), but rather to raise the prospect of other models of mimesis — and in particular, of addressing active forms of mimesis without models or copies.

Accordingly, my essay on Melville's "Bartleby" might be deemed representative for the entire volume. For in it I suppose that Melville's image of the narrator's Law Offices stands for a certain vision of the logos and mimesis itself — particularly as it depends on the production of copies based on originals. The questions to be asked as readers, then, are not only where the scrivener's dispossession of those Offices is effected, but how, as readers, we must follow that same gesture to perform the trajectory of Melville's text, and how this can entail an emptying out of the interiorizing model of a certain notion of the human (portrayed, in fact, as hellishly machinal and predictive)? In short, what alterations must occur in our model of reading itself, and hence "mimesis," to allow us to follow this historical transformation of signifying systems?

PART I

Dialogue and inscription

❖❖

Othello, Bakhtin, and the death(s) of dialogue

❖❖

'Tis the curse of service:
Preferment goes by letter

When Othello ends his final soliloquy with a dagger thrust to the throat, it is seldom noted how oddly his Venetian audience responds to this gesture. Rather than addressing the Moor's pathos-ridden end, they draw attention to what could be called the materiality of the speech itself. Othello's soliloquy (he has been dictating an imaginary letter) concludes:

>   Set you down this;
>   And say besides, that in Aleppo once,
>   Where a malignant and a turban'd Turk
>   Beat a Venetian and traduc'd the state,
>   I took by th' throat the circumcised dog,
>   And smote him – thus.   [*He stabs himself.*]
> Lod. O bloody period!
> Gra.   All that is spoke is marr'd.
>
>   (5.2.351–8)

It is these last two remarks and their impact on reading Othello's soliloquy and the problem of any suicide speech that I want to address. While Lodovico responds with astonishment to the act of suicide, he apostrophizes less that death than a deadly *punctuation* mark: "O bloody period!" He cannot stop himself from drawing attention to the speech itself, and to a completed sentence at that. Given the supposed impact of the thrust, it is almost mad. The grammatical metaphor acknowledges the facticity of Shakespeare's own writing, while the speaker registers amazement at Othello's self-constructing oratory, just when its aesthetic effect collapses into transgressive blood and ruin. This may imply astonishment that death could emerge from the formal beauty of the verbal performance, but it definitely acknowledges a performance. Yet "period" can also mean a circuit, a *periodos* or going round, as if Othello's reflexive self-murder tried to close a circle or circuitry all but imprinted in the opening and closing *letter* of his name. This circle or "O" may suggest less the completed rehabilitation of Othello's old image ("Then must you speak / Of one") than a voiding of the fiction of the self, like a zero. More resonant still, "period" retains its association with a woman's menstrual blood, a feminizing image that is in fact persistent beneath the text's martial pretense in the motif of Othello's posture of service to the state. In the final soliloquy, as the Moor reconstructs himself in a hypothetical letter as if dictated to the "state," a circularity seems at stake that has temporal and, in a way, even Nietzschean overtones. Yet if Lodovico's remark is odd, potentially the comment of a wry theatre critic on the speech's style, Gratiano's follow-up shifts into a *meta*textual vein altogether. Rather than having a discrete antecedent, discourse itself ("*All* that is spoke") is *marr'd*, as with a knife in the throat. It is unclear, that is, whether what is just "spoke" is undone by the deed, or if the fact that all speech is already "marr'd" — constituted by marks, letters, sound, recurrent anterior repetitions or, finally, others' words — alters how we assess what "death" even means for the speaker. The utterance notes a radical *duplicity* in Othello's language ("Soft you, a word *or two*"), one we will call for lack of a better word "dia-logic," that puts his staged pathos, and even his death in question. How, after all, does one represent, or represent to enact, one's own suicide? How does one shift from word to action? What in the speech are "his" words? Who is "Othello" at this point? Is that "death" itself already redundant, *de trop*? Why is the speech dictated as a letter to and before the hypothetical "state" as absent reader? What is the "state"? What happens to Iago's silence here? Who even speaks the text and from where? Can a "word" ever be, or ever not be, a deadly act?

I should say, at once, that in addressing Othello's soliloquy I am aware of choosing a text that, on its surface, would appear the least "dialogic" in the usual sense, one that might, as a suicide, signal the end of all possible dialogue. But by invoking this term, I am less interested in a Bakhtinian reading of Shakespeare, than in Shakespeare's *reading* of Bakhtin or, rather, how *Othello* can be said to critique a reading of Bakhtin that has become almost institutional. It is a "reading" that lies behind a crisis in the term's current use, at a time when "dialogue" has in places become a shop-worn formalism with dubious critical thrust. Somewhat caricatured, this translation sees Bakhtin's "dialogue" as a term for inter-subjective communication or even communion of self and other yielding a sort of domesticated field of difference (semantic or social) which appears, now, as the product of a need in the early 80s for a figure ("Bakhtin") who preserved a rhetoric of the self before the incursions of post-structuralism. To some extent what is involved is a correction coming out of the polemic distortions of the 80s. At that time, energetically managed by American slavicist editors, this appropriation quietly depended upon suppressing inquiry into Bakhtin's *rhetorical strategies* (the anxiety over the problem of "pseudonyms" being only the most obvious case).[1] Problems related to any critical rereading of Bakhtin include: what the "social" itself actually connotes, why a Bakhtinian criticism has not emerged, why his terms in fact deface the very concepts they seem first to cite (sign, dialogue, ideology), and why "carnival" has itself proven all too legalized (as the *Rabelais* warns)?

My own focus, however, will be to ask why the trope of dialogue produced in the 80s as a humanist and communicationist icon must now be read as a post-humanist and materialist figure that assumes its own dissimulation – and dissimulation in general as its ground? It will also be to suggest that it conceals a self-cancelling logic in which Bakhtin's own model of "dialogue" might best be understood, today, according to a strategy of defacement and *inscription*.

My argument will be that *Othello* dismantles the ideology of dialogue as an inter-subjective communicative model, displaying Shakespeare's reading of the most radical, and currently suppressed, elements in Bakhtin's text. Shakespeare's dialogism displays discourse *not* as communication or inter-subjective commerce, but as power, dissimulation, and entrapment – as a battle for mastery and the violating circulation of a public word that is always menacingly positional. Circularity in the play will appear in different guises, heard in the letter "O" and in strategic words like circumscribe, circumstance, or circumcised: it may imply alternately or inclusively reflexivity, a temporal recurrence not without Nietzschean overtones, the voiding of the subject, or the circulation of "social" language.[2] If Iago cannot

---

1 These questions have been posed by the two recent collections, *Rereading Bakhtin*, ed. Gary Saul Morson and Caryl Emerson (Chicago: Northwestern University Press, 1989), hereafter referred to as *RB*, and *Bakhtin and Cultural Theory* (London: Manchester University Press, 1989), hereafter referred to as *BCT*.

2 The "materiality" of the *sign* announced in V. N. Voloshinov, *Marxism and the Philosophy of Language*, trans. I. R. Titunik (New York: Seminar Press, 1973), hereafter *Marxism*, is so unequivocal ("*consciousness itself can arise ... only in the*

quite be called a self, neither can Othello, since his identity (which his blackness doubles) must be read as itself an aesthetic (linguistic) construct. In question is whether "dialogue" merely describes verbal exchange or is itself a trope, and if so, whether it is an openly representational trope or an anti-mimetic one?

The reading of Bakhtin produced in the early 80s yielded, in measure, a counter-figure and specular other to post-structuralism that might be briefly examined.[3] It is arguable that the ideological constraints of that production blocked a more careful reading of "dialogism" that might have proven irreconcilable to the prevalent communicationist, historicist, or humanist versions. However modified, this Bakhtin was to yield an affirming model of communication and a differential rhetoric of self and other partly derived from Buber (Holquist, Todorov), yet largely reflecting the academy's investment in a phenomenological model. Holquist's literary biography is only the most obvious attempt to use an account of authorial production to legitimize this ideology of "dialogue."[4] It did not seem to matter that just this reading is itself clearly barred by Voloshinov's *Marxism and*

material embodiment of signs" [11]), and unequivocally destructive of the phenomenological model (called "subjective expressionism"), that the constant return to this interpretation argues less an ideological investment than a failure to *read*. I will use *Othello* to explore the implications of this materiality ("from one link of a semiotic nature [hence, also of a material nature] we proceed uninterrupted to another link ... nowhere does the chain plunge into inner being").

3 The counter "post-structuralist" Bakhtin had influenced early readings in both humanist (Holquist) and marxist circles (Eagleton, Jameson). One may review it in David Carroll's "The Alterity of Discourse: Form, History and the Question of the Political in M. M. Bakhtin" (*Diacritics*, 8: 2 [1983]) and Robert Young, "Back to Bakhtin" (*Cultural Critique*, 2 [1985]).

4 Holquist's insistence in *Mikhail Bakhtin* (Cambridge: Harvard University Press, 1984) that Bakhtin's text is imbued with "a radical Christology" (82) has lost influence, but provided a rationale for placing the "pseudonyms" under the signature of "Bakhtin." This reading appears based on a literalization of the immediacy of dialogue, on "two actual people talking to each other in a specific dialogue at a particular time and in a particular place" ("Introduction" to Mikhail Bakhtin, *The Dialogic Imagination*, ed. M. Holquist [Cambridge, Mass.: Belknap, 1982], xx, hereafter cited as *DI*). In the introduction to *Rethinking Bakhtin*, Morson mounts a quasi-Oedipal counter-reading, where "Bakhtin" — now rid of the texts signed Voloshinov — finally emerges in this trajectory as a sort of right-wing moralist whose dialogism itself is suspect (*RB*, 31–49). This time Bakhtin opposes all "theoretism" (read, that is, contemporary "theory"), and finally become the neo-con Bakhtin of the 90s. This product is iconized in Morson and Emerson's *Mikhail Bakhtin: Creation of a Prosaics* (Stanford University Press, 1990).

the Philosophy of Language, under the name of "subjective expressionism." What had been suppressed was a material self-differing "word" precedent to any speaker – one that can say, like Iago, "I am not what I am." It has been noted that the translation of "dialogue" as double-talk fits all too well Bakhtin's theorized relation to "official" language and the Stalinist censor. What is sometimes forgotten is that the "official" language undone in Bakhtin and Voloshinov is also that of philosophy, linguistics, poetics, and psychoanalysis. Unmarked in their critical difference, terms like "social" and "sign" can only be misread, or assimilated to the familiar concepts that Bakhtin, precisely by using these *names,* would dismantle.[5] That Bakhtin does not, or cannot mark the difference in these terms – no longer words precisely – has always presented a problem for his readers, one only heightened by the forbidden ironic implications of a pseudonymous strategy. One commentator notes of the success of this reading: "the ease with which everyone can endorse the central elements of the Bakhtinian programme indicates that the hard work has not really begun. What is this 'dialogism' that so many celebrate as liberating and democratic …?" (*BCT,* 3). If this domestication has taken its toll, one reaction to the resulting critical impasse is retrenchment, since the investment in it has been substantial. Thus one finds Morson and Emerson in their recent *Mikhail Bakhtin: The Creation of a Prosaics* (1990) relinquishing the pseudonymous works altogether from Bakhtin's "authorship" in order to preserve the purity of "Bakhtin," now presented (finally) as a sort of right-wing moralist, the anti-theoretician void of both marxist and (originally) sociological concerns. The editorial gesture is instructive since the ensuing figure that is produced represents a final avatar of this original translation, now pared down, Bakhtin as a literary technician without many cultural complications. The circle has come full turn.

To speak of the "death(s)" of dialogue, then, may be to ask not only where this ideology of dialogue might be dead, but where a figure of "death" inhabits dialogue in a determining way that has been ignored, one place of which is the question of the "dead word" itself in Bakhtin's text.

---

5 This remains one of the more sensitive questions in "reading 'Bakhtin'" and is not unrelated to how we approach, still, the problem of the "pseudonyms." Each term, starting with "sign," may be approached as dismantling the conceptual site it names, among other things by moving it outside the binaries that held it in place.

1. Othello's black poetics

If *Othello* is privileged as a text, its difference – apparent in the extraordinary figure of Iago – seems marked in the blackness of Othello's face. Bracketing for the moment a reading of that blackness in an African context that is kept intentionally vague (without identified origin), what blackness marks here is a doubled otherness within the artifice of the familiar. It is not accidental that the Moor's discourse is notable, excessively musical ("more," too much) yet also emptily formal. However blackness might be read as a figure, it works to mark a rift in the speaker as such, effacing the otherness of the familiar that covers a break, or rhetorical gap. As a "general" rather than prince or king, the Moor simulates command yet represents a figure of service, not a *sovereign* subject (or speaker). The black *face* that represents the text's subject marks, then, an imploded doubling present both in Othello's too perfect appropriation of the Venetian codes and Iago's most enigmatic line: "I am not what I am." Moreover, just such doubleness seems echoed in the text's critical readings.

While the play is too canonical to question aesthetically, it oscillates in traditional criticism between being praised as the most perfect and powerful of Shakespeare's tragedies (almost obeying the classic unities, Dr. Johnson points out), yet is covertly recoiled from as without sense, irredeemably empty beyond its "domestic" ravaging. There seems a faction who will almost, with Lodovico at the end, utter: "This object poisons sight; Let it be hid." The main characters can appear *so* symmetrical as to seem numbingly allegorical (largely Christian), yet then manifest no transcendent import at all, and in turn seem almost to merge, as when Iago and Othello are linked by their respective "service," or the "innocence" of Desdemona spreads in turn to Iago's "motiveless" artistry. Interpretations of Othello's "barbarian" nature follow a similar split, sometimes making of him a passionate innocent, other times a pompous and formal boor, lacking instinct. Deciding between these alternating interpretations is less interesting than asking why they are invariably produced and what each is designed to contain or respond to.[6] Part of the problem is that

6 Shakespeare's adaptation of Cinthio's tale is revealing. He erases specific human motivations to make Iago into an abstract figure, and he takes Cinthio's hot-blooded saracen and makes him at once more black *and* more stately and re-strained. Not only are all *names* Shakespeare's additions – in a text where names

there is in a sense no problem at all, nothing occurs outside of Iago's fiction making, which stages the text as a play within itself — "nothing" really occurs, up to the triggered murder of Desdemona. I propose to read the text as less about jealousy than interpretation and signs (the relation of seeming to being), or Othello's inability to master in any other way than murderous literalization the total inversion of familiar meanings that Desdemona's supposed "infidelity" implies. If we can pretend to call *Hamlet* a subjective "tragedy," *Othello* appears to be one that occurs in the space where "subject" and "object" collapse, its word is "inter-territorial" in Voloshinov's sense, hence in a sort of circulation announced, too, by the "O(s)" in Othello's name. Thus Iago appears at once to be the ideal spectator (outside), inscribed in the text, and its sole agent.

Whatever the materiality of language may mean in this play, the public word is already "janus-faced" in the Star Chamber scene, as it is in Voloshinov, a "two-sided" figure in the absence of interiority altogether. "Social" language in *Othello* suggests at first the values, codes, or romanticizations of the "state" (Venice) that Othello's discourse moves through, quotes, and literalizes. Othello's blackness thus marks a self-difference inhabiting familiar language (that of Venice, of Shakespearean English), which his literalizations often obscure, providing a reversed or doubled instance of colonizing the colonizer.[7] The Moor's mode may be called one of self-manifestation, the aesthetic presentation of what is reflexively read as if from the

---

are determining, and end with "O" — but each figure is adjusted by substraction. Iago's lust for Desdemona is put onto Roderigo (not present in Cinthio), and his daughter is taken away, leaving his impulse undefined ("motiveless"). Rather than having lived together for years, Othello and Desdemona are just wed and, unconsummated, transported to Cyprus, brought together without knowledge of one another aside from their (mutual) seduction by storytelling. Emilia no longer knows of the plot. Chance plays no role, as all becomes part of Iago's machinations.

7 Phyllis Natalie Braxton, in "Othello: The Moor and the Metaphor" (*South Atlantic Review*, 55:4 [1990]), notes that Othello "is represented as traveling constantly," though his "origin is not named" (8), rendering his blackness not that of "a black of any one particular background" (9) but a matter of *color* and figuration as such. We may recall, in this, his role as "general." Noting that, once defined, "he is no longer the Other" (9), Braxton argues against a racially defined reading for one in which "color" as such (black) looms as a semiotic mark. What is a *black figure*? The point would be to acknowledge where racist codes — recurrent in Iago's mockery — betray a figural site that clearly resists codified racial definition.

outside: "I must be found," he says reflexively, active-passive: "My parts, my title, and my perfect soul / Shall manifest me rightly" (1.2.30–2). Othello's putative *immediacy* is also stately and controlled since it covers a rhetorical rupture. As such, he may always also *represent* the speaker representing himself in another's words without any other position. Yet to Iago he represents a "master's" position, if only simulated: authority comes, here, by surrogacy, and the highest figure in office, the Duke, operates by deferral and duplicity from his absent center.

Does this represent a position familiar in Bakhtin or Voloshinov? The "sign" in Voloshinov is without any interiority, since it refers to other self-differing signs without interior as well. Like the "state" in *Othello*, the idea of the "social" in Voloshinov functions at times as a material, citational, or even *aesthetic* figure.[8] "Social" language appears authorized by an irony its possessors wield, a doubleness that eludes Othello because he incarnates it. This "state" itself represents beneath the order implied in the word a form of violence, of which Othello is an implement. The "state" has no center. From the perspective of a "state" which has only surrogates, what Bakhtin calls "official discourse" is a fiction (as may be the unity of the state): it is, instead, or also, a "state" of being or language that is none. Here, Venice represents the epitome of a sheerly commercial entity, a Bakhtinian market-place ruled by economic necessity. As Brabantio discovers, the "words" of the senate are, in Voloshinov's sense, "janus" faced figures determined by circumstance: "These sentences, to sugar, or to gall, / Being strong on both sides, are equivocal. / But words are words" (1.3.216–18). Rather than situate discourse as a set of determined values, Voloshinov's "social" is essentially duplicitous, unanchored, influencing by a web of citation. In Bakhtin the "social" never represents what we call historical reference as such. The circularity which is heard in the "O" of *Othello* appears, now, not to be resolved by an escape into the word "state" with its static overtones. It is confirmed rather than resolved by a voiding circularity in social

8 Thus the letter and the materiality of the word converge as an always anterior, exterior, material or aesthetic effect. Othello might be called the most "aesthetic" of the tragedies, since its sheer exteriority is clear in Iago's production from within of every event before the audience. Voloshinov accounts for the *aesthetic* field of the word by remarking: "Language, so viewed, is analogous to other ideological phenomena, in particular, to art – to aesthetic activity" (*Marxism*, 48).

language that represents a problem similar to the one we find in Voloshinov's allegorical and tautological "sign."[9] As Iago demonstrates, since no word has intrinsic authority, a reading of its inflections is part of the calculation of self-presentation and control. Using the "state" in *Othello* to read Voloshinov's *Marxism and the Philosophy of Language*, we may say the latter's narration itself appears unexpectedly rhetorical or even ironic. That is, as a text, it presents itself as a phenomenology of "sign," precisely of what undoes any phenomenological model of consciousness ("subjective expressionism") by positioning the materiality of language before the effect of consciousness. Moreover, the narrative of *Marxism* moves as if outward, from "sign" and "inner speech" toward reported speech, detouring through a historical flashback to the philologist's word, formalism, the alien word, and the "dead word" (chapter two); yet it is also, as we hear from Bakhtin, "simultaneous." It cannot move outward if it is without interiority to begin with, being a material sign, and the detour through the "history" of the "dead word" becomes in itself the prototype for "another's word," the word of the other, which is always anterior — a problem that returns for us in Othello's soliloquy.

These successive dead words are historical "myths" because they represent as historically superseded epochs (such as formalism) what is arguably the *perpetual* formalization of anterior language as such, the other's word (*chuzoe slovo*). Language, in Bakhtin, whatever the description, operates as a scene of perpetual *in*scription, in which the otherness of the word is intertwined with its sheer anteriority. The difference means transposing what seems immediately before one — like another person talking in dialogue — into the perpetual dilemma of agonistic reading and circulation. If the temporality of "sign" leads directly into the collapse of representation in carnival, it is a figure that

9 The "O" of Othello suggests a reflexive, circular, and then emptying design — partly temporal, partly linguistic — that is present in the logic or exposition of "sign" elaborated in Voloshinov. There "sign" appears a simple term, but it distinguishes itself from the Saussurean figure it seems to cite, reversing the latter's sense (it is without bifurcation or content). This circularity is examined in Samuel Weber's introduction to the German translation of *Marxism*, translated as "The Intersection: Marxism and the Philosophy of Language," *Diacritics* 15, 4 (1985), a piece to which my own reading of Bakhtin is indebted. Nor is it accidental that the emblem for this, in the play, is the handkerchief, the most minimal and desemanticized of objects yet, as such, a "Thing" whose maternal source places it at the self-subverting limit of any fetish theory, a figure disowning the metaphorics of a maternal phallus.

is produced by what it is producing, the anticipatory reaction to another anticipatory reaction (*MPL*, 38–9). Voloshinov's "sign" subsists in the rhetorical cancellation of the concept it names, the binarized "sign" of Saussure that it seems, at first, to give new currency to, only without any bifurcation into signifier and signified, and without content.[10] Thus Iago speaks of manipulating signs: "I must show out a flag and sign of love, / Which is indeed but sign" (1.1.156–7) – signs that he stands outside of and which Othello, in reading, literalizes.

If the materiality of the "social" word finds a corollary in the most material elements of language, sound or letters, it is not accidental that the "state" continues to communicate throughout the text by *letters*.[11] Letters link the authority of the state to the "dead word" and writing to the (alphabetical) letter itself. As Iago asserts, speaking of promotion yet also priority: "Preferment goes by letter." Power circulates not through the discourse of masters but through anticipatory self-inscription in the (perpetually) other's word, a process Iago seems to master. The "state" that presents a unified aesthetic image in the codes of Venetian courtship, martial splendour, political adjudication, revenge, and love, relies on public "reputation" (as Cassio notes) for power. In his contradictions, Othello represents the martial violence of this aesthetic state that must imprint its law on the anonymous Ottomite hordes (whose double-O reflects his own).

If Othello's blackness can signify a collapse of the representational system he incarnates – a sort of black-hole within its terms – his relation to the "state" seems based on his sheer mimesis of Venetian codes that is itself all too literary. Mimesis here is identified with a relation to the past, with the re-presentation of an already formalized

10 Raymond Williams in *Marxism and Literature* (London: Oxford University Press, 1977) noted a tendency to misread Voloshinov, or miss his radical impact, due to his retention of terms like "sign" and "ideology" where he meant to annotate new semantic fields. What is not noted is the active practice of desemanticizing these terms, creating figures that, like Derrida's, are "neither word nor concept."

11 References include: Iago's noting "the curse of service: / Preferment goes by letter" (1.1.35–6), the Duke's "bitter letter" (1.3.68), the letter Roderigo produced (5.2.308–9) after his death, and Othello's soliloquy. After striking Desdemona, Lodovico asks "did the letters work upon his blood" (4.1.275), connecting again "blood" with the violence of marks ("O bloody period!"). A connection must, then, be made between inscription (or letters) and the "dead word," sheer anteriority.

or mnemonic moment – and not something co-present. In the wooing scene reported before the Signiory, it is cultural images from romances that are consumed by Desdemona. Thus Desdemona would "Devour up my *discourse*" in tales of "the Cannibals that each other eat, / The Anthropophagi, and men whose heads / Grew beneath their shoulders" (1.3.143–5), narratives Iago dismisses as "bragging ... and fantastical lies" (2.1.223–4). This cannibalization of discourse persists in Othello's account of the courtship, which depicts a remarkably passive or reactive scene of seduction that Desdemona seems covertly to direct. He moves upon her "hint" to do so, reading signals indirectly planted ("I should but teach him to tell her my story / And that would woo her") while the stories or verbal representations supplant and *defer* contact. Instead, language stands between the two negotiators' reading "hints" and counter-projections, circling a third image or cultural cliché: "She loved me for the dangers I had passed, / And I loved her that she did pity them." The circuit, called a "process," seems to close around a *verbal* narrative (dangers, that she did pity) standing between two narcissistic readers, each exchanging the other's reading of their own projected role. Each takes as object a representation, loving the love of that representation first, words which maintain an implicit chasm. His "story" shows Othello, above all, to be less man of action than a *bovaryste*, an imitative reader of adventure romances, an African Quixote in a Venice that is, for him, fabled, and commodified. Othello represents to the "state" an efficient machine of violence that – incarnating this rift – is his greatest social asset.

2. The story of "O"

The double circularity present in the name "Othello," in the suicide, in the "social" word, appears to hint at a sort of Shakespearean nihilism (in a distinct and, indeed, positive sense), a null-point that at times precedes figuration itself – a moment close to the "psychosis" of Iago, yet present in the way a Borges or Coleridge, say, will celebrate Shakespeare's identity too. In the opening scene in Cyprus, the absence of any sail ("I cannot 'twixt the heaven and the main / Descry a sail" [2.1.3–4]) suggests a field without metaphor. When Iago notes "'Tis the curse of service: / Preferment goes by letter," he connects the problem of *service* to what precedes figure, to the material bearers (pre*fer*/meta*phorein*) of linguistic sense, letters. The usurpation of "service" that Iago announces on his own behalf corresponds to that of material language and letters in the text moving to usurp the role of active agents. There will be in the course of *Othello* a clear crisis of action and agency that Iago remains a "motiveless" source of. Iago is the figure from whose language calculations every person serves as agent, precipitating the act (or deed) of murder, and the impossible "act" – one of mechanical implementation and volition – of the suicide. Othello is, however, never shown as the man of action (master) he is advertised as, short of smothering Desdemona, an act that leaves no scar or mark. He thematizes a rupture between sign and signified that he cannot read, but recoils from in the possibility of Desdemona's infidelity. When the Turks are overcome, it is not even by his hand. When we hear that the "tempest hath so banged the Turks / That their *designment* halts" (2.1.21–2), this "designment," or undoing of sign's logic, is attributed not to any *cause* – a word that threads the text – but to a tempest, a temporal disarticulation of cause, effect, antecedent, and sequence. The letter of preferment, the "O," appears to be a dubious cipher for the subject or sign, since it echoes as an emptied point, a nullifying yet recurrent site in which circulation and circularity resound and clash, duplicate and separate. Linked to Iago as well, it is attached to the numerous Italian male names (most given by Shakespeare), like Cassio, Gratiano, Brabantio. The "*Ottomites*," the Venetian *other* as hordes of identity-less Turks to be inscribed on, double behind and replicate the site of Othello's fabricated identity – as in the soliloquy's "turban'd Turk." When this specular system risks collapse, short-circuiting, it is depicted by Othello as "the fountain from which my current runs or else dries up" (4.2.59–60).

The central example of short-circuiting can be located in the logic of service. When Iago projects a reversal of masters and servants in the opening scene, what he actually undoes is the figure of "service" itself ("I follow him to serve my turn upon him. / We cannot all be masters, nor all masters / Cannot be truly followed ... In following him, I follow but myself" [1.1.42–58]). Iago's is *not* Bakhtin's "unofficial" word usurping or doubling against the "official" to bring it down. The system does not erect anything self-sufficient ("myself"), and does not assume mastery as such, since that depends on the perpetual subversion of another's lead, an illusory mastery (such as Othello's) that is itself led. Iago speaks of the "curse of service" with this circuitry in mind. He addresses Othello as a false master who, in fact himself a servant, will seek his image in Desdemona ("O my fair warrior"), another servant ("the captain's captain"). Othello's line about Brabantio – "My services which I have done the Signiory / Shall out-tongue his complaints" (1.2.18–19) – inscribes his verbal hyperbolism as something itself credited in and by the service of the official sign (signiory). If Desdemona's example of service *feminizes* both Othello and Iago by its relation to their own (as the "O" too does), Iago's line, "I am not what I am," migrates across the text, clearly assimilating Othello. This is remarked as Othello is later portrayed inversely in Iago's line, "*He's* that he is." In this line, the first person Othello is placed in the mocking language of identity, only in third person status – what is not that of any subject. Iago's "I am not what I am" remains under-read, since it not only inverts the biblical "I am that I am" in the abyss of self-difference (this could not read, for instance, "I am not what I seem"), but also renders any assertion of the first person its own linguistic annihilation. "I" never is what I "am," once that is *said*. Iago inhabits a site where language begins by cancelling. To say "I am ..." dialogically inscribes one in the representation of another that negates the utterance. "Othello" becomes, or in a sense always was, the third person to his own "I," the romantic or narcissistic construct, "Othello." What Iago initiates is a different "devouring" of discourse that eviscerates identity (and links him curiously to Desdemona). When the text arrives at Othello's late line, "That's he that was Othello; Here I am," the two grammatical sites (dis)converge as a temporal dislocation that sustains dialogic difference from the "I" as its own premise.

Iago's short-circuiting of "service" parallels the assertion in the text of the material elements of language – the servants and vehicles of meaning – over authorial semantics, a gesture echoed in the ascendency of animal and lower bodily imagery. When Othello is racially castigated as "an old black ram" (1.1.88) and "a Barbary horse" (1.1.111–12), the animal tropes recall the material vehicle of the signifier that carries (*phorein*) semantic import, like the errant Pegasus in Plato's myth in *Phaedrus*. This recurs in images of feet and *legs*, of which Cassio's is in the last act cut off or "in two," while Othello looks for Iago's cloven feet. When Iago taunts Brabantio about his likely progeny – "you'll have nephews neigh to you, you'll have coursers for cousins, and gennets for germans" (1.1.112–13) – the material base of language is what positionally generates (gen ... , germ ...) Iago's fabrications. The subversion of "service" by service ("follow but myself") marks a reflexive moment where material traces (letters, sounds, values, "dead" words, "official" or others' words) assume the priority over speaking subjects. Iago's discourse appears as a peculiarly dialogic laboratory for this event. Here the most invested and formally evolved language, that of the aesthetic state, disintegrates for Othello into psychotic ejaculations that dismember face itself ("Pish! Noses, ears, and lips? Is't possible? – Confess? – Handkerchief? – O devil" [4.1.42–3]). If Othello *seems* locked within a literalized language from the (black) position of outsider, Iago seems to be on the outside (inside) of it, subscribing to no positional site. There will appear a moment, then, when Iago and Othello emerge from the same pre-representational site. Iago, subverting service and refusing the dialectic or pretense of mastery in a manner recalling Bataille's notion of "sovereignty," opens the anarchy of a radical aesthetico-political critique of the dialogic word as such.

In fact, the Rabelaisian lower body as a figure of *materiality* emerges in a remarkable word-play connected to circularity. In the opening of Act III a Clown punningly transmutes the letter "O" into a covert Rabelaisian trope compounding the anus and the lips of speech as passed gas ("wind"). Wind in the text is associated with breath and speech, ranging from the tempest to Desdemona's smothering:

Clo. Are these, I pray you, wind instruments?
[1.] *Mus.* Ay, marry, are they, sir.
Clo. O, thereby hangs a tale.
[1.] *Mus.* Whereby hangs a tale, sir?
Clo. Marry, sir, by many a wind instrument that I know. But, masters, here's money for you; and the general so likes your music that he desires you for love's sake to make no more noise with it.   (3.1.6–13)

Hanging is a suspension, here of the temporal narrative (tale). The "wind instrument" or passing of wind reduces the "tale/tail" to hanging beside an evacuating rim, the now narrative "O" as mouth and anus, a cipher in and outside the body. The Clown steps outside of narrative time with a quip that negates even the "music" of Othello ("any music that may not be heard"), rendering that too a mute writing. This chain of figures (circuitry, breath, lips, speech, anus, tale, hung) points to the arrest at any moment of the text's elaborate double talk, the stepping outside of the narrative progression. It also connects the "O" cipher to the lower bodily stratum in a covert figural chain that makes of language production both wind and excrescence. Why does Shakespeare's Clown intervene, here, suspending narrative in writing the "O" as anus?

If Iago subverts semantic mastery from within the cited words of the pseudo-master(s), then the line, "In following him, I follow but myself," marks a further turn. "Myself" is in play as a reactive effect that needs a primary text ("I am nothing if not critical"), nothing *in* itself. The dismantling of (inter)subjectivity in *Othello* arrives at the point rhetorically resisted (and affirmed) in Voloshinov and Bakhtin, the moment of the speaker *without one's "own" word of any sort*.[12] A collapsed circuit is indicated by the way in which the pseudo-master follows the pseudo-servant following the "master," only to follow a self that is reactive. What Bakhtin calls the "dialogic word" harbors an *anamorphic* logic in which the container is the contained, and the obverse, of which Iago's "motiveless" discourse is a prime agent and example.[13]

Iago's discourse is perhaps the most complex in Shakespeare. Like his "plotting," it inter-dialogically and de-dialogically effaces any reflective distance of the reader in a rhetorical assault that converts anticipation and the other's word into a past tensed inscription of the other in the sheer movement of self dramatization. Iago's will to power as representation problematizes the figure of agency altogether, since it appears to be the latter's negative source. Coleridge's overrated alliteration — "the motive hunting of a motiveless malignity" — may not do justice to Iago's moral wit, his role as playwright *en abyme* within the ("real") play (inverting outside and in), or his "honesty," if by that we mean deconstructing before oneself one's aims as another's.

12 While the monologic, priest's, philologic or formalist word is, as Voloshinov notes, an "abstraction" (*Marxism*, 72), one remains confronted by the rhetorical reversal at the end of *Marxism*, the surprising bid for "one's own" word. The radical absence of this possibility, which haunts and is resisted in all of Bakhtin's writings (and is converted, occasionally, into the opposite), is precisely explored in *Othello*.

13 I am using the term anamorphic in a sense developed, in part, from Lacan's logic of the gaze by Ned Lukacher in "Anamorphic Stuff: Shakespeare, Catharsis, Lacan" (*South Atlantic Quarterly* 88, 4 [Fall, 1989]), where the concept anticipates a linguistic problem of materiality in which "Shakespeare's literary anamorphosis" (877) blocks catharsis itself through the "stuff" of the "sheer positedness of language" (879). Anamorphosis dismantles the possibility of a further outside, as it dismantles any cathartic expression, much as Bakhtin's resolute exteriority of the "word" implicitly bars any interiority of the self. Examples of Bakhtin's anamorphosis might include the mock-temporal narrative that has "dialogue" come after a (non-existent) "monologue," or novel after epic, where the "second" term contains and precedes the first it seems to emerge from.

Part of that distinction is called *not* "being" what "I" is, experiencing "I" as another, reappropriated or doubled, from a space not named. If Othello sees himself implicitly as "Othello" (an aesthetic construct, a "he"), Iago — in which name one hears "I" and *ego* — arguably inhabits an "I" that is also ventriloquized from a (reversed) non-position. To be "nothing if not critical" is to perpetually depend on negative reversal and intervention: Iago is always also in the position of an intervening witness, outside. Such dialogic self-difference is noted not as a negation but as the affirmation of non-being ("*I am* not what I am"). This statement contains an unending movement that suicide proves an almost irrelevant termination of, if we read the suicide of Othello as that of a conventional "I." One could not speak of a "word" of Iago, according to the *faux*-typologies Bakhtin's Dostoyevsky book pretends to. His word appears already representing itself, as another's before another, spoken by a "he" before a "he" assumed as an "I" (by another). If Othello's face is black — preceding the subjectivity it constructs and presents — Iago is face*less*.

In Iago's cinematic dialogism "social" embedding seems perpetually cited with authority only to become simulacra by that fact. Typically, the positing of "facts" yields anticipatory retort, from which the retro-fact (now fiction) turns into the affirmation (also momentary) of a reversal, itself distanced or discarded in turn. It is interesting to scrutinize how Iago generates his language (or the reverse), since it suggests an accelerated dialogic laboratory. No "word" can be subscribed to, since it is restlessly negated in a duplex economy that reflects the urbane or commercial code of the Star Chamber itself. To move in the sheer space of "others' words" is not a paralysis, though, since if self-difference is the principle of language, Iago is its most aggressive itinerant. Interestingly, the normative social functions of hypothetical "truth" (itself utilitarian) and "honesty" (externalization) appear manifest in Iago — "honest, honest Iago" is more than an irony. The following seems a fairly unexceptional passage of ratiocination: "The Moor, howbeit that I endure him not, / Is of a constant, loving, noble nature" — affirmation, suspending self-opposition ("howbeit"), authorizes a reversal in identification, meant to provide a rotating, retro-active cause: "And I dare think he'll prove to Desdemona / A most dear husband. Now I do love her too;" — a "fact" disassembled, a counter-moment hypothesized as mimicry ("Now"), then again erased, until an untruth becomes undecidable ("I do love her too"), merging with the first

position: "Not out of absolute lust," − conditional reversal, followed
by a parenthetical counter-fiction, imprinting a momentary self in the
text: "though peradventure / I stand accountant for as great a sin,"
− this identifies with the simultaneously denied position, now splitting
against itself to simulate a public *norm* (sexual lust) that is fictional but
simulates identity. It moves behind what others acknowledge, as
resting point (this motive is specifically deleted from the Cinthio tale
by investing "lust" in Roderigo). A further dissociative "cause" is
then posited, at first provisionally:

> But partly led (*conditioned*) to diet my revenge,
> For that I do suspect the lusty Moor (*fiction reversing all the above*)
> Hath leap'd into my seat;   (2.1.294−6)

The circularity of Iago's thought is that of recasting from effect to
cause, as the effect of an effect. Rather than an "I" stating opinions in
counter-point, Iago's discourse discriminates and "counter-casts"
figures to confirm the negative possibility of a hypothetical position,
that then seems as if confirmed before himself miming, still, another's
other. (This displays the restless negativity of language the ideologists
of dialogue most dread.) Iago stands beyond any psychological profile
in the space of a psychosis dramatizing or producing subject positions,
like a playwright. The only conversant to check Iago is Desdemona, in
banter, when she moves into a mode of double talk with Iago. If
discourse is "feminized" in the world of the play, the male privilege
or position is always simulated. Male power subsists in the repression
of *naming* that truth − and Desdemona is strangled when thought to
have disclosed it and used that power. "I(ago)" dramatizes it(him)self
by miming how *others* would respond to a situation ("gnaw my
inwards," "evened with him, wife for wife"), framing "other's words"
against him(it)self in a machinal migration impossible to cease.
Ultimately he does the same with his "own" words (like a shark biting
its own tail), when he becomes self-mocking in parenthetically
suspecting Cassio "with my nightcap too."

Here Shakespeare's dialogism − like Bakhtin's − is not based on the
agency of a self, mystified or otherwise, since the "social" word is at
once positional and subject to desemanticization. What emerges
might be called a *technological* reading of (the) word, based on
dissimulation, power-plays, and a battle for mastery.

3. Trialogues

Where in Bakhtin's work had language as will to power been, however, precisely spelled out? Have we been reading Bakhtin, or an element in his text, from the very first? Does "dialogue" exist or is it a trope codified in reverse, naming itself from its own after-life to manage a different sort of scandal?

In fact, Iago seems not to be unique as a speaker, but only to *accelerate* the "discourse scenario" outlined in Bakhtin, a scene not of communication but what might be called reading and power were not these terms themselves threatened with foreclosure at the outset. Bakhtin's premier example of dialogue turns out to be *not even dialogic as such*, at least not in the proper sense. Such a model that names itself the opposite (almost) of what it is might seem intrinsically ironic, so much so that to name it simply "dialogic" could show Bakhtin's attempt to disfigure in advance the ideology of dialogue, which he knew would be attributed to him. If Iago's dialogism displays a mock-self that is always a positional retro-effect of effaced citation, the threshing machine of discourse that harvests I's in its wake projects backward as cause (or "I") what is the (circular) effect of a self-cancelling operation. Precisely such an operation is described in Voloshinov's writing, where "dialogue" is *not* dyadic at all, and is not as Holquist reassures us "two actual people talking to each other in a specific dialogue at a particular time and in a particular place" (*Dialogic Imagination*, xx). In fact, it begins with three participants, of which the Listener is not even addressed, and the utterance itself is closest to lyric or even overt apostrophe – the antithesis, it seems, of what we think of as social discourse. One may call this model trialogic, except the third figure (the addressee or hero) need not even be human or alive, a problem that implicitly embarrasses, or vampirizes, the first person as well.

As I noted in the preceding chapter, the only full description of the discourse scenario in Bakhtin is found in Voloshinov's "Discourse in Life and Discourse in Art," and it is worth rehearsing in this context a bit differently since one encounters it almost nowhere in Bakhtin's voluminous commentary (indeed, it seems to represent an indigestible or unincorporable factor). Here, again, a single utterance is made to represent the "social" word as such, a word without semantic content or even response. The model is strangely narcissistic. As with Voloshinov's later example of the curse-word from Dostoyevsky's

Diary in *Marxism*, it is "a word virtually empty semantically" (102), a place-holder or zero term, that is nonetheless paradigmatic of utterance as such, of any word. Why does Voloshinov choose *apostrophe*, the lyric model rejected broadly in Bakhtin later, as the very premise of dialogue?[14] Why, moreover, has the entire Bakhtin industry avoided encountering or at least reading this ur-text of dialogue? The example is the utterance "Well!" made before a second person, at the sight remarked before of snowfall. A dislocation asserts itself at once in the temporality of the snow *falling* in May, projecting the past or dead word (wintry snow) into the proleptic spring ("*they both were looking forward* to spring and *both were bitterly disappointed*," 99). The "third" participant is not the listener but the addressee of the apostrophe, who may (and perhaps must) not be even human: "Who is the third participant? Who is the recipient of the reproach? The snow? Nature? Fate, perhaps?" (103). This third (who "remains nameless") is produced by "an attitude of a kind verging on apostrophe to that object as the incarnate, living culprit, while the listener – the second participant – is, as it were, called in *as witness and ally*." Now, in this scenario, again, the very model of dialogue, of the social word, there is at first *no* dialogue as such, no retort. While "social," the first person may be thought, herself, to be violently brought into representation or language together with "an inherent *tendency toward personification*." That is, what we habitually think of as the dialogic "other," the second person, is in fact here shut out of direct communication, is not an addressee at all but a "witness or ally" – with the implication that this would be so *even if he were "directly" addressed, since the position itself would only migrate*. In fact, the second person or listener is called a "reader" (105) of the exchange, one who is outside and must construe or misconstrue, read it like a (mute) text that is structurally closed, one who does not hear but who *over*hears, and then can (only) formulate a retort in which a counter-reading is anticipated (with reference to itself as a past text). This exchange, doubly *triangulated*, implies a mechanically pretended yet inescapable battle for recognition in which positions whiplash or rotate and the "I's" own emergence is at risk, cut off in the very utterance. (While the scenario may not imply

---

14 The text in question is V. N. Voloshinov's decisive "Discourse in Life and Discourse in Art" is found in *Freudianism*, trans. I. R. Titunik (Bloomington: Indiana University Press, 1987), 93–117. For a full treatment of this text, see my, "'Well!': Voloshinov's Double-Talk," in *Sub-Stance* 68 (Fall, 1992).

murder, it can easily be misread as suicidal.) Like Iago's "I am not what I am," the voice that emerges in personifying its addressees must be implicitly personified itself, and becomes in essence a third person instantaneously, a "he," a representation, defaced, "dead." The utterance, which brings the speaker into being, implies her representational death as its price, preceding "life" with death. Since the speaker is situated in this triadic site, every utterance, including "inner speech," is social, *external*, material, and triangulated in advance. Yet the "social" comes into existence — it is everything — at a price, since it is in this sense self-cancelling too: the first person is always also another, "dead," and communication — which is here asserted — is momentarily barred. Here the second person prepares a retort that anticipates the reading of his reading, the ceaseless mode of Iago's speech. There, multiple positions appear simultaneously rotated by a speaker (as if he were his own "reader"), and in struggling to usurp the absent position of centered speaker, a compulsory model of aggression is unleashed as the defining moment of utterance itself. There is nothing neutral about any of the three positions. Bakhtin stresses that every utterance is a "dialogic" retort to the extent that a second person is usurping or miming the first person as speaker (Iago's "service" position *vis-a-vis* Othello). This occurs though the first person or master now appears as a retro-construct of that reader in turn. It is the role of the Star Chamber to at once formalize and expose the public or collective social fiction of the *third* figure as juridical yet blind Other. Rather than exemplifying the social in the manner of Terry Eagleton, Voloshinov's model seems to perform what Baudrillard might call the "end of the social" — at least as a metaphysic or ontological reserve.

Apostrophe or prosopopeia here defines the site where social exchange shifts from an idyllic account to a deadly material structure ("All that is spoke is marr'd"). It projects a living voice onto the addressee — what was mute or dead to begin with, like a character in a script — but in bringing the first person into speech, it rewrites him as a third person, a representation. Before such violence, the "I" must dissimulate itself at the onset, as one might before a tyrannical violence or the persecution of a Stalinist censorship. Iago can suspend and defer this "death" by always inhabiting it in advance, turning the "he" into a transient "I," whereas Othello is always trapped in this model, as if projecting himself as a third person, a seamless *aesthetic* construction. Othello thus appears in his suicide speech like one who, never having learned his own "death" (which would have let him read Desdemona), is left vainly pursuing or literalizing it well after it matters. Desdemona becomes, on the other hand, a reverse Eurydice, the supposed semantic referent or addressee stalked and killed, rather than one to be retrieved from the dead by Orpheus. Othello's destruction of Desdemona, and himself, at Iago's bidding, can appear an allegory of the self-cancelling structure of Voloshinov's social utterance.

The representation of one's own voice as another's, of "I" as "he," projects the *other's word* as always an anterior trace (snow in May), and it is here worth recalling that Menippea's foremost genre is the dialogue of the "dead." In Bakhtin, the "living" word may be an oxymoron, since it implies less an immediate access to life than a trope for that language most saturated with conflictual, "dead" or anterior traces ("voices"). If the pop translation of dialogue as a communicationist model was designed to contain the otherness of Bakhtin's text, it appears to have been with good reason. Emerging only with the "death" and prosopopeia of the speaker (the "polyphonic" author), the "dialogic" scenario must appear self-cancelling in a curious sense. "Dialogue" – like Iago – is not only not what it seems (that is, is not dyadic), but is not what it is. Recurrent metaphors of self-cancellation occur in *Othello*, up to and including the suicide itself. These include the tempest's sinking of the Turkish fleet, as well as numerous tropes, like, "And by how much she strives to do him good, / She shall undo her credit" (2.3.358–9), "for honesty's a fool that loses that it works for" (3.3.382–3), "It is a monster / Begot upon itself, born on itself" (3.4.161–2), "the green-eyed monster, which doth mock the meat it feeds on," "This sorrow's heavenly; / It strikes where it doth love" (3.3.166–7), or Desdemona's final line on who killed her, "Nobody – I myself" (5.2.124).[15]

Strictly speaking, the trialogic scenario that Voloshinov sketches seems, if anything, to render the speaker virtually mute, since the utterance is addressed to one who, being personified, is not its recipient, and the person who can listen only *over*hears it as a "witness," herself shut out of the address, a silent reader of it. Instead of communication, the model might be that of one trying to hear another whose words are not quite audible or contextualizable and,

---

15 The "O" attached to many Italian names echoes as well in the near *authorial* signature of Desdemona's "Willow Song" (Will-O).

since that other is a double, not being able even to hear oneself. This structural muting is displayed in the scene where Othello *witnesses* – that is, overhears and misreads – Iago's staged exchange with Cassio. When the Speaker addresses a third person, the Listener always overhears a figure inaccessible, distanced, translated. With the imaginary ability to withhold recognition (response), the Listener seems empowered in turn over the Speaker, and is appropriated to that role in turn. Hearing Iago's exchange with Cassio about Bianca, Othello writes Desdemona in as the subject:

> *Cas.* Alas, poor rogue, I think, [i' faith], she loves me.
> *Cas.*   Alas, poor caitiff!
> *Oth.* Look how he laughs already!
> *Iago.* I never knew woman love man so.
> *Cas.* Alas, poor rogue, I think, [i' faith], she loves me.
> *Oth.* Now he denies it faintly, and laughs it out.
> *Iago.* Do you hear, Cassio?
> *Oth.*   Now he importunes him
>   To tell it o'er. Go to, well said, well said.   (4.1.108–15)

If social context is supposed to ameliorate the cycle of reading in Bakhtin, we forget that this triadic scene defines the "social" itself in his text. Giving value to words in context, the "social" accelerates the sheer "janus-faced" exteriority of word to the point of its own dispossession (as in "carnival" or before the Star Chamber).[16]

4.

As if citing Voloshinov's model, Othello's discourse often recurs to apostrophe, suggesting more than the implied animism associated with the racial motif of African descent. Not only does this occur in numerous addresses ("O now, forever / Farewell the tranquil mind! Farewell content!"), but in exclamations that all but personify the impossible non-letter "O" itself in wordless anguish ("O! O! O!"). Othello, trapped in and produced by this language, this letter's evacuating rim, has no way out of it. The use of apostrophe accelerates near the murder scene ("Let me not name it to you, you chaste stars. / It is the cause" [5.2.2–3]), where Desdemona is to pass, *unscarred*,

---

16 When the handkerchief itself is called a "thing," the pursuit of a site outside language results in figures like that of the finger *itself* – the fetish possibility of pointing or mute indication ("make me / The fixed figure of the time of scorn / To point his slow and moving finger at" [4.2.52–4]).

from life to death (*and* back). The hinted at necrophilia ("Be thus when thou art dead, and I will kill thee, / And love thee after") confuses the *monumental* form of the sleeping Desdemona with the eroticized (addressed) dead. Having Desdemona pass unmarked from life to death is presented as a *re*storation to purity ("the cause"), hence a putative return to the unmarr'd, or unwritten, from the sullied, as though the living were the dead, and one had to restore to death the living. Thus "death" proves difficult to enforce in the text. The dead keep popping up, returning to speak yet again, and the dismantling of dialogue enters a site of speaking death. This movement completes the emptying out of "word" begun in the Star Chamber. Desdemona returns to life on the bed, a prosopopeia of herself, only to lie in a reflexive accusation ("Nobody — I myself") that strips Othello not so much of guilt as *agency*. Cassio will not be killed, nor will Iago when stabbed, and Roderigo pops back to life and "spake, / After long seeming dead" (5.2.327–8), while his letters also speak *for him* after death. On the other hand, Othello has difficulty just being killed; he is twice disarmed and must stage manage his own murder, even calling his audience back into the room and (apparently) turning up with yet another secret dagger. It is almost impossible to leave the "living" province of the already (un)dead word, making the line between them tenuous and the act of suicide itself a dilemma from the point of view of language (how, indeed, does one "die" from the site of the undead?). If to die in the text (any text) does not stop one from talking, the idea of an *escape* into suicide is problem-ridden. It can only depart from the reflexive system by repeating or fulfilling it. Indeed, we might say suicide re-enacts the attempt of the undead to *return* to a nostalgic pretext of life (which is, properly, dead).

Othello's dismantling of "dialogue" moves from formal music to psychotic agrammaticality, from the "social" word of the Star Chamber to sheer apostrophe. The text proceeds even to annotate in the soliloquy the *return* now not of the other's word in circulation, but of one's own as another's, of anteriority as such ("That's he that *was* Othello"). Othello, as the other's (Venice's) effaced other, turns finally toward the sheer anteriority of the "state" signified in the letter he pretends to dictate. In his final soliloquy, the "state" as the composite trope for this deadly field of material language is as if performed before itself, witness or addressee.

One question remains before returning to the suicide as a speech act. *Othello* poses the problem of agency itself — Iago's and Othello's

– which often turns on a play on the word "cause." Presented as a war-like figure of action (the opposite, say, of Hamlet), Othello is remarkably passive, or reactive, throughout. When Iago speaks of the wars in Cyprus as what "even now *stands* in act," he links action to what may be called a stasis ("stands"), or state, that also suspends any discrete act, a figure that – as we might expect from Hamlet more succinctly – makes the "acting" of the play a metaphor for the barred passage from cognition to action itself. Thus events in the text take place almost reflexively (the Turkish fleet being sunk), and since nothing "happens" outside of Iago's manipulations, the text anatomizes where the aesthetic field of language or fiction shifts violently to the "deed." The play up to that point seems a kind of *fore*text, a plotting precedent to any event, to the text itself as an event, something that "*fore*does" calamity (5.1.129). Indeed, Iago could be plotting a piece of writing, a play called "Othello." On the other hand, the murder is enacted almost as a non-event, the merest withholding of breath without "scar," becoming retro-actively *the* act in every consequent sense ("Thou hast done a deed – " [5.2.164]). That the "act" is also given a sexual meaning, in Emilia's and Desdemona's banter ("That she with Cassio hath the act of shame"), links the name Othello both to the Greek verb *ethelo*, for will or desire to have happen (to it) – a verb which Heidegger tells us is itself reflexive ("to allow something *reference* back to itself") – and to Blake's use of the verb-name in the *Book of Thel* to mark a transition from a virgin Mallarméan possibility into the violating choice of writing.[17] Cassio's name gives the logic of "place" a further twist, due to the circulation of variants on the word *cast* – to fix, throw, dismiss, contain, fall, chance – all of which are woven into the dialogue. Mocked by Iago as "a great arithmetician" (1.1.19), Cassio is first called a "*counter*-caster," a bookish calculator, whose discourse occurs at a point where language seems formalized.[18] Thus Cassio is connected to a series of "cast"

17 In his essay on Heraclitus' *logos*, Heidegger notes that "*ethelo*, does not mean 'to want,' but rather 'to be ready of itself for ...'; *ethelo* does not mean merely to demand something, but rather to allow something a reference back to itself" in *Early Greek Thinking*, trans. D. Krell and F. Capuzzi (New York: Harper and Row, 1975), 73. Shakespeare's choice of this name implies the reflexive agency that puts the circularity of the sign itself in the foreground, inscribing Othello as already the reactive product of a site of exchange.

18 This foray into *numbering* comes apart when the Duke reads the letters reporting the Turkish fleet. Though all disagree on the numbers, the "main article"

words which, like the term "cause," also suggest enclosure, falling, and chance.[19] Cassio inadvertently usurps the "place" of Othello, first as Iago's fiction, and ultimately as fact when he is appointed commander, a concretized figure of chance who undoes Iago's plotting by surviving *with his severed leg* – a term or figure that echoes the materiality of language, legacy, reading itself (*legere*), and which here is separated, dismembered, and cut off.[20] Thus the word "cause" careens through the text, moving behind these terms, oscillating in sense from cause as figural origin to a proleptic principle one *follows* ("Let me not name it to you, you chaste stars. / It is the cause" [5.2.2–3]), and in the process reverses the temporal flow of agency. The trajectory of "cause" seems to bracket the logic of causality as such, a suspension Bakhtin says is Dostoyevsky's nihilistic "criterion" for distinguishing the essential from the inessential: "there is no causality in Dostoyevsky's novels, no genesis, no explanations based on the past, on the influences of the environment or of upbringing, and so forth" (*Problems*, 29).[21] Rather than contrast the Moor as man of action to the undecidable Hamlet, *Othello* can recall the Mallarméan reading of Hamlet with Desdemona's murder becoming a figure of violating ideal possibility.

Yet what use is this suspension of "causality" to the reading of Bakhtin – where the state of aesthetic possibility, rather than preceding action as such, appears in the sheer double-sidedness of "carnival" as the reign of reversible external signs? Can we read the

---

of an assault comes through ("as in these cases where the aim reports / 'Tis oft with difference" [1.3.6–7]). This moving behind number is connected with "cases" that allow for difference, a threatening truth that accords with no formalization, made apparent through varying combinations.

19 Variations on the word "cast" are particularly insistent, from Cassio and his being called a "counter-caster" (1.1.31), to his being "cashiered" (1.1.48), to "Cannot with safety cast him" (1.1.149), to "these cases where the aim reports" (1.3.6), "Seems to cast water on the burning Bear" (2.1.14), "Our general cast" (1.3.14), "You are now cast in his mood" (2.3.273), "hath cashiered Cassio" (2.3.375), "Your case is better" (4.1.69), and "whereon it came / That I was cast" (4.2.323).

20 See my treatment of the severed foot in Poe's "Cask of Amontillado" in chapter 5.

21 The suspension of causality that is the reverse side of Iago's motivating every occurrence, recalls the criterion Bakhtin asserts for Dostoyevsky's "principle of simultaneity" in *Problems in Dostoyevsky's Poetics*, trans. C. Emerson (Minneapolis: Minnesota University Press, 1984), hereafter cited as *PDP*: "almost a criterion for distinguishing the essential from the nonessential" (29).

soliloquy, then, as Othello's attempt to supercede the traps of "dialogue" identified with Iago, and to do so by using that technology against itself – a suicide of (and by) language?

5.

How can Othello's final soliloquy, then, attempt to move outside of or beyond the suspended temporality of Voloshinov's logic of the sign? What in the speech absorbs, repeats, or turns against language as dialogos? *Who* speaks the soliloquy – and from where?

Ned Lukacher, in "Anamorphic Stuff: Shakespeare, Catharsis, Lacan," argues that Shakespeare's concern with language's materiality ("stuff") makes his text radically anticathartic, lacking, as it does, any space outside. Lukacher states: "It is as though Shakespeare must deny both himself and his audience the aesthetic pleasure of cathartic identification and purification. It is as though Shakespeare discovers through anamorphosis an anticathartic aesthetic that insists upon displacing the role of catharsis, upon performing a catharsis of catharsis" (878). Such a blockage of catharsis as an economy of expulsion, healing, or ecstasy, is consistent with an "inter-territorial" word that cannot move from inside ("inner speech") to out, since it is always already external ("a theatre without outside"). While Othello projects a logic of self-manifestation ("My parts, my title, and my perfect soul / Shall manifest me rightly" [1.2.31–2]), his "recognition" scene operates, in fact, as a reverse spectacle without true other or audience, and Lodovico's cited exclamation ("O bloody period!") acknowledges the multiple carnage of this circular system. When Gratiano says of the deathbed scene, "The object poisons sight. Let it be hid," he draws the curtain, again, before what Kristeva would call an *abject* system that "poisons" – that is, it both produces and inverts or confutes – sight (reading) or the eye ("I") itself. There is no coming to light in Othello's unravelling of Iago's plot, in the way that the image of self-consciousness seems to attend Oedipus' blinding. The murder of Desdemona is called a putting out of a "light" which was, in a sense, never in play in Othello's *figural* blackness, and which, like a psychosis, may be said to precede metaphor itself. Othello is caught in the dilemma of demanding others speak of him as he is ("as I am"), which becomes what he seemed. When Othello has smothered Desdemona, the inner chamber is depicted as an outside ("Look in upon me then and speak with me" [5.2.257]), while the outside or next room is called by the text "Within": "Come, guard the door without" (5.2.241). Othello's inability to remain alone occurs in what might be termed an anamorphic space, an inner exterior (or the reverse) without any outside. What *Othello* dismantles is any possible model of interiority. Citing itself, the suicidal speaker recedes as a perpetual citation of a citation, quietly assuming the discourse of the then silenced Iago.

The closing scene shifts the concept of "circularity" from the social as "other's word" to the return of the "dead word" – or pure anteriority – that Voloshinov narrates and conceals in the genealogical allegory of formalism in *Marxism*. The "other's word" (*chuzoe slovo*) becomes doubly elusive, since it never was the immediate access to any other person. Rather, the trialogic word was always also passed through citation, the mnemonic trace echoed in the epic's "absolute past." Bakhtin's "word" begins in an apostrophe that is always also an encounter with a received or "dead" word. This, of course, duplicates the relation of the actor to the script. To say that Shakespeare's text reads its own status or even muteness as script is not surprising (he indicates it frequently, as in Lodovico's exclamation). In Othello's last scene, the "inter-territorial" word passes from social circulation to one in which the "I" (Othello) surveys the (eternal) return of anterior traces, the simulacra of his image. The various circular figures in the text seem to convene and break in the soliloquy. Not only does the speech have a peculiarly Nietzschean moment first remarked on by T. S. Eliot, but it reminds us where the same must be said of Bakhtin's text. The "janus-faced" word that begins by relying on social value and proceeds to empty that ends by putting the value of values itself in question – one implication of "carnival" that is frequently skirted. The nihilism implied in the emptying of Othello's identity, or of Bakhtin's "word" by extension, can be read, on the whole, as a transvaluative project.[22] It is this I want now to examine.

The line, "That's he that was Othello; Here I am," for instance, differentiates the anterior "he" ("was") from the "I (am)" that "now" claims it. That there is no representation possible for Othello's anguish or dilemma, for his anamorphic and exitless trap, makes even the status

---

22 Properly speaking, the place to read this narration of a field that suspends narrative would be in the essay on "chronotopes," where it is not entirely successful. As for values, the connection to the *Genealogy of Morals* is palpable.

(or "state") of suicide questionable; what functions as a perfect aesthetic image (tragic recognition, recuperation), must be simultaneously disowned as simulation. Incarnating this break, the tragic impossibility of tragedy or catharsis, seems to be one culmination of the play. The more the Othello-image of the soliloquy appears successful when presented before the ideal eye of "the state," the more remote and disowning becomes its speaker. "Othello," at this point, cannot stop the machinal doubling familiar in Iago's discourse from asserting itself. Like another giant tragic warrior, Ajax, "tragedy" is short-circuited since what would elsewhere signal a tragic *ek*stasis of consciousness from itself is linguistically undercut by the sheer exteriority of the figure. Death here names an escape from consciousness of "death" (that is, language), escaping another death (the present) into a merely literal erasure ("in my sense, 'tis happiness to die" [5.2.290]). Such would restitute an aesthetic image ("Speak of me as I am") before a hypothetical "state" deprived of the power to act (the Signiory). Given the chiasmus-like return to "life" (death) from undeath (life) involved, we might say that *suicide* for Othello is an indifferent trope by which he seeks to name the chiasmic inversion that has produced his interpretive dilemma. Though an interesting piece of performance art, the Othello-speaker seems to require help even in sustaining the desired interpretation ("nothing extenuate / Nor set down aught in malice"):

> *Oth.* Soft you, a word or two before you go.
> I have done the state some service, and they know't.
> No more of that. I pray you, in your letters,
> When you shall these unlucky deeds relate,
> Speak of me as I am; nothing extenuate,
> Nor set down aught in malice. Then must you speak
> Of one that lov'd not wisely, but too well;
> Of one not easily jealous, but, being wrought,
> Perplexed in the extreme; of one whose hand,
> (Like the base Indian), threw a pearl away
> Richer than all his tribe; of one whose subdu'd eyes,
> Albeit unused to the melting mood,
> Drops tears as fast as the Arabian trees
> Their med'cinable gum. Set you down this;
> And say besides, that in Aleppo once,
> Where a malignant and a turban'd Turk
> Beat a Venetian and traduc'd the state,
> I took by th' throat the circumcised dog
> And smote him – thus.   [*He stabs himself.*]   (5.2.338–356)

If the auditors comment on the materiality of the speech, it is because that speech's aesthetic spell separates it from its speaker. It moves through address, narrative, recuperation, partition, and execution — terminating the language machine "Othello." What is often disregarded is that "Othello," the "I" of the soliloquy, may be without specific locus since in doubling himself, he is become "like" Iago, no one, a cyborg. What Othello would escape is the inescapability of the state of representation, the sign, death, or "life" — that is, the "state" which is the hypothetical reader and agent (through Othello's hand) of (self) execution, "traduced" by the turban'd Turk. This irony must be edited from Lodovico's exclamation. Like a recording, Othello seems to stammer a logic of replication that must begin again and again by asserting a spurious unity ("Then must you speak / Of one ...," "Of one ...," "of one ...," "of one ... "). In circular fashion, Othello may desire to project becoming with the stamp of "being" ("as I am") — yet finds instead of circularity the irreducibly mute character-letter "O." The speech accelerates the triadic model of "dialogue" to a permanently rotating, exponentially duplicating structure without set positions ("Othello," "I," spectators, "turban'd Turk," "the state," Iago, Desdemona, each act as surrogates, speakers, readers, witnesses, and agents). What "Othello" rightly wants to suicide (to use Artaud's active verb in writing of Van Gogh) is the hermeneutic reading of "dialogue" that had entrapped him to begin with, and which his murder of Desdemona represented, yet which he must literally die with, thereby invoking again. In one sense, suicide is less an escape from than an endorsement of that system in which Othello was entrapped, itself made arbitrary and stripped of pathos.

Iago has at this point withdrawn from discourse: "What you know, you know. From this time forth, I never will speak word" (5.2.303–4). To never more speak "word" — notice, he does not say "*a word*" — recalls the construction of Bakhtin's Russian text, where *word* circulates without an article and appears as a person or "hero." Iago's withdrawal is not a matter of leaving the theatrical space free for Othello to return to his true self — it is all too obvious that he remains mutely present, watching. His withdrawal represents a further foreclosure, since Othello now also takes up the place of Iago outside of his (Othello's) own discourse. Othello is at once in and out, passing back and forth with no other, his own double. As a position, Iago is beyond the pseudo-pathos of death, a remainder, without "cause," as the promise of incommensurable tortures hopelessly recalls. Othello's suicide conceals the model it repeats: Desdemona's lie of self murder ("Nobody – I myself"). The soliloquy returns less to the Moor's identity than to an image of it, spoken through Iago's language-power, then turned against the latter's earlier disavowal of suicide to Roderigo (Othello as the "circumcised dog" reverses Iago's, "Drown thyself? Drown cats and blind puppies!" [1.3.335–6]). The "tragedy" of Othello's closing lines – its inability to be tragic – is inseparable from its permanent irony, passing through multiple positions and belonging to none, caught in the voiding circle of a repetition without cognition, "O," consciousness here being (deathful and deathlessly) "*of o*ne" that is another. What seems most elusive, and most banal, is Othello's literal death, indeed Lodovico and Gratiano at first do not grant it status.

The music of Othello's language seems inseparable from its aesthetic formalism, the constructed mosaic of doubly borrowed discourse. It invokes the "I" of the state against Othello the traducer – and translator – the "malignant and ... turban'd Turk," or Ott*o*mite. In speaking to or for and wanting to execute on behalf of the "state," Othello positions his "I" in the most anonymous and lethal site. Speaking with the determination of the Law for unity ("of one," "in Allepo once"), he still seems oblivious to the duplicitous and dispersed identity of the "state," which he borrows the name of. Thus the opening, "Soft you, a word *or two* ..." announces a doubling against a borrowed "official" image that returns us to the *bovarysme* of the wooing scene. The triadic scenario of "dialogue" operates in reverse, a virus Shakespeare wantonly injects into the verbal order. The first person now addresses a third (himself) before a second (the state), that in turn is an addressee, rotating to (simultaneous) counter-positions as the first speaker, identifying with the second, enacts the murder of the first person as third (the "turban'd Turk"). What should be a routine aesthetic act (the model of "all that's spoke") is "marr'd," and impossible to contain. What is disfigured in the black face of Othello is that the origin of speech in the speaker's representational death is here re-staged as (mere) literal suicide – as Othello, in one sense, misreads what is demanded of him, and literalizes another's death. That death is left open to interpretation as either the most controlled and predictable moment of the machine-like "state," or Othello's effort to elude that by miming the same ineluctable movement – options that are indistinguishable. One can wonder if what the play might have taught Othello – the shallow nature of his interpretive system, his lack of sovereignty, and the reversible play of sign structures — is here wasted by his return not to past or true nobility, but to the stupid literalizing tendencies of his former way of reading, used to trigger the dagger thrust (as editors tend to fill in the missing agency of his demise). The empty demand, "Speak of me as I am," grafts a now positionless "I" onto "one" whose anterior image still has currency (Lodovico: "he was great of heart"). The very picture of the constructed subject, "Othello" *is* none, and at any point could utter with Iago "I am not what I am," a fact we are distracted from by the speech's music and spell. As one could say of any author, there is no "Othello" ("That's he that was Othello"), but a "he" that simulates "I" at every point it states itself. Self-hatred covers hatred of the misprision of taking an aesthetic construct ("Othello") for a self, one that, defined as identity and "occupation" rather than dialogic self-difference, now appears to be stupid ("O fool! Fool! Fool!"). He is stupid, of course, for responding with hermeneutic and reactive violence to figurative shifts ("Sir, she can turn, and turn, and yet go on / And turn again" [4.1.253–4]).

To return to the opening discussion, Lodovico remarks not only where the aesthetic (Othello's narrative) veers into bloody death, or fiction into deadly fact. This, after all, is the topic of the play. It notes where Othello's "death" cannot be confirmed altogether and where the "soliloquy" is a scripted text spoken by an actor, even in the play. Among other things, the "tragedy" of *Othello* is to permanently oscillate between the black or white interpretive extremes outlined earlier, as between grotesque bathos and a too noble (if too late) suicide; a spectacle that also "poisons" sight or readability. The death that appears to escape from this system is also a discontinuous metaphor that only confirms and repeats it. Othello, a mercenary of this *state*, being double, is condemned to stammer out its law — "of one," "of one," "of one" — like a broken record, a law it itself discredits.

Shakespeare's reading of Bakhtin turns out to be that of Bakhtin himself, albeit one suppressed by the pieties of translators' evasions. This reading would elaborate a positional, duplicitous, and anamorphic concept of "dialogue," in which the triadic structure of the "social" is defined as a deadly battle for mastery (subject construction) and entrapment (of a lethal Other) based on mimicry and usurpation; one in which the death preceding dialogue dictates, now, the death of the ideology of dialogue that is its contemporary evasion. In fact, this thoroughly materialist and even pragmatic view of language dismantles many of the idealist premises that Bakhtin's translators ironically restore and reminds us, again, that "dialogue" as double-talk extends to Bakhtin's style. If we read Iago's plotting against Othello as mere resentment before the latter's power, we overlook where the Moor never represented a sovereign subject to begin with, or where that illusion is itself an *aesthetic* image based on surrogacy. In this scenario the "self" is a retro-discursive effect based on the ceaseless return of the anterior moment, trace, mark, letter, or other's word. The reading of Othello's soliloquy outlined here – which could now be a called Bakhtinian – would argue in the text for the disputed word "Indian" over "Judaean," since the speech disbands any claim to *in*wardness as other than the considerable pathos of its lack.

If T. S. Eliot was correct in reading Othello's soliloquy as a sort of Nietzschean posture ("Shakespeare and the Stoicism of Seneca"), this suggests something different from the deluded pathos and escapism Eliot attributes to Nietzsche. Rather, the insight might well hold because the soliloquy stages itself before an (eternal) recurrence of anterior figures – a "nihilism" that might be called, with all sorts of additional discriminations, Bakhtinian. One might extend this Shakespearean or Nietzschean reading now to Bakhtin's "dialogue" itself, the reading most likely to have been suppressed by Bakhtin's American, slavicist explicators in the 80s. Bakhtin appears less as a new methodology than as a transvaluative and destructively parasitical text, one whose interaction with inherited concepts could be called intentionally ruinous (as in Kristeva's phrase, "the ruin of a poetic"). Bakhtin's own terms – sign, history, dialogue, the social – must now, in the 90s, be read as the radical emptying and alteration of the conceptual fields they appear to name. Yet this scrupulously "social" or triadic reading of *dialogue* has in fact been the model Bakhtin used throughout his analysis of Dostoyevsky. These texts display a conception of dialogue more in line with C. Auguste Dupin than Martin Buber, Gadamer or even Heidegger. The black face of Othello already announces this field of play.

I return to one final question. A good deal rides on how we read "ideology" or "value" in Voloshinov. Situated socially, Voloshinov's deployment of the term "value" as the semantic desideratum in language linked to ideology is an example of the stylistic duplicity that the "pseudonyms" already announce. Since it simultaneously involves a reversal of the familiar concept, rather than yielding a "science of ideologies" Voloshinov's text can be shown to undertake an unmarked reading of Nietzsche's *Genealogy* — itself echoed in several arguments (the discussion, say, of the priest's word). As seems explicit in the figure of "carnival," the two-sided word depends on "value" (judgment and retort) for its semantic import, yet by implying its opposite it puts the value of values in question: a "two-sided" reversibility we have already witnessed in the Star Chamber scene (and it is worth noting that the Signiory is no more "cynical" than it is matter of fact and joyous when displaying this pragmatism). While perhaps not desirable, it is possible to read Voloshinov as a failed Nietzschean reading of Marx's *German Ideology* with the latter's definition of language as "practical consciousness." He would be projecting less a marxist "science of ideologies" that is supposedly descriptive, than a foray into that *aesthetic ideology* which marks his own linguistic materialism — a reading of Bakhtin as a post-marxist. As such it would be an attempt that is sacrificed, like Othello in his suicide, in a uniquely fertile if indecisive soliloquy on verbal and historical difference (Bakhtin's seemingly endless and often shapeless writings). Reading "dialogue" through *Othello* reminds us that Bakhtin's "laughter" is indeed untragic and entails, in many respects, a ruse. The dilemma for Bakhtin's readers today is, of course, complicated by our need to recover his alterity from our own reading habits, where the mechanics of "re(*dis*)covery" itself are deceptive. That the ideology of dialogue is today floundering, or dead, does not mean it will not come back to life — perhaps as a triadic and materialist model of agonistic defacement and ideology critique? — and may indicate less the weakness of Bakhtin's own rhetoric than its effectiveness. That is, if part of his role had been that of conceptual saboteur. Bakhtinian writing may be said to appropriate and dismantle "official" philosophic vocabulary, much as Henry Louis Gates Jr. says *black* "signifyin(g)" works against and within the discourse of the master terms — utilizing rhetorical doubleness to undo semantic "signification," yet all the time unable to mark this difference outwardly by any change in the word itself. Hence the uncanny pseudo-familiarity of terms like "dialogue" or "novel" or "ideology," and so on. Like Othello, the "word" of Bakhtin or Voloshinov may be black within a "white" discourse, disguised by the formal music of the text. Shakespeare's anamorphic logic reminds us of the snare (Iago's "web") that reading Bakhtin either mimetically, sequentially, or within the fiction of his historical authorship still entails – and what a more materialist conception of his "word" implies. For Bakhtin, even the term "dialogue" must be read suspiciously, that is, dialogically, as strategically ensconcing double talk. One way that the term can be redescribed today is as (a strategy of) defacement, so clear in Bakhtin's own example of Stavrogin in the last chapter of the *Dostoyevsky* book (called, summarily, "Dialogue in Dostoyevsky"). Another is through the problem of another's word – which is always also to say, the past or dead word.[23] As such, it may and perhaps must be rethought today through the implications that the term "inscription" provides. As a material figure of anteriority that occupies a site of a thing-like facticity, the term evacuates any pretext to immediacy, inter-subjectivity, or humanist "self and other." It returns us, on the contrary, to a historical site where the speaker itself emerges apostrophically.

23 In the text from *The Possessed* cited in the *Dostoyevsky* book, Stavrogin and Tikhon circle Stavrogin's confession ("If someone forgave you this (he pointed to the sheets)" [264]), that is, a written text between them. Tikhon suggests giving it to a nameless reader ("a stranger, a man you'll never know"), while Stavrogin attempts to maneuver Tikhon into playing the role of confessor in order to entrap or humiliate the latter, so he would lose his power to "forgive" (and hence reverse roles). Stavrogin, anticipating the latter's withdrawal, tries to coerce him a second time ("If you forgave me, it would be much easier"), to which Tikhon responds by reversing the tables again ("if you forgive me too"). This metatextual dialogue is twice removed from any immediacy, since in the "confession," of course, a text is circled in advance of any reading of it, as if "dialogue" were always the preliminary maneuvering before a blind in-scription. The very text meant to exemplify "dialogue in Dostoyevsky" turns around strategies of inscription and disinscription. See *PDP*, 264–6.

P.s.: Plato's scene of reading in the *Protagoras*

For Detienne and Vernant Plato is the original author of that Platonism which has never "ceased to haunt the metaphysical thought of the West." Perhaps there is such a Plato – the "terminal" Plato, as he is called, of the later writings. But traditional metaphysics begins when certain strands of Platonism are abstracted from Plato's works as a whole (for example by Aristotle, the first major (mis)reader of Plato) and the counter-discourse of his irony is ignored. Only recently have certain critics begun to correct the metaphysical reading and prepare the way for a reassessment of Plato's thought. This "other" Plato requires *a critical and perhaps even literary analysis* of the dynamics – the *metis* – implicit in so many of his early and middle works ... One may even wonder if Plato himself was not a philologist in this Nietzschean sense: a reader, interrogator, and transvaluator of the Greek World.   Robert Pogue Harrison, "The Ambiguities of Philology"

Description, it appears, was a device to conceal inscription.
Paul de Man, "Hypogram and Inscription"

How does the model of dialogue previously developed – that is, of dialogue as a dissimulative agon, triadic in structure and essentially anamorphic, turning on the inscription of empowered traces – work in the most pivotal of dialogic writings, Plato's? How, moreover, does it intervene in the received iconography of Plato as the father of metaphysics, or help address the "'other' Plato" mentioned above by Robert Pogue Harrison? If the very idea of a reversal of Plato is itself a firm part of modernism's notion of itself, would any shift in reading this production not intervene in a wide series of constructions and meet with institutional resistance – not only from the traditionalists but from those invested in the notion that there has all along been this paternal, "terminal" Plato to overthrow? Michel Foucault addresses the puzzle of Plato's role in our construction of modernity, in a review of Deleuze's *Logique du Sens*, when he asks: "Are all philosophies individual species of the genus 'anti-Platonic'? Does each begin with a declaration of this fundamental rejection? Can they be grouped around this desired and detestable center? ... Plato, then, is the excessive and deficient father."[1] Does this paternity not seem, now, a trifle too Oedipal, too centered, *too* familiar – too much of a useful icon? What if Platonic metaphysics were itself a *mis*reading, calculable as such?

In the following discussion, I will limit myself to a fairly isolated problem in the "early and middle works," which Harrison recommends as the texts we must return to. It concerns the representation of Protagoras, the great sophist presented in the dialogue of that name (later resurrected and caricatured by Socrates in the *Theaetetus*) and associated commonly with relativism, humanism, and pragmatism through his famous text on the *metron* ("Man is the measure of all things ... "). In brief, I want to ask whether what seems perhaps the surest drawn of Plato's dramatis personae does not conceal, in fact, a position less that of a historical character than of a *figure* of material language in Plato? A figure that raises questions about an "other" Plato in general that leads directly to a crisis of reading in this text and beyond.

1. Plato's web

Protagoras is not routinely considered enigmatic as a character in Plato. If anything, he has seemed too precisely sketched, too concrete, too life-like – as if the sheer powers of descriptive writing, of mimesis itself in Plato, were part of the text's aesthetic preoccupations. Willamowitz goes so far as to accept his near historical accuracy in the *Protagoras* (despite the scene of the dialogue preceding Plato's birth), and others assume the character Protagoras' mythos of world origins in the dialogue is taken directly from the historical figure. The latter is, by some accounts, the first myth or narrative presented in Plato's writing – a transitional moment in the production, on which device all of "middle Plato" may depend. And yet it is itself deemed rather flat and didactic, decidedly unplatonic. In general, the sophist appears as

---

1 Michel Foucault, "*Theatrum Philosophicum*," trans. D. Bouchard and S. Simon in *Language, Counter-Memory, Practice* (Ithaca: Cornell University Press), 168. See also Robert Pogue Harrison, "The Ambiguities of Philology," *Diacritics* (Summer, 1986) 14–21. Throughout this essay I will mostly use the translation of Plato's *Protagoras* by W. K. C. Guthrie, *Protagoras and Meno* (New York: Penguin, 1956) with occasional modifications, *Platonis Protagoras*, ed. J. Adam and A. M. Adam (Cambridge University Press, 1968), and texts in *The Collected Dialogues*, ed. E. Hamilton and H. Cairns (Princeton: Bollingen, 1961).

a smart, if relatively banal or "commonsense" figure dueling with Socrates before the circle of Athenians. Less obvious, perhaps, is how that audience itself comprises in this scenario a public *Other* given the empowered social role of judging the "outcome" of a contest. The dialogue is routinely valued for its "literary" qualities, and is otherwise considered philosophically slight and even marginal – neither belonging, as is said, to the aporetic or early Socratic dialogues nor to the middle "constructive" philosophy of Plato in the usual taxonomy. The pretext of the public encounter is the teachability of *arete* ("virtue"), and a sort of strategic verbal combat proceeds that increasingly (if covertly) appears as double talk before the audience – that circle of Athenians who implicitly confer the power of truth. Less obviously, the group in Kallias' courtyard seem invested with the power to silence, and worse, to kill – a fact echoed in covert references to Socrates' own death. The implicit specular opposition that the two agonists more or less assume is further complicated by the manner in which the sophist must both screen himself and solicit a following from the public audience. This is routinely overlooked in commentary and becomes, in the course of the dialogue's account, difficult to frame. There is little wonder, then, that the "conversation" breaks down repeatedly at its center, or that it seems in its progression never quite to "begin," or tries to "begin" again and again until its end. The text also seems to virtually fall through every representative *genre* of discourse – a technical meltdown within and of "dialogue" itself generally unnoticed by commentators, who tend to focus on colorful "historical" personalities and the devious plays on logic. There seems, then, a sort of reflexive crisis within the *Protagoras* that is screened by the descriptive brilliance and sheer banality of the arguments.

The *Protagoras* enjoys an odd reputation – odd, let us say, in the sense of *atopos*, place-less or uncanny, a term first used by and of Socrates in the opening (309b). What one commentator has called Socrates' "hedonist calculus" at the end, when he equates pleasure with the good, a "crack in the 'unity' of Plato" (Raven), might almost be applied to the whole dialogue. What occurs seems at times to function as a metatext in which "dialogue" itself is revised from the usual hermeneutic model of ironic pedagogy or the "fused horizons" of understanding (Gadamer) to an agonistic encounter of violent dissimulation and social usurpation more Nietzschean than "Platonic." This *atopos* dimension extends further. On the one hand, the text is celebrated as Plato's most masterful *mimetic* writing, a "dramatic masterpiece" in which Protagoras himself is treated like a historical personage, and where "Socrates" seems so unscrupulous and even nasty at times that some assume such a *de*idealized portrait must present the real thing. Guthrie speaks of "one feature of the *Protagoras* which cannot fail to puzzle, if not exasperate, a reader: the behaviour of Socrates" (18). Indeed, here Socrates seems marked by *difference* from his usual portrait, appearing *in extremis*, brilliantly manipulative yet malicious.[2] The mimetic spell cast by the writing draws commentators toward a sort of abject literalism. As Harry Berger Jr. notes in his often challenging reading of the text in "Facing Sophists," "commentators often write as if they are eye-witness reporters" at a sports event rather than readers of a text:

The (*Protagoras*) is one of Plato's more engaging dramatic performances. In fact it is so much like a sporting event or a show that commentators often write as if they are eye-witness reporters giving us their views and reviews of the event. The debate is divided up into a number of rounds differing in length and character. The nominal topic is *arete*, which can mean excellence, power, skill, or virtue, and in fact one of the points in dispute is whether it is to be conceived primarily in technical or ethical terms; whether it is teachable the way knowledge as know-how is teachable, or the way knowledge as wisdom is teachable. But this topic keeps turning new facets toward us as the debate proceeds ... Later, after a long and hilarious parody of literary interpretation, Protagoras claims courage differs more than the others, and is not a virtue at all. Socrates brings him to his knees with a complicated set of moves, including a much disputed defense of the hedonist position that pleasure and pain are the criteria of good and evil, and that *arete* is a form of

---

2 Gregory Vlastos agrees: "(Socrates) is not a wholly attractive figure in this dialogue. His irony ... seems clumsy, heavy-handed here. His fulsome compliments to Protagoras, continued after they have lost all semblance of plausibility, become a bore. In his exegesis of the poet he turns into a practical joker, almost a clown ... [It is] a labored one-man charade, throwing in some philosophical edification on the side, as when he drags in (by a misplaced comma) his doctrine that no man sins voluntarily" (*Protagoras*, trans. B. Jowett and M. Ostwald, preface by G. Vlastos [Indianapolis: Bobbs-Merrill, 1956], xxiv). Whatever makes the *Protagoras* break down the pretext of "dialogue," it is often situated oddly in the narrative accounts of Plato's production. That narrative routinely contains three phases: the aporetic or "Socratic" dialogues, a middle or "constructive" Platonic phase – with Socrates as mouth-piece – and the "terminal" Plato. The problem is that the *Protagoras* will often be presented, as by J. R. Raven's *Plato's Thought in the Making*, at or as a fold between the early, "Socratic" or aporetic writings and the middle "Platonic" phase. It is neither, but itself in passage between two scriptive epochs – a kind of *fore*text to the advent of "Plato," or metaphysics.

knowledge, the knowledge underlying an art of measurement that enables you to maximize pleasure and minimize pain. He then returns to argue that since courage is concerned with the expectation of evil or pain, in particular with knowing which evils are to be feared and which to be faced, it must be a form of virtue. (69)

Thus the spell of the text, like the charisma of Protagoras, involves that cast by the seductions of mimetic writing itself. Not only does a certain specular doubling appear to occur between the elder sophist and the younger Socrates, but it is expressed through recurrent strategies of entrapment or what Berger interestingly calls "saving face."[3] At the end, Socrates apparently wins the contest by compelling Protagoras to exchange positions with him, yet he does so by arguing for the teachability of *arete*, thus assuming the sophist's original position and forcing Protagoras to appear to take his. Socrates publicly "wins" due to a series of dubious logical shifts, we might say, by becoming more Protagorean than Protagoras (thus losing?). Yet at this point another "voice" is brought into play. One which draws attention to a problem thematized throughout – that of having a voice, or one's own *phonen* at all, as Socrates complains after what Berger calls the "parody of literary interpretation." What is here given a voice, however, seems to be language itself, what is called the *exodos ton logon* – "the outcome (or outside) of the words, the arguments, the *logoi*." What we may not notice is that, aside from identifying language as an exterior figure (*exodos*), any text that can give discourse a "voice" also marks where speaking characters may behave or be like words in turn. Socrates' almost mad prosopopeia of this "outcome" does not say much, but rather points, deictically. This double prosopopeia (by and of speech) supersedes and precedes speech by pointing a mocking finger of blame, even castigating the mock-specular combatants for having reversed positions: "It seems to me that the preset outcome of our words is pointing at us, like a human adversary, the finger of accusation and scorn. If it had a voice (*phonen*) it would say: 'What an absurd pair you are, Socrates and Protagoras'" (361a). An absurd pair (*atopos*), P and S, Protagoras (or Plato) and

---

3 The doubling between Socrates and Protagoras is reflected in various binaries – that Socrates teaches outdoors, Protagoras within; that Socrates accepts no payment, that Protagoras does; or, in the text, that Protagoras argues for the teachability of *arete*, Socrates against, and so on. It may not be arbitrary that apocryphally or otherwise the same sort of death by public trial is attributed to Protagoras as Socrates.

Socrates – always imbricated in each other's positions at the behest of some chiasmic principle in language itself! Because Socrates stages this reversal he is praised as he decamps, claiming another appointment elsewhere, which he had earlier reminded us of while calling himself a new "Prometheus" (a character *in* Protagoras' myth). Nonetheless, the opening demonstrates that what has or has not occurred here, at a spot just *before* the text's own first exchange, is far from clear. For in that opening Socrates sits down, as if himself an old man suddenly, in the place not of his nameless interrogator, but of the anonymous companion's *slave*. (Whatever it means to "speak" from the invisible seat of the material servant or slave, there is an entire semiotics for the uses of slaves in Plato.)

I have withheld engaging in the actual arguments to draw attention to formal elements that are often lost in reading this text. One thing that goes unremarked is that the public or social space of the *agora* that assures the *mise en scene* dramatic color and stability – next in this only to the *Symposium* – appears nonetheless reflected into a different form of exteriority associated with language, and reading itself. The *Protagoras* seems possible to call Plato's dialogue *of dialogue*, not only as a reflexive text about social discourse as combat and strategies of entrapment that appear staged in a persecuted space before an empowered community, but also as one whose exchanges seem repeatedly broken off and which before being half-way through *falls* virtually through all discursive genres to the point of putting genre itself (or merely "dialogue") in question. The movement is almost too symmetrical to miss, moving from long to short, and hedged with distracting images of muting and silencing all along. These include the peculiar trope of Prodicus, whose booming voice makes it impossible for Socrates to hear what he is saying, but also the silencing and dispossession performed by the assembly itself who expel talkative members (demanding "not only death but alienation of property and in a word the ruin of their estates" [325 b–c]). I am alluding to a movement that readers nonetheless routinely fail to note, a virtual "China syndrome" meltdown of discursive forms from the long set pieces – *mythos* and logos, elenchus or epideixis – through dialogue, dialectics, question and answer, *anti-logos legein*, or eristics, down to explicit reference to the pithy utterances of the seven sages and the *inscriptions* at Delphi ("inscribing those words which are on everyone's lips: 'Know thyself' and 'Nothing too much'" [343a]). Moreover, after a total breakdown, it moves beyond that to the citation of one poetic text in turn citing another. One casualty of this fall through and subsequent suspension of "genre," however, may be any genre-based rule or law for interpreting this hyperbolic dialogue itself. The frames of narration and double-talk seem impossible to keep in place before the odd mimetic and specular spell of the performance – a spell attributed, in Kallias' house, to Protagoras' Orpheus-like voice.

What must be added here is that, as the most social and mimetically persuasive writing in Plato, the *Protagoras* also creates a space in which the official dialogue – that between the two protagonists, Socrates and Protagoras – appears structurally staged before the unknowing third "Other" that the social group represents. A rift opens in the strategic utterances of the two, possible to read as at once direct argumentation (consistent with social expectation) and sheer duplicity (knowing strategies calculating the other's duplicity as well). This creates what might be called a crypt in the "public" space of the agora itself, one in which the exteriority of the writing itself operates to create yet an "other" textual *mise en scene* that leads us to the central reading scene itself.[4] This structurally creates a double space in the "dialogue" in which *each* protagonist reads the other's dissimulations, unable to expose them without disempowering his own pretense of authority before the socius.

2. Screens of the sophist

If Socrates' account of the entry into Kallias' courtyard is typical of the text's literary and descriptive power, there is a catch in the fact that he repeatedly compares himself to Odysseus in a Homeric *katabasis* into Hades. Here an intertextual dimension is marked and suspended at once:

When we were inside, we came upon Protagoras walking in the portico, and walking with him in a long line were, on one side Kallias son of Hipponicus, his step-brother Paralus the son of Pericles, and Charmides son of Glaucon, and on the other side Pericles' other son Xanthippus, Philippides son of Philomelus, and Antimoerus of Mende, the most eminent of Protagoras' pupils ... As I looked at the party I was delighted to notice what special care

---

4 Such a "third" – which can become confused with the position of an external reader – may be read in Lacanian terms as the symbolic, a move which casts the "Other" as both an empowered yet impotent presence dissimulated before. On the "ignorance of the big Other" see Slavoj Zizek's *Looking Awry* (Cambridge: MIT Press, 1991), 72.

they took never to get in front or to be in Protagoras' way. When he and those with him turned round, the listeners divided this way and that in perfect order, and executing a circular movement took their places each time in the rear. *It was beautiful.*

'After that I recognized', as Homer says, Hippias of Ellis, sitting on a seat of honour in the opposite portico ...

'And there too spied I Tantalus' — for Prodicus of Ceos was also in town ... But what they were talking about I couldn't discover from the outside, although I was very keen to hear Prodicus, whom I regard as a man of inspired genius. You see, he has such a deep voice that there was a kind of booming in the room which drowned the words. (314c–316a)

I ignore where the voice of Prodicus is enigmatically cancelled by the excess of its own sound, sense cancelling sense, a metaphoric booming echoed when Socrates later likens Protagoras' machine-like discourse to a gong ("like a gong that booms out when you strike it and goes on until you lay a hand on it" [329b]). I choose to ignore this since, for the moment, it seems to direct us toward a play of the signifier in the "ear" that will open onto an *other* scene in the text. While Socrates' invocation of Hades is meant in part as social satire — likening Prodicus, say, to Tantalus, past or dead figures — the text also solicits a representational order that resurrects the dead. The move exceeds that of the *Theaetetus*, say, where an older Socrates ventriloquizes an already dead Protagoras, caricaturing Protagoras' text for future readers. Here the well-known list of Athenians in the *Protagoras* are themselves marked as representational and ghosted, as when Pericles' sons are depicted as present even though the text plays off its foreknowledge of their coming deaths in the plague. The narrated *katabasis* suggests a going-under of a unique sort: a virtual immersion into what could be called pure anteriority as such. In Plato, where every dialogue is a Menippean dialogue of the dead that the reader forgets is openly marked as such, it is valuable to recall which "dead" Socrates one is dealing with in a given text, that is, how his death, or return is remarked, or which doubles of him are circulated (as occurs in the *Symposium*, or *The Sophist*). The invocation of Hades, however subtly, suggests where the mimetic pretext ("like a sporting event") veers increasingly toward problems of a death*less* scene of representation, which Protagoras and Socrates appear at moments inversely privy too. If personifying the dead suggests the trope of prosopopeia, Hades marks where that figure is universalized with respect to any subject position. It is at this point that the descriptive language of the text is partitioned from itself, opening a representational space whose only corollary is the double-talk of the agonists themselves. The very casualness of this scene, all too descriptive, links us to the idea of anteriority, of the past, but in a way that assimilates the present audience (such as that of the dialogue), and future reader who, too, in reading (Plato, for instance), enters that scene and that history. Something in the *dialogue of dialogue* here blocks or precedes the emergence of the subject, or face — this is variously present in the first speaker remaining anonymous, in the *exodos ton logon* at the end, in the young Hippocrates' face blushing when becoming visible at dawn, in the critical reading scene, or in Socrates' likening *arete* itself to a face (*prosopon*) with five parts (329c). Yet it is Protagoras' own introductory speech that situates this problem as that of the speaker's linguistic emergence in history.

Protagoras' self presentation is socially marked in a totalized yet also traceless way, and this will be Socrates' problem in trying to respond to it. To make his own dissimulation invisible he draws attention to it, sets it aside as (itself) another's. It sets the terms of the debate, yet does so by what amounts to an open or very public *fore*closure of discourse that cannot but resonate beyond the individual strategy of this character. This he does by providing himself with an enviable genealogy reaching back through and assimilating the great names of history itself. In doing so he legitimizes the strange and negative term "sophist" and empties it of the popular connotations, which Socrates had Hippocrates blush at in realizing (312a). The sophist says that while others and earlier sophists — among them the greatest *names* of history going back to Homer and Hesiod — concealed themselves for fear of a tyrant's persecution, or of the people themselves, by assuming "disguises (*proschemata*)" and appearing to be poets or gymnasts or artists, he himself comes forward openly and without disguise, calling himself openly a sophist. The system put in place by "father" Protagoras, who both enforces and strips the illusion of paternity, is well worth considering:

I appreciate your forethought (*promethe*) on my behalf (*hyper emou*), Socrates. A man has to be careful when he visits powerful cities as a foreigner, and induces their most promising young men to forsake the company of others, relatives or acquaintances, older or younger, and consort with him on the grounds that his conversation will improve them. Such conduct arouses no small hostility and intrigue. Personally I hold that the sophist's art is an ancient one, but that those who put their hand to it in former times, fearing the odium which it brings, *adopted a disguise* (*proschema*) and worked under cover. Some used poetry as a screen, for instance Homer and Hesiod and Simonides; others religious rites and prophecy, like Orpheus and Musaeus and their school; some even – so I have noticed – physical training ... All of them, as I say, used these arts as a screen to escape malice. I myself, however, am not of their mind in this. I don't believe they accomplished their purpose, for they did not pass unobserved by the men who held the reins of power in their cities, though it is on their account that these disguises are adopted; the mass of people notice nothing, but simply echo what the leaders tell them. *Now to run away and fail to escape, but to be discovered instead, turns the attempt into sheer folly,* and cannot fail to arouse even greater hostility, for people think that the man who behaves like this in addition to his other faults an unprincipled rogue. *I therefore have always gone the opposite way to my predecessors.* I admit to being a Sophist and an educator, and I consider this a better precaution than the other – admission rather than denial. *I have devised other precautions as well,* so that (if Heaven will forgive the boast) I come to no harm through being a confessed Sophist, though I have been many years in the profession. Indeed I am getting on in life now – so far as age goes I might be *the father of any one of you* – so if there is anything you want of me, I should prefer to say my say in front of the whole company. (316c–317c; my emphases)

Protagoras introduces himself in the form of a denial then – the (proschematic) denial of any screen or *proschema* – even as he claims a position as "father" in age and authority to all present (a *pater*, say, like "Plato" to the West?). The word *proschema* reverses the claim it also fosters when attributed to others, since it can be translated not only as disguise, veil, screen, or pretext, but also as *prefiguration* – recalling that the name Protagoras means not only *first in* but *before* the *agora*. Liddell and Scott translate *proschema* as "*that which is held before*: hence, I. *a screen, cloak,* Thuc.: *a plea, pretence, pretext, ostensible cause*" or "*a screen* or *disguise.*" The Protagorean "I" inscribes itself in a history of renowned names, history itself become a heady series of *names* that seem here almost interchangeable due to the anonymous position of the "I" behind the series. Here an effaced duplicity inhabits the facade of paternity itself, in a mock-genealogy that implicitly eviscerates genealogical logic by subtly making names temporally interchangeable. Presented as all too historically situated, it turns out that the *Protagoras* stages an encounter between putative generations (say, P's and S's) that is genealogically undermined and in which the definition of (a) history may be at issue. In a text that exiles woman, "father" Protagoras invisibly assumes the coded position of woman in a *proschema* that is also the denial of *proschemata*, according to the cultural cipher which reads woman as veil or figuration itself, and which makes this supposedly "historical" Protagoras a screen, "literature" as such. That the text erases the familial, Oedipal narrative it has Protagoras and then Socrates strategically pretend to, is further marked in the scene upon entering Kallias' courtyard. There a eunuch slams the door on Socrates "mistaking" him for a sophist, thus introducing an anti-generational and even *neutered* logic into the specular pretexts ("I believe the porter, a eunuch, overheard us, and it seems likely that the crowd of Sophists had put him in a bad temper with visitors. At any rate when we knocked at the door he opened it, saw us and said: 'Ha, Sophists! He's busy.' And thereupon he slammed the door as hard as he could with both hands" [314c–d]). What does the "eunuch" know, who introduces an anti-generation and neutered logic that saps the specular pretext? If the *proschema* speech is apotropaic, nothing in the dialogue seems to escape its system.[5]

If the public space of the agora is itself gradually shifted to a different version of exteriority, that of material inscription, two passages in Protagoras' logos seem to provide this with a particular gloss. While pretending to argue for the teachability of *arete*, the sophist turns to increasingly minimal examples of what any learning might mean, coming finally to that of poems automatically learned by heart: "they set the works of good poets before them on their desks to read and make them learn them by heart (*ekmanthanein*) ... so that the child may be inspired to imitate them" (326a). Here the verb for such machine-like memorization (*ek-manthanein*) – like the figure of Mr. Memory in Hitchcock's *The Thirty-Nine Steps* – draws attention to an *ex*ternalizing effect that seems associated with writing itself. Learning, to begin with, is imprinting. Moreover, the image of memory oriented toward anteriority is quickly supplemented by another minimal act of learning, that of *copying* models. Here, the learning of laws is rendered analogous to children learning to spell,

---

5 Protagoras' example of punishment, for instance, is based not on revenge but future *deterrence* ("turning away," *apotropes*). Whoever is punished becomes a sign for others, yet in doing so turns the eye *away*: "No, punishment is not inflicted by a rational man for the sake of the crime that has been committed (after all one cannot undo what is past), but for the sake of the future, to prevent either the same man or, by the spectacle. ..., someone else ... at all events the punishment is inflicted as a deterrent (*apotropes goun heneka kolazei*)" (324b). The logic seems to register an apotropaic mechanism in the text itself. This excess produces itself as a sign for others viewing the spectacle; yet in being executed, as in dying to become a sign, one cannot (be) read (oneself).

and specifically to making letters from stencilled *outlines* that one places beneath the implement. These are called *hypogrammata*. Quite aside from the term's use in the argument as a passing example, the word *hypogram* resonates with a number of other possible meanings. Not only is the term used by Saussure as an alternate name for anagrams, but it is strikingly appropriated by de Man to take on the more explicit associations of subscript or subtext, as well as the implications of signature itself.[6] Moreover, as a term of underlining the eyes cited in an example from Lucretius, it also is transformed into the giving-of-face of prosopopeia as well: it is a term that can straddle or dissolve the interface of representation itself. Hypogram as a word transformatively opens a space of contested signification that passes from signature and subtext to letter and the very emergence of the voice:

> When they have finished with teachers, the state compels them to learn the laws and use them as a pattern (*paradeigma*) for their life ... You know how, when children are not yet good at writing, the writing-master traces outlines with the pencil (*hypographein grammas te graphidi*) before giving them the slate, and makes them follow the lines as a guide in their own writing. Well, similarly the State (*polis*) sets up the laws (*hyponomous hypograpsata*), which are the inventions of good lawgivers in ancient times, and compels the citizens to rule and be ruled (*archein kai archesthai*) in accordance with them. (326c–e)

Does this reference to *hypograms* plunge the text, potentially, into an "other" scene being played out in the *Protagoras* – a shuttle-term dissolving the representational pretext our more or less Platonic aesthetic holds in place? A reader like Berger attempts to restore the historical foundation and "save face," or at least the faces of Socrates and Protagoras (and by implication the reader). He accordingly stabilizes the performative circulation of ironized words by making the "father" of the discourse the historical Athenian community itself. The move is promising, but the text seems to position that community and its "we" in almost automated terms themselves. When we meet Protagoras his adepts are lined up, following his movements with mechanical steps, and he notes later that the mass of men mechanically follow others' words ("the mass of people notice nothing, but simply echo what the leaders tell them" [317a]). Indeed, while references to

---

6 See "Hypogram and Inscription," in *Resistance to Theory* (University of Minnesota Press, 1984), 27–54, hereafter cited as *RT*. I discuss this term at greater length in chapter 7 when addressing Melville's "Bartleby."

automaton figures recur throughout the text, like that of Pericles' sons grazing for knowledge on their own ("they simply browse around on their own like sacred cattle, on the chance of picking up virtue automatically (*automatoi*)" [320a]).[7] What emerges between Socrates and Protagoras becomes a battle behind the scenes for who can usurp the position of conferred power that increasingly turns on the revision of communal texts and installed readings – not unlike Plato.

3. Hyperbaton: reading Plato reading

What does it mean to ask where Plato addresses "reading" itself – and if that scene is itself too literal or even routinely dismissed as a parody, might it not dissimulate something impossible otherwise to address, and this by the same system of making that too obvious as we saw in the *proschema* speech?

First the scene. Following the breakdown of the dialogue of dialogue, Socrates threatens to leave and is restrained. Protagoras is then pressured to try to *begin* yet again (something in the text like a comic "death drive" seems to irrevocably forestall beginnings). He does so by proposing to read or critique a Simonides poem, into which the previous terms of discussion will be "transposed." The text will itself absorb, reflect, or in turn read the meta-exchange which, under the judging eye of the Athenians, has been hyperbolically interrupted. After checking that Socrates indeed admires the poem and approves of it, the sophist strikes. He asserts that Simonides, who seems in the text to cite and criticize Pittacus' apothegm ("Hard is it to be noble"), in doing so contradicts what he *himself* will say in the same poem. In this way, Protagoras asserts his authority as interpreter, wounds Socrates, and usurps the esteem of Simonides in one fell swoop. What is less obvious still is that the section remains a logical reduction of the previous breakdown of types of "speech," turning instead to pre-

7 Berger's attempt to circumvent the familiar *mimetic* reading of Plato in "Facing Sophists: Socrates' Charismatic Bondage in Protagoras," *Representations*, 5 (Winter, 1983), starts promisingly, yet as Berger's mock-Bakhtinian reading of "*saving* face" suggests, it is the *face* of the mimetic reading he returns to – dismissing the reading scene ("a long and hilarious parody of literary interpretation"), the myth, and the *proschema* speech in the process. Berger returns to a model that creates a new *interior*: "The Protagorean dialogues reveal that neither Socrates nor Protagoras 'is, or becomes, just in and by' himself ... What binds and bounds the faces together, making them one as any self/other is one, is the new interior they constitute between them" (68).

inscribed texts. Coming after the meltdown of genres and embedding within its virtually interrupted parenthesis the reference to inscriptions at Delphi, the focus on the attempt of one text to "overthrow" another threatens the *mise en scene* and its nested frames ("In my judgement he wrote the whole poem against the saying of Pittacus and on its account, in a deliberate effort to damage its fame" [343c]):[8]

'My question to you therefore will concern the subject of our present discussion, namely virtue [*arete*], but *transferred to the realm of poetry*. Simonides in one of his poems says to Scopas son of Creon of Thessaly:
Hard is it on the one hand to become
[*genesthai*] /A good man truly, hands and feet
and mind / Four square, wrought without blame.
Do you know the piece, or should I recite it all to you?'
'There is no need' I said. 'I know it and have given it quite a lot of study.'
'Good. Now do you think it a beautiful and well written poem?'
'Yes, both beautiful and well written.'
'And do you think a poem beautifully written if the poet contradicts himself?'
'No.'
'Then look at it more closely.'
'But really I have given it enough thought.'
'Then you must know that as the poem proceeds he says:
    Nor do I count as sure the oft-quoted
[*nementai*] word /
    Of Pittacus, though wise indeed he was /
    Who spoke it. To be (*emmenai*) noble, said
    the sage, / Is hard.
You understand that this is the same poet as wrote the previous lines?'
'Yes.'
'Then you think the two passages are consistent?'
'For my part I do' said I, though not without a fear that he might be right. 'Don't you?'
'How can a man be thought consistent when he says both these things? First he lays it down (*hypotheto*) himself that it is hard for a man to become truly good, then when he is a little further on in the poem he *forgets*. He finds

8 See Eric Havelock, *Preface to Plato* (Cambridge, Mass.: Belknap, 1963), chapters 2 ("Mimesis") and 5 ("Epic as Record versus Epic as Narrative"), on how *mimesis* itself shifts in meaning from implying representational distance to the collapse of representation itself. Derrida's elaboration of mimesis in the companion piece to "Plato's Pharmacy," "The Double Seance," derives from the Heideggerian distinction between *aletheia* as *adequatio* and as unconcealedness, yet rewrites mimesis as itself actantial, transformation, and event-like, a model all too applicable, in fact, to (this) Platonic dialogue.

fault with Pittacus, who said the same thing as he did himself, that it is hard to be noble, and refuses to accept if from him; but in censuring the man who said the same as he does, he obviously censures himself. Either his first or his second statement is wrong.'

This sally evoked praise and applause from many of the audience, and at first I was like a man who had been hit by a good boxer: at his words and the applause things went dark and I felt giddy. (339a-d)

A covert double talk occurs between the two agonists and through the poetic texts in which, out of the eye of the audience (and, for the most part, Plato's readers), the roles each assumes correspond, at first, to the initials of the poet's names (ostensibly, Socrates/Protagoras: Simonides/Pittacus). Protagoras will claim that by attacking the utterance of Pittacus – the rather banal, "Hard is it to be noble" – Simonides attacks the very thing that *he himself says* later in his text, thus contradicting himself. It is an accusation covertly aimed at Socrates (the other S) for attacking Protagoras (another P) about the teaching of "virtue," which Socrates himself also clearly does. After arguing that their *difference* lay in Simonides' speaking of "becoming" rather than, as with Pittacus, of "being" noble, Socrates at the end of his long response ventriloquizes Simonides' supposed reply to Pittacus, explaining his reason for attacking: "as it is you have made an utterly false statement about something of the highest import, and it passes for true. For that do I blame you" (347a). Having opened the Pandora's box of a cryptogram concealed by lying too openly on the surface, rather like the *proschema* speech's "honesty," where does this doubling stop? The very thing that this exchange appears to underline – a specular misprision between the two – seems itself implicitly dismissed by this very exchange that fosters it, since that instantly becomes another signalled strategy in turn. Even Socrates' amusing parody of Protagoras' *proschema* speech in the interlude – when he speaks of the Spartans who, while seeming to be stupid or non-verbal, do so to "disguise" the fact that they are the best philosophers and the envy of Greece – falls further into the hall of mirrors, since it instead confirms the absolute image of a persecuted position that must invert and dissimulate itself without trace.

The symmetry, in short, is not itself secure. In defending Simonides Socrates allies himself with a figure often considered the first sophist. Moreover, Socrates' strategy rests on working out a conceptual distinction between "being" and "becoming" in the poems, like a comedic send-up of late Platonic metaphysics. Socrates' reading will mimic the sophist's method of applying a rhetoric term – effectively opening interpretation in general to the sophisticated address of rhetorical systems acting irrespective of grammar. What is applied is the trope of *hyperbaton* (usually translated as inversion or transposition, and one of Longinus' foremost figures of the sublime). Its use involves shifting the antecedent of the adverb "truly (*aletheos*)," into what could sportingly be described as a repositioning of truth. In section twenty-two of Longinus' *On The Sublime*, *hyperbaton* is presented as perhaps the central trope of the sublime. Translated variously as inversion or transposition, what is peculiar about the figure is that it also exemplifies the danger of suspense, of hanging in suspense (temporally), or in a parenthesis that can generate so many additions or variations that it may seem to connote a numerical sublime, or inversely sheer interruption.[9] This inversion or transposition of *aletheos* determines the dialogic exchange in the poem by positioning one utterance "before" another, yet it also applies to that "inversion" Socrates is performing with Protagoras in (at least) a dual sense:

It occured therefore to Simonides, with his philosophic ambitions, that if he could floor this favourite maxim with a triumphant knockout he would become the favourite of his own day. In my judgement he wrote the whole poem against the saying of Pittacus and on its account, in a deliberate effort to damage its fame.

9 *Hyperbaton* will represent the overt disarticulation of what nominally defines the sublime (*hypsos*) with reference to *pathos*. The danger of the sublime is not the *uncanny*, not a repressed figure with the power to obliterate, the simulacrum of a sacred origin or its double. What is sublime is the destruction of the sublime itself, that the collapse that would dramatize "risk" or "danger" with *hyperbaton* is engineered to interrupt and defer any "going-over" or actual movement across. Emblematic of any utterance, it yet fulfills itself – seeks its *jouissance* – as a parenthesis engendering more parentheses, like the flight of Xeno's arrow. What is called "inversion" intends a reversal yet encounters suspense, both as arrestation and regression. Longinus describes the speaker utilizing this trope: "carried away by jealousy or some other feeling – there are *countless emotions*, more than one can say – often put forward one point and then (made to) spring off to another with various illogical interpolations, and then wheel around again to their original position, while, under the stress of their excitement, like a ship before a veering wind, they lay their words and thoughts first on one tack and then another, and keep altering the natural order of sequence into *innumerable variations* – so, too, the best prose-writers by use of *hyperbata* imitate nature and achieve the same effect" (22.1; H. Fyfe translation). While anchored in the expression of emotion, the figure yet flies off in the direction of sheer number ("countless emotions," "innumerable variations").

Now let us all examine it together, to see whether I am right. At the very beginning of the poem, it seems crazy if he wished to say that it is hard to become a good man, that he should then insert "on the one hand" [*to men*]. This insertion seems to make no sense, except on the supposition that Simonides is speaking polemically against the saying of Pittacus. Pittacus said "Hard is it to be noble," and Simonides replied, disputing the point, "No; to *become* a good man is hard truly" — not, by the way, "to become truly good" he does not refer the "truly" [*aletheos*] to that, as if some men were truly good and others good but not truly so. That would strike some people as silly and unlike Simonides. *We must transpose, invert, or carry-over* — we must posit a *hyperbaton* [*hyperbaton dei theinai*] for — *the word "truly" in the poem,* thus as it were implying *the saying of Pittacus before it, as if he spoke first and Simonides were answering* his words. This: "O men, hard is it to be noble"; and Simonides replies, "That is not true, Pittacus; not to *be* but to *become* a good man, foursquare in hands and feet and mind, wrought without blame, that is hard truly." (343c–344a; my emphases and amended translation)

Why, indeed, is this reading scene even here, twisting between dialogues of mute texts within other mute texts? What may be unseen is that a figure of interpretation and priority is put in play as the example — indeed, model — of the (historical) revision staged between Socrates and Protagoras, or even between the "early" or "Socratic" dialogues and a "middle" or constructive Plato. What, if anything at all, occurs in this interlude after which the argument (again) resumes ("which we broke off in the middle" [348 a])? What is (or is not) decided here? The collapse of mimetic frames — like that of genres — may be difficult to contain. Does the text, here, involve Pittacus, or only manipulate that example, as *example*, to trump Protagoras against his own (false) reading? Or is it situated to inscribe the audience, and if so which, the Athenians or Plato's subsequent readers? Who, here, is inscribed in whose text?

Hyperbaton could be called the trope of the dialogue itself — a term that might also be translated as going-across, or even as translation (*Uber-tragung, Uber-setzung*). The figure marks where the text, or its Socrates, seems to be virtually going-*hyper* amidst the ruptured nest of frames both within and beyond the work potentially. Indeed, what seems to collapse the surrounding frames in a sort of *mise en abyme* is a counter model of dialogic power based on reading, or at least on a positioning of anterior figures and on usurpation. Somewhat confusingly, not only does a (first) second text (Simonides, Socrates) offer to displace the authority of a supposed first (Pittacus, Protagoras) but the positional reversal appears as a cipher of history itself or its epochal shifts, though even such shifts seem already evacuated by Protagoras' *proschema* speech. Here, the external or public space of the agora seems itself transposed into the externality of memorized texts or inscription (*ek-manthanein*). As in the dialogue, there is no space at all for interior or private meanings (as pointedly demonstrated in the needling exchange with Prodicus concerning the word "hard" [341 c–d]). This will turn out to mirror a certain dispossessing play of signature, of the *hypogram*, even of letters.[10] A certain radical exhibitionism by the text can be pointed to – this display of the phallus of inscription, of the dialogue of dialogue, of *arete* as face, of signature, of reading – that seems virtually reproduced in the embarrassed blush appearing on Hippocrates' face at sunrise, at the dawn of "the West." It may seem opportunistic to seize on the adjective *aletheos* to which Socrates applies his *hyperbaton* and find an analogy in Heidegger's precariously instituted reading of an epochal "transposition" within the word *aletheia* itself in Plato (and his subsequent mock-renunciation before the philological objections of Paul Friedlaender), nonetheless, for Heidegger what is at stake is Plato's shift from one concept of "truth" to another: from *aletheia* heard in pre-Socratic fashion as unconcealment to Platonic "truth" as representation (or *adequatio*); a shift that for him inaugurates metaphysics as such.

The double talk has yet another fold though. It recalls to us that no arbitrary curtailment of reference or even self-reference is being enforced. For instance, when Socrates explicates the term "willingly" as applying to Simonides himself, he describes a scene that reflexively refers to his own death: "The word 'willingly' applies to himself. His view was that a good man often forces himself into love and praise, as when someone's mother or father or native land is unsympathetic to him ... Simonides had in mind that he himself had often eulogized a tyrant or someone of that stamp not of his own free will but under compulsion" (346a–b). Yet the reflexive, autobiographical inflexion can be turned in various directions, including to the trace of Plato, who must of course be present in any positional agon in which the textual priority of Socrates and Protagoras, an S and a P, is at stake, and in which scene we may have to read Plato's own reading of (his potential posteriority to) Socrates – certainly something other than a question

10 Of course, it is worth recalling that in the *Theaetetus* the concept of "primal letters (*stoicheia*)" is broached in association with Protagoras.

of fathers or sons. This marks Plato's ghostly transgression (back) into a signatorial combat for empowerment. Is the anonymous "P" of a certain Plato itself proximate to the anonymous "I" of the sophist who inhabits every great name of history (which would include, then, the future)? Why is there a seeming proliferation of P-names across the dialogue (Prodicus, Pericles, Paralus, among others), as if no "frame" quite closes out this autobiographic mark? Does the work display — or display by effacing, *proschematically* — Plato's signature, providing we can read "Plato" as a linguistic materialist?

One problem is that the frames themselves become more anamorphically distorted with every pass. While the signatures at first seem to align themselves ($S = S$, $P = P$), this is simultaneously deranged by the triangulating addition of yet another "P" to the receding apparatus we may at first call SPSP (Socrates critiques Protagoras' critique of Simonides' doubling critique of Pittacus). Here, in the hub of *difference* (being/becoming, old/young inside/out, P/S), are we reading a certain "Plato" reading not only reading itself but reading Socrates reading (another) "Plato" (reading)? Opening this *combinatoire*, not only has Socrates become the first sophist to ventriloquize Simonides (thus preceding Protagoras) but the P-signature is here suspiciously aligned not, it seems, with Protagorean dissimulation but "being" itself or a prior text (Pittacus' "Hard is it to be noble"). Rather than assert the power of anteriority, the reading scene unsurprisingly defaces the legitimacy of that mock-origin we saw in the logic of the *proschema*.

A complication arises when we feed the third P-signature (Plato) into this loop, for as the (then) "younger" figure in this mock-familial triad, he must first appear himself in the position of the younger challenger, Socrates himself. Yet this occurs while, as if by an inversion, "Socrates" implicitly becomes the elder or authoritative Protagoras — *as if* this transition, or hyperbaton, could also be read through the presumed position of the *Protagoras* in Plato's own archive or production, that of being as if in between the "Socratic" and middle or Platonic works. It is also at the point, say, of a "historical" shift on which outcome the opening of an age of metaphysics as event routinely seems to depend.[11] More interestingly, the configuration

---

11 The juxtaposition of *hypo*gram — signature, underwriting, infratext, letteral outline — and *hyper*baton indicates the representational economy of a text that involves the play of deficiency (*hypo*) and sheer excess (*hyper*). In the dialogue,

corresponds with odd precision to those maneuvers which Derrida explores when interrogating the question of priority and anteriority in the well-known "Envois" section of *The Post Card*; here the scriptive positions of Plato and Socrates are put into play in a variety of temporal, authoritative, and erotic combinations. Indeed, the reading scene of the *Protagoras* can be seen either bemusedly or quite aggressively to anticipate Derrida's work, or to (re)write that *in advance*. Caught in its trans-historical tractor-beam, it places within its textual gaze an entire tradition that will produce the iconic "Plato" as well. It produces, for instance, a *mise en scene* that arguably anticipates or inscribes the inversions of sender and receiver, debt and priority that Derrida explores – and with considerably more economy. In a typical passage of Derrida's "Envois" section in *The Post Card* we read:

The charter is the contract for the following, which quite stupidly one has to believe: Socrates comes *before* Plato, there is between them – and in general – an order of generation, an irreversible sequence of inheritance. Socrates is before, not in front of, but before Plato, therefore behind him, and the charter binds us to this order: this is how to orient one's thought, this is the left and this is the right, march. Socrates, he who does not write, as Nietzsche said (how many times have I repeated to you that I also found him occasionally or even always somewhat *on the border* of being naive; remember that photograph of him with his 'good guy' side, at the beginning in any event, before the 'evil,' before the disaster?). He understood nothing about the initial catastrophe, or at least about this one, since he knew all about the others. Like everyone else he believed that Socrates did not write, that he came before Plato who more or less wrote at his dictation and therefore let him write by himself, as he says somewhere. The entire 'overturning' remained included in the program of this credulity. This is true *a fortiori*, and with an *a fortiori* different each time and read to blow up otherwise, from Freud and from Heidegger. (20)

Ignoring the contretemps with Nietzsche, which names the "catastrophe" as a certain misreading of Plato, we encounter a bit later:

this is the catastrophe: when he writes, when he sends, when he makes his (a)*way*, S is p, finally is no longer totally other than p (finally I don't think so

---

we seem to trace the hyperbolic attempt, and failure, of a certain "I" or first person to speak. In the "hedonist calculus," a text forecasting a later text of the *Philebus*, its calculations are situated between what is explicitly called excess (*hyperbole*) and deficiency (*elleipsis*) (356a). When Socrates remarks that he is himself surprised (*atopon*) in "forgetting" Alcibiades, it follows the recollection that the ephebe "spoke up for me (*hyper emou*) at some length." The phrase also indicates where the "I" itself is as if spoken for, or behind (*hyper*).

at all, S will have been totally other, but if *only* he had been totally other, truly totally other, nothing would have happened between them, and we would not be at this pass, sending ourselves their names and their ghosts like ping-pong balls). pp, pS, Sp, SS, the predicate speculates in order to send itself the subject." (30)

Yet the system's ability to (de)generate itself — at least according to Plato's reading of "reading" — may have more variations when Plato appears to read or factor in Derrida's reading of Plato with(in) its "*renversement.*" Moreover, though routinely and quite necessarily dismissed as "trifling," the reading scene draws attention to the fact that there is no law for rereading Plato today that will legislate how to take this scene or curtail its mad formal drift. How, even, do we close off the "historical" frames collapsed by the *proschema* speech, which transposes the future (reader) into Hades? Derrida chooses to examine the system he will designate as Socrates-Plato, using the initials Ps or Sp — invoking under this rubric not only the primary/ secondary process, or subject/predicate, but also the issue of debt and succession, of (a) Socrates standing *behind* and dictating to Plato, of Plato "writing" Socrates, making Socrates into (the implement of) writing. By allowing ourselves this unencumbered speculation, is Socrates' inversion of *aletheos* itself a perversely anticipatory parody of Heidegger's *Plato's Doctrine of the Truth,* as when the latter attempts to locate a historical and epistemic shift or transposition (*verlagern*) in representation itself, one that is staged by "Plato" in the word *aletheia,* and that as a shift from unconcealment to meaning *adequatio,* mimesis, and that as occurring specifically in the *Republic*'s allegory of the cave?

The dialogue can thus seemingly be rewritten (again) by aligning Plato's signature with the *Pi* of Protagoras', particularly where the latter reveals himself in Plato as a safe and seemingly banal screen for what precedes figuration *as material language itself.* This, of course, is a possible reading, though one almost barred by Plato's long-clichéd condemnation of "sophists," and the centrality with which that opposition is usually dealt as a founding gesture of philosophy.[12] Yet

12 Friedlaender, for instance, notes that "a great many of the ideas and images that later became important for Plato are already anticipated in the myth of Protagoras" (*Plato: An Introduction,* trans. H. Meyerhoff [Princeton: Bollingen, 1969], 177). Rosemary Desjardins argues untraditionally that the Socrates (and hence, with all sorts of slippage, Plato) of the *Theaetetus* ends by supporting the Protagorean thesis that is routinely assumed to be there dismantled. See Desjardins, *The Rational Enterprise: Logos in Plato's Theaetetus* (Albany: SUNY University Press, 1990), 85–90.

the dialogue's own Socrates finds, in the process, that he must himself *posit* as fact, or even uphold the pretext of *prior* authority in order to (pretend to) rewrite or usurp that and draw on a power in circulation already or supposed to be: "You cannot knock down a man who is lying on the ground, you can only knock him down if he is standing, and put him on the ground" [344c]). The text folds back again.[13]

It would seem that the one overt place where Plato appears "autobiographically" inscribed in his text is not the reference to him by name in *Phaedo*, but in the dialogue *of dialogue* itself. It might even seem – and not only tongue in cheek – to be a staged or mock agon on which, nonetheless, an entire epoch technically depends (will Plato write further? will Socrates be dominant?). Does the "history," which a current reader stands at one supposed end of, hang as if in the balance in this idiotic reading scene, on its pivotal outcome (*exodos*), the ascension, inscription, and usurpation of S(P) over and in P(S)? Might that epoch simply *not* (have) happen(ed), be revoked or erased – as occurs if we construct, now, an "other" Plato – or might Plato *not* "write" the rest of the production, not "father" metaphysics at all? Is every possible history inscribed in the *proschema* speech still? Can the production be read (or rewritten) differently, in which case could an epoch of metaphysics be said never to have occurred as such, to be a retro-projection from "modernism"? What does it mean for (a pre-Platonic) "Plato" to read (a post-aporetic) Socrates here, or the reverse? Does Socrates' accusation at the end of the reading scene, spoken through a ventriloquized Simonides and as if to Pittacus as a front for his own non-double, "Protagoras" – that is, that an S blames a P for saying something covertly yet radically untrue, though invisible as such – in fact end up as a rebuke by Socrates that is addressed to Plato's own "constructive" philosophy (the entire itinerary of truth, *eidos*, and immortality, offered under "Socrates'" aegis)? Who, moreover, represents the third figure or *tyrant* before whom dissimulation and name-changing is compulsory in the text's system – the Athenians, the anterior and circulated work whose

---

13 It is interesting that Protagoras' dubious myth of origins is given its final rewrite in *The Statesman*'s myth of origins, where, however, we encounter the image of time reversed – reminiscent of the *Second Letter*'s reference to a "Socrates grown young" (314c). In that myth, time is not only reversible, with the living growing younger into death and the dead revivified, reaching an antescene to creation itself, but the turning point is said to come at a "standstill," termed *atropos* (269b–273e).

authority is to be displaced, or Plato's "Platonizing" readers before whom the scene is systematically occluded?

The *proschema* speech suggests that the tyrant or guardian invariably doubled or dissimulated before assumes different forms. If one such is the weight of anterior words (Pittacus' text), another is the literal addressee, the tyrant Scopas of Simonides' text (whose tendency to flatter tyrants is mentioned). If Scopas as tyrant, as reader and overseer (as the name suggests, *Scop-*), places yet another S-name at the outer rung of this nested series, it is one that seems to reproduce the SP system (ScoPaS), making that momentarily the tyrant. Here, it seems, the series of *letters* themselves can generate numerous combinations or inversions (psps(s)pss(p)pps, p(psp)ssspspss, and so on), establishing or erasing different possible histories (or futures) – depending on where or if it can be closed. In such a context, it can hardly seem accidental that Simonides added a new letter to the Greek alphabet, and specifically the letter *psi*, welding the *pi* and *sigma*.

Is Plato here amusing himself, by choreographing a cryptogrammatic skit in this scene which no "serious" reader can even acknowledge, or is a certain destining uncontrollably in play and marking *itself*?

One problem is that the "first" text in this series to be overthrown, Pittacus', is itself suspect. For if we look closely, rather than being a hyperbolic claim to being, it is in fact an *excuse* for not-being – "Hard is it to *be* noble." It's difficult to be, to be noble – excuse me for this lack or failure, or allow this excuse to itself excuse some other act or non-act. The utterance itself may come *after* an accusation, or at least as a retort in an absent dialogue. As a Greek reader might have known, the utterance was in fact famously a *response* in context, and that to yet another double, yet another P-name. That name is in fact absent from Plato's work – deleted even from Socrates' list of the seven sages (343a) on which he is usually found, as in the *Second Letter*. It is Periander, minister of Corinth. For it was when Periander usurped power in his city that Pittacus, also a minister and fearing his own similar ambition, made his utterance and *stepped down* from power.[14]

---

14 By and large, Simonides' poem seems to be read as a discourse on the ethical mean. Leonard Woodbury, in "Simonides on *Arete*" (*Transactions and Proceedings of the American Philological Association*, ed. F. Walton, lxxxiv [1953]), calls *arete* in this usage an "ideal more bourgeois than chivalrous" (162) and notes: "at the beginning of the sixth century, Pittacus, who ruled Mytilene by right of an extraordinary magistracy, hearing that Periander of Corinth had converted a

Periander, the absent "I" at the text's dead center, seems almost as a
name to resonate through other names or words bearing the prefix
peri (Pericles, *perituchousi*). The prefix implies circularity – as, say,
that mentioned in the *Meno*'s reference to consciousness' only
recognizing what is already in memory, the image of a turning-man
(Peri-ander) repeating what is already imprinted, a machine like that
the *Theaetetus* calls a *peritrope*.[15] This absent center – the absence of a
first text, of Being, of the *pater*, of Protagoras or Plato, of the "I" –
names the dilemma of Socrates before the sophist as well. Socrates is
unable at first to disclose the sophist's *proschema* as a dissimulation of
paternity since it denies him a positive position to usurp; it outpaces
any merely ironic strategy he can come up with as the exchanges
disintegrate. There is no *first* site here, no text whose authority is not
conferred by a blinded audience over the site of an unmarked yet
radical absence; just as priority in history itself – of the pre-Socratic
over the Platonic, of Socrates himself over Plato – is less suspended
than exposed as the effect of counter-inscriptions, and the response to
this by Pittacus is linguistically empowering in turn, particularly since
it is abdication in advance of a false usurpation. More interesting, then,
is to return to "father" Protagoras or the allusion to the eunuch, and
hence implicitly to the strategy of abdication as being what steps aside
from the non-position of the King. At the end of the hypogrammatic
chain leading to Pittacus (and "Periander") – a kind of chain letter
both in the text and the subsequent interpretive history of Plato –
there appears a strategy of *proleptic abdication* that occurs repeatedly in
the dialogue, as in the mythos with Prometheus giving power to his
brother, or in Pericles' abdication before raising his sons (319e–320b).
Such actions are designed to be recuperative. In the first case,
Prometheus' abdication to Epimetheus – a yielding of Forethought to
Afterthought that dislocates any temporal present as well – produces

similar office into a tyranny, begged to be relieved of his powers, pronouncing
the famous apothegm, that it is difficult to be good" (153). Plato's text rewrites
the figure of the "noble" ("Hard it is to be noble") as a signature of and in the
place of Being as well.

15 The circular movement that is linked to a mnemonic trap of cognition in the
Meno finds expression in the end of the *Theaetetus* in the self-cancelling *machine*
called the "peritrope": "Socrates: We are supposed to acquire right opinion of
the differences which distinguish one thing from another when we have already
a right opinion of them, and so we go round and round: – the revolution of
the scytal, or pestle, or any other rotatory machine (*peritrope*), in the same
circles, is as nothing compared to such a requirement" (210d–e).

the image nonetheless of cities poised on the verge of self-destruction ("They sought therefore to save themselves by coming together and founding fortified cities, but when they gathered in communities they injured one another for want of political skills, and so scattered again and continued to be devoured" [322b]). While in Pericles' example the *natural* wandering of his sons ("like sacred cattle") turns quickly into the story of Alcibiades' corruption of his half-brother Cleinias, which Pericles himself cannot halt and in fact ends up accelerating and being caught up in.[16] The metaphoric system of "abdication" is echoed in metaphors that depict systems which are in some sense self destroying, as in Socrates' trope of the physician whose cure makes the disease worse (340d–e), or the astonishing image in the hedonist calculus of a "good" that is "overcome *by itself.*" What "law" or dissimulation intervenes − like Zeus' in the mythos? − to divert the underlying system of specular loss and destruction into the constructive edifice of "Platonism"?

Part of the point of raising these questions, of course, is to ask what determines the proper way to now read "reading" in Plato? Must it be dismissed as "trifling" compared to the philosophic text, or can we read this scene as a reflexive moment in Plato that interrogates where historical trajectories, signifying chains, and destinations interlace, and where (future) "interpretations" are (repeatedly) decided? The complicity of interpretive institutions in the iconization of "Plato" is also at issue. Does the signature of Plato − read through "Protagoras" − denote the absence of the very Plato elsewhere constructed, one evacuating the position of the "father" and marking it as *proschema*, secured by a strategy that rewrites truth as will to power? Does the *Protagoras* itself constitute a *ps.* of sorts, generally unread, an after-remark explosively addressed to a post-Platonic readership, visible only after the monumental Plato has more or less subsided as a construct or prevailed? Is the trope of "inversion" being made a principle of (textual) history − yet also, thereby, indicated as a sleight-of-hand too?

---

16 The downward spiral begun with Pericles' sons (*automatoi perituchosi*) continues in the subsequent anecdote involving the two brother systems − Pericles/ Ariphron, and Alcibiades/Cleinias − where Pericles himself ends potentially (due to a grammatical equivocation) in the position attributed to the corrupter-brother, Alcibiades. Pericles' attempt to recuperate a doomed, anti-generational structure with a benign tropological one of fraternal substitution collapses: "Ariphron gave him (Cleinias) back: he could make nothing of him" (320a).

4. Knocking before dawn: the aesthetic and Protagoras' *metron*

If we ask now why Protagoras is associated with reading in Plato – and not only reading, but signature and materiality in general – the question leads us back into the text, and specifically to its frame narrative and opening. Unlike the elaborately devious opening of that other "literary" masterpiece, the *Symposium*, that of the *Protagoras* (which we might, now, abbreviate as the *Ps*) does not draw much commentary, though it is arguably more complex. The text opens with a nameless voice asking where Socrates is coming from – the question of anteriority in general. While citing the cliché of erotic pursuit ("Where have you come from, Socrates? No doubt from pursuit of the captivating Alcibiades" [309a]), this cliché is itself replaced, and suddenly supplanted by another figure, the sophist:

FRIEND. Where have you come from, Socrates? No doubt from pursuit of (*peri*) the captivating Alcibiades. Certainly, when I saw him only a day or two ago, he seemed to be still a handsome [*kalos*] man; but between ourselves, Socrates, 'man' is the word. He's actually growing a beard [*hypopimplamenos*] ...

SOCRATES he came to my assistance and spoke up for me at some length. For as you guessed, I have only just left him. But I will tell you a surprising thing [*atopon*]: although he was present, I had no thought for him, and often forgot him [*epelanthanomen*] altogether.

FRIEND. Why, what can have happened between you and him to make such a difference? You surely can't have met someone more handsome [*kallioni*] – not in Athens at least.

SOCRATES. Yes, much more.

FRIEND. Really? An Athenian or a foreigner?

SOCRATES A stranger [*xeno*].

FRIEND. Where from?

SOCRATES. Abdera.

FRIEND. And this stranger struck you as such a handsome person that you put him above the son of Clinias in that respect?

SOCRATES. Yes. Must not perfect wisdom take the palm for handsomeness.   (309a–c)

Before we assume that this is the same Socratic argument we hear in the *Symposium*, that of wisdom's superiority to beauty, we should take note of the difference. Here it is the stranger, the outside figure, who interrupts the erotic pursuit and supplants Alcibiades as most beautiful. And yet, Alcibiades – the figure sometimes for nature itself – is also one who "spoke up for me at some length (*hyper emou eipe*)," someone who speaks for (*hyper*) me or "I," and has just become a "man" as is shown on his face, altered from beneath by a beard (*hypo-pimplamenos*) – like a hypogram ascendant. Here the stranger from Abdera (a name in which the very alphabet seems to begin) has the effect of erasure, of causing Socrates to forget, and be stunned, *atopon*, supplanting the youth with an *old* man.

In reading this charming opening we may forget certain things too. For example, we may forget that twice in the text an "appointment" elsewhere is alluded to outside the scene that will follow. What we seldom connect with (at least critics do not) is that this manipulative "appointment" ("I have something to do" [335c]; "I ought long ago to have kept the appointment I mentioned" [362a]) turns out to be none other than the chance meeting here reported and the subsequent contract of narrating that event (which alludes, in its turn, to that fictional appointment). What occurs suggests the familiar Moebius strip of the inside folded up into the outer frame, a perpetual and never quite begun beginning placed already after the end in an anamorphic fashion which – though itself buried, left unremarked by the critical apparatus – alters either the "spot" in which the text may be said to occur within the narrative of Plato's own production, or even the history of interpretation that fixes it in place (the *Protagoras* as marginal, brilliant, drama, unphilosophical).[17] Indeed, in one sense, this curious fold already produces the text, at its "opening," in the form of a certain remainder – as occurring after a point of exhaustion, haunted, *atopon*. And this, too, is immediately marked, if only to begin reweaving the text itself again, as a replay, from the hyperbolic rupture that it has already experienced and is about to retell. It does this in the mysterious figure of the slave boy in whose seat Socrates sits, and then in the runaway slave of Hippocrates – a figure absorbing this previous slave – about whose pursuit Hippocrates begins the initial narrative when arriving at Socrates' home before sunrise, at a time *at once too early and yet too late*. In this sense the text is without

17 Berger comments on this effect: "The narratorial speech act becomes a repetition of the act it narrates, and as the two interlocutory communities join forces, the narrated past moves forward to surround and imprison the narrator" (79).

outside, or else can be called purely exterior itself, folding back into the opening – a meta-dialogue itself about (its own) narrative. It may not be accidental that it produces, by many accounts, the first myth or allegory in Plato.

Socrates explains then how Hippocrates approached him before dawn, with a *knocking* that precedes visibility or the sun, and which we will associate with Protagoras:

Last night, a little before daybreak, Hippocrates son of Apollodorus, Phason's brother, knocked violently on my door with his stick, and when it was opened, came straight in in a great hurry and shouted out:

'Socrates, are you awake or asleep?' I recognized his voice and said:

'That will be Hippocrates. No bad news I hope?'

'Nothing but good (*agatha*)' he replied ... 'Protagoras has arrived.' (310a–b)

As we hear, again, Hippocrates was seeking out his runaway slave, a figure of material excess and subversion, since in running away the "slave" (like the hypogram) also ceases to be an invisible servant, like a frame narrative or insistent letters in a sentence. The runaway's name is mentioned also as Satyros (an allusion to Socrates' appearance, as noted in the *Symposium*), and it is in the seat of the companion's slave that Socrates sits while narrating, thus creating an association between the narrating Socrates and the runaway figure. The knocking – and we hear of Hippocrates' brother *Phason* ("my brother mentioned it to me"), a name suggesting a verb of speech itself – is accompanied by the question preceding the emerging consciousness of philosophy's absolute subject: "Socrates, are you awake or asleep?" The text places us reflexively before consciousness, before the dawn, before figuration or face – and it records a *measuring* series of alternations, aural, preverbal, differential, suggesting the act, of entering. From it we hear will come "nothing but good," nothing but the itinerary in Plato, perhaps, from which the "Good" itself will emerge from the problem of this knocking, this outside.

Yet why is Protagoras associated with "reading" in Plato? Part of the answer may lie in the text attributed to him in the *Theaetetus*, that is, the text that has gained him the iconic label as the representative of relativism, or pragmatism. The simplest reading of Protagoras' famed dictum, "Man is the measure of all things ...," is itself the calculated literalization by Plato through Socrates' caricature and ventriloquism in the *Theaetetus*, a reading designed to contain or even mask something that erupts performatively in Plato's earlier text bearing his name. This common reading can be called that of subjective relativism, a making of *man* as the measure, and hence what seems also to be an overt humanism. It is hardly expected, then, that this can also be translated as a radically materialist, linguistic, and *post*-humanist text, which may be the case.[18]

In the frame narrative Protagoras is associated, however ironically or enigmatically, with beauty (*kalos*). In a certain sense, this quite literally replaces the erotic pursuit of Alcibiades with Protagoras as a figure of what may momentarily be called the *aesthetic* — particularly if we choose to understand by that something material and linguistic as well. When the sophist is first seen leading his entourage at Kallias' the sheerly *formal* movement is called by Socrates "most beautiful (*kallista*)," and, recalling the use of Agathon's house in the *Symposium* where the subject is "the Good," the name Kallias itself echoes this (*kalos*) in a way not immediately apparent or perhaps interpretable. One may suspect that a different definition of the aesthetic is itself a hidden subject, one certainly unexpected in such a rational and essentially banal set of arguments turning on defining and teaching *arete* — what becomes, in the process, at times a purely emptied term. Protagoras supplants the pretext of the pursuit of beauty with something else, something materially emerging with the knocking and potentially focused on a prefigural and material moment: the aesthetic as the base of cognition or perception itself (*aisthanumai*). Aspects of this interpretive impasse come through if we focus on the non-word "measure (*metron*)" itself, which can be expanded as an act of cutting, criticizing, hierarchizing, even reading (*Dichten ist Messen*, says Heidegger).[19] Ignoring the caricature of humanist relativism in the *Theaetetus*, then, we might try to reread the text by reversing the predication of Protagoras' dictum to read not that "Man" is the center (individually or collectively), the measure of all things as such, but that Man — an *empty* term, a linguistic subject position or place-holder

18 The relevant passage on Protagoras' double-text "*Truth*" in *Theaetetus* reads: "Socrates: In the name of the Graces, what an almighty wise man Protagoras must have been! He spoke these things in a parable to the common herd, like you and me, but told the truth, his *Truth*, in secret to his own disciples" (151e–152d).

19 Heidegger's dictum is found in "... *Dichterisch Wohnet Der Mensch* ...," in *Vortraege und Aufsaetze*, II (Neske: Pfullingen, 1967): "Das Dichten is vermutlich ein ausgezeichnetes Messen. Mehr noch. Vielleicht muessen wir den Satz: Dichten ist MESSEN in der anderen Betonung sprechen: DICHTEN ist Messen" (70).

momentarily without definition – "is," or is supplanted, disarticulated, or situated by an activity that encompasses (and produces) "him" reflexively, one which at base can be called measuring. Such measuring resituates the human against something that is perpetually exterior to and before it, as itself a forgetful if semiotic figure and effect that is retro-projected as a site. Moreover, the *metron* also strips the human of face momentarily, requires it haltingly or failingly put that on, perpetually, yet again, in the act of language. Again, the received canon plants over the elusive name Protagoras a label (subjectivist) that may very well be the predictable reverse of one major implication of his text, since there need be nothing *subjectivist* in this materialist, semiotic, and linguistic model. And if we do represent *metron*, say, by the knocking that opens the text or as a series of alternating marks or bars – say, / / / / – that is also by something prenominal, prefigural, or even preletteral. The aesthetic, or material, is that which gives rise to perception.

If we attach to the name Protagoras the figure of *pragmatism*, as well, we may ask where a trace of this is left in the dialogue. I allude, specifically, to where the word *pragma* is used when Socrates is trying to entrap the sophist by suggesting that to each word (justice, virtue) one "thing" corresponds: "Now let us consider together what sort of thing (*pragma*) each is. First of all, is there such a thing (*pragma*) as justice or not?" (330b–c). While the move is irrelevant for the argument, the reference to *pragma* seems oriented toward a certain thingness or facticity in the text itself. What may be odd is not Socrates' trickiness in that discussion, which shifts the usual Socratic question, "What is 'X'?" to the different question, "Is there such a *thing* as ...?" As commentators have noted, this may be the first emergence in Plato's writing of the trope of the ideas itself, and is in some sense odd if the term, *pragma*, suggests at the same time a facticity, which is the opposite of any transcendence. Moreover, the text seems to be marking in its reference to *pragma* a certain thingness refracted through the reading scene associated with inscription, or what could be called the *pragma* or "stuff" of language. Protagoras becomes potentially a figure for a linguistic materialism that is as anti-mimetic as his famous dictum is. If a certain "other" Plato leaves his signature in the anonymous "I" of Protagoras, it is a Plato who must be himself rewritten as a linguistic materialist, one for whom the construction of the great philosophemes must be addressed not as philosophic doctrine, but precisely as constructions generated through the handling of figuration itself, or the semiotic space of the speaking and dead Socrates. How, though, does an ethical and epistemological figure like the "Good" find itself derived from the trajectory of a personified material sign?

5. The self-cancelling Good

Several metaphoric sequences seem to occur in the *Ps* where what we might call a logic of self cancellation appears to operate. Such might not be limited to the mythos' tale of the cities' self destruction, or the allegory of the brother pair of Alcibiades and Cleinias, or tropes such as that of the doctor whose cure worsens the disease (340d–e). It also applies, and perhaps foremost, to what is presented as a mere passing image in the hedonist calculus of a "good" that is *overcome by itself* (355c). This last figure, though used as a logical absurdity ("What ridiculous nonsense, for a man to do evil ... because he is overcome by the good (*hettomenos hypo ton agathon*)!" [355d]), is suggestive given the course of the dialogue, as though it were one (more) place in the text where an underlying problem breaks through. On the surface, the figure trades against the hedonist calculus' exchange of four names (*onomata*), pleasure for good, and evil for pain, particularly when applied to Socrates' recurrent ethical hypothesis of an *involuntary good*. What is at stake in a "good" that overthrows itself – a system that machinally produces a counter-moment that effectively cancels the very thing proposed as its telos, like the interpretive formalization of a truth?

However contrived, what emerges may be precisely the logic of the "good" as that (which) occurs through Socrates himself. For one thing, the figure of *Socrates* – Socrates as ghost, as personified revenant – becomes the site in Plato of what could be termed a narcissistic and materially reflexive sign, a site openly called "in between" (*mesos* and *metaxu*) in the *Symposium*'s dialectic, and which is transposed to appear itself as the telos of the dialectic. In that dialogue, it has been pointed out, Socrates appears to be the very model of the Good, as he seems elsewhere transposed into the semiotic chain leading through the master-philosophemes themselves: Being, the Idea, the immortal soul, the King, *arete*.[20] The logic of the *involuntary* good, however, presents

20 As Friedlaender notes Plato perceives the eternal forms in and through Socrates. Thus "Socrates," "*Eidos*," and "immortality" are, as it were, three different aspects of the same figure (30).

certain problems in itself, and it is important that the early Socrates relies on it so extensively. It may be rewritten less as an *ethical* argument (which is itself weak) than as the covert projection onto ethics of a linguistic or aesthetic promise that might be called the claim of any word to being, a promise particularly present in the "absolute" subject, Socrates.[21] For instance, the Socratic dictum that "virtue (*arete*) *is* knowledge" may be less an existential assertion of ethics, as it sometimes seems, than a description of how *arete* functions as a cognitive trope, one to which the pretext of an "involuntary good" is connected. This seems clear in Socrates' repeated references to a *virtue* that pragmatically refers only to and is gauged by the subject's well-being, a virtue that is given the reflexive structure of a narcissistic sign which we see attributed to Socrates as Eros, or Hermes, or the Good in the *Symposium*. Such a notion of "virtue," which here functions semiotically, suggests a different system than that of an ethics of *the other* as such, since no "others" are at first involved in what is best for "my life" ("taking forethought for my whole life" [261d]). While the Ps fails to define "virtue," it nonetheless does expose a critical dimension of the term that it presents as a sort of unveiling and which cannot be entirely separated from other events in the text itself (the reading scene, the play of signature, the implied *metron*). *Arete* is not only emptied out of familiar sense early in the dialogue, but becomes associated with a principle of exteriority that may be essentially material and linguistic in nature. This emerges clearly when Socrates likens *arete* to a "face" (*prosopon*) with various parts, and it unexpectedly appears as the figure of prosopopeia that precedes

---

21 Philippe Lacoue-Labarthe and Jean-Luc Nancy address Socrates as "the subject of irony" in their account of Platonic dialogue in German romanticism in *The Literary Absolute*, trans. P. Barnard and C. Lester (Albany: SUNY Press, 1988): "(F)or the age of metaphysics, Socrates (the figure and the person) has always represented the anticipatory incarnation or prototype of the Subject itself ... This amounts to making Socrates the subject-'genre' through whom – and as whom – *literature* is inaugurated (and inaugurates itself, with all the force of the reflexive, since irony is also precisely this: the very power of reflection or infinite reflexivity – the other name of speculation). To be entirely rigorous, one must therefore say: Socrates, the Subject in its form or its figure (the exemplary Subject), is the eponymous 'genre' of literature ... And consequently a 'genre' beyond all genres and containing this 'beyond' within itself – or in other words, at once a general theory of genres and its own theory." (88) The seductiveness of the mimetic character, Socrates, conceals where his site also functions as a representation *of representation* in Plato's text, and the undoing of mimesis.

representation itself. Here the parts of the face itself appear as stand-ins for different sense organs ("mouth, nose, eyes and ears"), and we are led to rewrite the dictum that *arete* "is knowledge" as one that involves less an existential ethics that sounds too good to be true than a form of knowing linked to *sense perception* and phenomenality itself. *Arete* at this point – that is, in Plato's evolving tropology – is both a figure of unrepresentability and a term of materiality that precedes the emergence of the subject:

"Well, that is easy to answer" said he. "Virtue is one, and the qualities you ask about are parts of it."

"Do you mean" said I, "as the parts of a face are parts – mouth, nose, eyes and ears – or like the parts of a piece of gold, which do not differ from one another or from the whole except in size?"

"In the first way, I should say; that is, they are in the relation of the parts of a face to the whole [*hosper ta tou prosopou moria echei pros to holon prosopon*]." (329d–e)

"Virtue" as *face* underlines the fact that the dialogue that has seemed the most brilliantly mimetic of all also precedes mimesis or face. Accordingly, it reaches into the underlying networks and signifying chains whose powers situate and constitute the text or its ability to position itself as a sort of trans-historical depot – a site of constant arrival and departure, a fold after which various histories seem launched or which return to it – and it stages a crisis in mimesis, which the rest of Plato's writing cannot quite contain (nor, in a sense, wants to).[22] It is not accidental that the locus of this crisis – and the place where it is best covered – is in the figure of "Socrates" himself. A figure who presents the image of a mimesis without models that alters throughout the writing and remains the putative locus of voice, as well as the signifying lack that will echo through concepts like the good, *arete*, the Idea, or the King. It is worth recalling the text's

22 At all events, Berger's attempt to save this "face" in a footnote protects his interpretation from the dissolving interface of Platonic script: "*Arete* as 'face' is the *arete* of public performance, of self-concealment and self-presentation. That Protagoras chooses to define the parts of *arete* in terms of face rather than gold implies his commitment to *arete* as a *techne* of saving face" (91f). Berger's last footnote comments upon the proliferation of the Greek word *prosopon* in the *Protagoras*, where it occurs eight of the fifteen times it appears in Plato. As a prefigural moment, *arete* as "face" denotes sense perception's dependence on the materiality of inscription. See also Kierkegaard's discussion of "virtue" in the *Protagoras* in *The Concept of Irony: With Constant Reference to Socrates*, trans. L. Capel (Bloomington: Indiana University Press, 1965), 92–7, hereafter cited as *CI*.

seeming obsession with origins that turn out *not* to be originary: Protagoras' false allusion to being a *pater*, the mythos' mock history of the world, the collapse of dialogue itself into inscription. Not only does Socrates' invocation of Hades redouble the text as a phantasmal scene or dialogue of the dead but, repeatedly, personifications and masks of various sorts are marked. It is as if representation itself were being defaced: the anonymous first speaker, Hippocrates' face caught before dawn, the *proschema* speech, repeated speaking through "other voices," the personified "outcome of the arguments," *arete* presented as face. Not only is the most descriptive text made to become a scene of inscription, but it emerges at a site as if between waking and sleeping ("Socrates, are you awake or asleep?"), before an integral subject can even be asserted. Kierkegaard remains a premier metaphoric commentator on the problem of *arete* in *the Concept of Irony*, where he links *arete* to a material movement of language, a sort of silent sound held to function as a tyrant:

the unity of virtue is like a tyrant who lacks courage to rule over the actual world, and so first massacres all his subjects in order to rule with perfect security over a silent realm of shades ... But what I must call particular attention to is the fact that this unity of virtue becomes so abstract, so egotistically terminated in itself, that it becomes the very crag upon which all the individual virtues are stranded and torn asunder like heavily laden vessels. Virtue traverses its own determinations like a whisper, a shiver, without ever becoming audible much less articulate in any one of them. It is like imagining an infinitely long row of soldiers, wherein each soldier forgets the password the very instant he whispers it in the ear of his neighbour. (*Concept of Irony*, 94–5)

Kierkegaard appears to read *arete* as a tyrannical figure of what precedes or dispossesses the living that it, at the same time, generates – a figure that also cancels what it gives rise to. *Arete* is, to begin with, unrepresentable and repeatedly assimilated to a pre-phenomenal trace ("silent realm of shades," "without becoming audible"). Such a term compulsively inaugurates a *series* it can, at each instant, outpace ("traverses its own determinations"), disband ("torn asunder"), or erase ("forgets the password the very instant he whispers it"). To some degree, the narrative present in the sophist's mythos (as a potential stand-in for narrative in general) is designed to manage this disruptive figure through history and the odd pretext of Zeus' law. What is interesting, here, is that what seems to correspond to the self-cancelling logic witnessed elsewhere may be called nature or *phusis* itself; a nature which will be elsewhere likened to "chance" ("Everyone knows that it is nature (*phusis*) or chance (*tuche*) which gives this kind of characteristics to a man" [323c–d]).[23]

In Protagoras' mythos we hear that the gift of a certain "law" intervenes to curtail the self-destruction of cities:

Secondly, by the art which they possessed, men soon discovered articulate speech and names, and invented houses and clothes and shoes and bedding and got food from earth.

Thus provided for, they lived at first in scattered groups; there were no cities. Consequently they were devoured by wild beasts, since they were in every respect the weaker, and their technical skill, though a sufficient aid to their nurture, did not extend to making war on the beasts, for they had not the art of politics, of which the art of war is a part. They sought therefore to save themselves by coming together and founding fortified cities, but when they gathered in communities they injured one another for want of political skill, and so scattered again and continued to be devoured. Zeus therefore, fearing the total destruction of our race, sent Hermes to impart to men the qualities of respect for others and a sense of justice, so as to bring order to the cities and create a bond of friendship and union. Hermes asked Zeus in what manner he was to bestow these gifts on men. "Shall I distribute them as the arts were distributed — that is, on the principle that one trained doctor suffices for many laymen, and so with the other experts? Shall I distribute justice and respect for their fellows in this way, or to all alike?" "To all" said Zeus. "Let all have their share. There could never be cities if only a few shared in these virtues, as in the arts. Moreover, you must lay it down as my law that if any one is incapable of acquiring his share of these two virtues he shall be put to death as a plague to the city. (322a–d)

Something must intervene in the cycle of scattering and the destruction of cities, and that is a gift imposed by a certain Zeus — one presented in the form of two elements, as presented through Hermes, a principle (universal participation) and a law (which executes with death). Moreover, it is this intervention that seems to make possible the very occurrence of the future or history (as Kierkegaard points out of this section's argument, the "Sophist negates original history,

---

23 While Protagoras' *logos* exempts those maimed or deprived by nature from the *law* that the myth's "Zeus" imposes, what is first called "nature" begins to be called "nature *or* chance." This exception proves problematic for *phusis*: "Who would be so foolish as to treat in that way the ugly or dwarfish or weak. Everyone knows it is nature *or* chance" (323d). The association of "nature or chance," as Vlastos notes, is demeaning for *phusis*. The disposition of a "nature" released of its usual *others* to become an automatic or chance effect returns us to the problem of material language itself.

Socrates subsequent history" [*Concept*, 96]). But there is something arbitrary about a "law," moreover, given by a Zeus practically ventriloquized by his own servant, Hermes, figure of signs. What law of Hermes – the intermediary figure, likened in the *Symposium* to Socrates, *mesos* or *metaxu* – seems to arrest the cycle of destruction in representation and history, a cycle that laces many points of the *Ps*? Zeus' law in the mythos is designed to arrest a process of unravelling begun when Epimetheus and Prometheus begin world history with an *abdicating* reversal of roles – and hence temporal order. Yet this is itself contradictory, as Louis Bodin has shown, since it involves the gift of *both* a principle and a law. It is a law that legislates "death" for those who do not display justice (*dike*) and respect (*aidos*), but also these have just been distributed universally in any case, which should make the law moot. It is Zeus' law ("*my* law") that stops the spiral of self-destruction the text associates not only with nature (*phusis*) but with chance and, hence, language itself. The ventriloquized Zeus seems to preserve history – the future, or present even – by presenting a *detour* or interruption in a self-cancelling system, in which what is called "nature" is itself only the remnant of a disempowered previous "law" itself. In this way, that future does not quite take place, just as the present of the dialogue occurs already in a representational Hades. Zeus' law as intervention or detour in a self-destroying *phusis* resembles potentially any production of "voice," of a first person subject and, in a certain extended sense, of the *eidos* itself as a formalized counter-ideal to this linguistic *phusis*. Socrates' hyperbolic example of the "good" overcome *by itself* remains more than suggestive, since it reproduces clandestinely a semiotic logic that seems to permeate the dialogue – becoming, incidentally, a figure that Shelley would use in several key texts. If we extend this insight, it would seem that the "idea" is less a founding figure for truth than a hypostasized trope – indeed, the hypostasization of figure – the inversion of a material or aesthetic site occupied in the dialogues by the mimetic Socrates, the formalized inversion of the linguistic thing (or *pragma*).

According to the myth the "art of politics" is introduced only after Epimetheus distributes (*neimai*) all the possible *gifts* to other living creatures, leaving none for "man" (322b–c). The problem with the logic is: men would save themselves from destruction, but must do so by a social contract that only leads to further annihilation. What may again be called a self-destroying system – here of the *polis* itself – has a semiotic contour. Interestingly, men stand to be "devoured" by beasts, again and again, that is by figures of materiality like the "slave" or the horses in Hippocrates' name. It is an odd "art of politics" — one might say an aesthetic politics — that erects itself not against other human communities, but a *devouring* of man by what is not human. This situation is not to be rectified by the gift of respect (*aidos*) and justice (*dike*) that are later mentioned. According to this system, cities must first exist for there to be "political skill" at all, but once banded together they destroy each other and themselves. The latter cannot emerge to begin with. Such an anamorphic logic can only be interrupted by a ruse. "Zeus," at Hermes' bidding, or Hermes (as sign) at Zeus', appears to impose or legislate two things: a principle and a law. This moment appears decisive as the only authoritative mime of *law-giving* in a dialogue replete with fake fathers, abdicating archons, and excuses in the place of command. The principle of universal participation of this "skill" or "art" is not consonant with the "law" or *nomos* that would supplement or enforce it, since the latter punishes ruthlessly the lack of what, according to the first principle, everyone *must* possess anyway. Why punish with "death" those who do not have what everyone must anyway, by decree, possess? It is Zeus who masquerades as Protagoras here in a duplicitous role. The duplicity of "*my* law" depends on the sign (Hermes) that purveys and originates it, as the auto-destruction of cities and *phusis* appears itself *interrupted*. The "law" technically preserves the (appearance of the) future of the world from a premature, even precipitous foreclosure, yet only as a detour. The future (present) exists because of this law, which is nonetheless fictional. The "law" describes the interruption of a self-cancelling nature, which may itself be the remnant of a previous *nomos'* destruction. In the myth, this is depicted as beginning with an original abdication that recalls that of "father" Pericles or Pittacus (or Protagoras or Plato). What occurs, though, when we precede the world's origin, history, and narrative as such? As "*my* law (*par' emou*)," Zeus' imposition appears to be the arbitrary "law" of a despotic speaker: *me*, mine, or *Meinung*. We are left with a legal fiction that, contradicting itself, interrupts a narrative seemingly generated by pivotal metaphoric repetitions of a self-cancelling *phusis*. When Socrates notes that Alcibiades spoke "on my behalf (*hyper emou*)," or Socrates himself on Hippocrates' or Protagoras' behalf (316c), the preposition *hyper* seems also to denote the infinite precession of one speaker's being "spoken" by the *phusis* of material language.

If what the *Protagoras* betrays is the signature of an "other," Plato is no longer the paternal icon. This altered reading also marks Plato's as a profoundly duplicitous text all along – as, indeed, dia-logic. The entire iconography of Plato as father of presence would appear superimposed over a more radical absence or even abdication, over Plato as "woman," as *proschema*, as linguistic materialist, as "Protagoras." What the *Ps* suggests is a Plato no longer inverted by Nietzsche in the parables of "modernism" but much closer to Nietzsche. Not unexpectedly, it is just such a Plato that Nietzsche in fact notes in a posthumous text. Nietzsche notes *parenthetically* a very different reading of Plato from the one any overthrow pretends to: "(Plato: a great Cagliostro – remember how Epicurus judged him; how Timon, the friend of Pyrrho, judged him – Is Plato's integrity beyond question? – But we know at least that he wanted to have *taught* what he himself did not regard as even conditionally true: namely, the separate existence and separate immortality of 'souls.')"[24] This would seem to challenge Derrida's occlusion of Nietzsche's insight on just this point as well: "He understood nothing about the initial catastrophe, or at least about this one, since he knew all about the others. Like everyone else he believed that Socrates did not write, that he came before Plato" (*Post Card*, 20). If by virtue (so to speak) of following the play of letters we have addressed the space of a certain *re-signifying* going on in Plato's text and the reading of it, this play amounts to a strange and perhaps irreversible intervention of sorts. Considering how many narratives seem to begin at this point, with the idea of Platonism or Plato as origin, it has the potential effect of touching one end of a spider web through which shocks are sent across the whole, or dislodging the small key-stone of a vaster edifice. If this old icon of Plato is taken away, subtracted, well, we are left to take responsibility for a Plato that *we* culturally construct, if only to pretend, then, to invert and project that again back as a paternal or first text. The *Ps* deforms all mimesis in advance – generates its rules, precedes its reign, veers into an (un)sublime space in which a materiality before all discourse is metrically (re)positioned, (re)personified.

24 Friedrich Nietzsche, *Will to Power*, trans. W. Kaufman and R. J. Hollingdale (New York: Random House, 1967), 233.

6. Post-scriptum

What irradiates through the *Ps* is, among other things, the possibility of reading the signature of an "other" Plato in the facade of Protagoras. If we do so, "father" Plato becomes as much a construction as "father" Protagoras. For if we can say that either father Plato or father Parmenides may be imbricated in the speaker of the *proschema*-speech – the latter name being equated in Plato with Being, the sun, the ideas, and so on – then even the famously histrionic gesture of the Eleatic Stranger in *The Sophist* when he pretends horror at the parricide of "father Parmenides" that his discussion of simulacra implies (241d) would have to be read a bit differently. Indeed, ironically. That is, it could be read more as self-consciously comic than mock-tragic, as Derrida pretends for rhetorical effect in "Plato's Pharmacy" when he says: "This parricide, which opens up the play of difference and writing, is a frightening decision. Even for an anonymous Stranger. It takes superhuman strength. And one runs the risk of madness" (164). Rather, the comic pretense of parricide that is exposed by the *Ps'* play would appear but a rhetorical move among others, one not dissimilar to that of the classically staged overthrow – hence prolongation – of the iconic "Plato." What else can we do with the fact that in the dialogue bearing his name this supposedly other paternal P, "father Parmenides," does not support the doctrine of the ideas but in fact deconstructs the notion of the *eidos* itself, put forth now by a young Socrates, and this with the *third man* argument that is presented, as Friedlaender points out, in Heraclitean (which is to say, Protagorean) fashion?

In contrast to Heidegger, Derrida's reading of Plato in "Plato's Pharmacy" is openly doubled, as we see when he notes: "Play and art are lost by Plato as he saves them, and his logos is then subject to that untold constraint that can no longer even be called 'logic'" (156). On the one hand, Derrida rhetorically upholds a traditional or iconic Plato to be dismantled; on the other, he points to an "other" Plato who installs the first figure as a construction through the economy of the *pharmakon*, installs a Plato who generates "metaphysics" as an effect that he also stands apart from. Nonetheless, Derrida's rhetorical stance of *opposition*, to a previous historical fold of representation, seems to stay in play at least strategically. And this requires some editing or stage managing. The strategy becomes visible, when Derrida alludes to the passage in the *Phaedrus* in which the myth of Boreas' abduction of the virgin Orithyia while "playing with Pharmacia" (229 d) is evoked by Socrates. Derrida's use of the text is, like Heidegger in one sense, precisely to mark a spot or kairos that seems to occur within Plato's own writing:

"This brief evocation of Pharmacia at the beginning of the *Phaedrus* – is it an accident? An *hors d'oeuvre*? A fountain, 'perhaps with curative powers,' notes Robin, was dedicated to Pharmacia near the Illissus. Let us in any case retain this: that a little spot, a little stitch or mesh (macula) woven into the back of the canvas, marks out for the entire dialogue the scene where that *virgin* was cast into the abyss, surprised by death *while playing with Pharmacia* ... Through her games, Pharmacia has dragged down to death a virginal purity and an unpenetrated interior" (70).

But a funny thing occurs here. Derrida does not continue to quote Socrates when, a moment later in the passage, he changes his mind about just where that spot is. Socrates is in doubt as to whether it is in fact elsewhere, inside the walls of the city, rather than here, outside ("though it may have happened on the Areopagus, according to another version of the occurrence" [*Phaedrus* 229d]). The idea of a "spot" here seems, once again, multiple, presenting an insecure point of rhetorical contact that drifts in different versions, the very place where a metonymic, historical, or narrative series appears launched. Yet it provides no secure locus for situating that which cannot, itself, be framed or revised again, a sort of Lacanian *point de capiton* in which a master signifier weaves together a skein of possible meanings as a decisive, historical, *combinatoire* that can nonetheless in turn be undone. Plato has Socrates double the site in a manner encompassing or dissolving the inside and outside division that Derrida rhetorically finds constitutive of Plato's effect, and at this spot, so to speak, Plato's text marks its own management of a *pharmakon*-site without inside or outside. Such doubling seems permitted by Derrida's text but also produces a Plato who exceeds that reading, turning the tables: a Plato as remainder. It is all the more apt that Derrida, as though absorbing the possibility that "Plato's Pharmacy" may be (mis)read as yet another overthrow or usurpation, returns later with the "Envois" section of *The Post Card*. In this text, as noted, any such ordering of priority and epochal supplantation is suspended and examined as a reversible structure through the problem of Plato's priority to Socrates. It is done, that is, by the model of S and P, which is literally and letterally put into play; done, again, as a rewriting of – hence, re-inscription in – the reading scene of the *Ps* itself. It is interesting that in doing so Derrida, like Heidegger and through him, must claim an originality of seeing *more than* Nietzsche specifically; he must occlude the possibility of this being already in play in the latter's reading, and must come in a sense before him: "He understood nothing about the initial catastrophe, or at least about this one, since he knew all about the others."

To put these texts in contact compels a further spiral, then, that does not efface Derrida into Plato so much as unbind a long held iconography of "Plato" himself. The question here might be that of another "Plato" that escapes – or at least sabotages – the generational position of Plato as origin, enforcer, tyrant, facticity, inscription, and platonist, though the result is not only a postmodern Plato that was always available. The *Ps* appears to rehearse (and release) in advance such future readings – to conceal or produce a Nietzschean Plato (truth as will to power), to dislocate the "mimetic" reading of dialogue, to open the eviscerating play of signature by reading (and perhaps overleaping) Heidegger's or even Derrida's reading of his text.

What, in fact, is at stake in this reading, we might say, is the overthrow of the entire trope and historical fiction of the overthrow, the overthrow of the overthrow, or that there was a paternal icon to overthrow that did not – in Plato – sustain itself in advance by abdicating that position dia-logically.[25] We can see how this works in practice: once we cast Nietzsche as a platonist, as Heidegger does in a reading scene that repeats that of the *Ps* in producing the "modernist" Plato, for example, we are not far from another reversal.

25 In the twenty-fourth lecture of *Nietzsche, Volume IV: Nihilism,* "Being as A Priori," we read: "the name *metaphysics* means nothing other than knowledge of the Being of beings, which is distinguished by apriority and which is conceived by Plato as *idea.* Therefore, *meta-physics begins* with Plato's interpret-ation of Being as *idea.* For all subsequent times, it shapes the essence of Western philosophy, *whose history, from Plato to Nietzsche, is the history of metaphysics* ... With respect to the founder of metaphysics we can therefore say that all Western philosophy is Platonism. *Metaphysics, idealism,* and *Platonism* mean es-sentially the same thing. They remain determinative even where counter-movements and reversals come into vogue. In the history of the West, Plato has become the prototypical philosopher. Nietzsche did not merely *designate* his own philosophy as the reversal of Platonism. Nietzsche's thinking *was* and *is* everywhere a single and often very discordant dialogue with Plato" (164). So basic has been the figure of this beginning and the implications of its "over-throw" or "reversal" (*Umkehren* as opposed to *Ueberwinden*), that it is odd it has not been examined as essentially recuperative in nature.

In that, we would come to read *Plato as a Nietzschean*. If Heidegger would overthrow the system Plato-Nietzsche, as he seems to want, he would then occupy the position previously given "Nietzsche" as closer-of-metaphysics. Yet instead, at this point – the point, say, in which the philologist Friedlaender jumps in, Prodicus-like, to forestall his transposition of *aletheia* – Heidegger himself appears in this rotation or peritrope as the metaphysician par excellence instead, which is to say, unlike Plato himself, platonic.[26] As we know, in order to read Nietzsche as a Platonist, as he does in the *Nietzsche* lectures, Heidegger must first establish (retrospectively) Plato as a reversal of some preceding truth that he (Heidegger) could as if return to, which he does in *Plato's Doctrine of the Truth*.

P.s. It would seem that metaphysics would here be synonymous with the positional claim of epochal transpositions, or their undoing, to begin with, which is another way of suggesting that "metaphysics" itself is always such a retro-projection, that it never quite was – or is always about to be re-installed.

26 Friedlaender literalizes the public reading of "Heidegger's historical construction" – blowing the whistle on and tip-toeing around a move he can not comprehend the stakes of (metaphysics' overthrow). To do this he returns to present a too literal reading of *aletheia* at the expense of what, for Heidegger, would be the entire *in between* of "history and metaphysics" itself, what lies between Plato to Nietzsche. Friedlaender, who claims "both aspects (versions of *aletheia*) have equal status for Plato," without any historical turn or shift, wants to return to the simple truth. Heidegger's reading of Plato through (or against) Nietzsche first (re)posits Plato's own iconic figure in order to allow the facade of his "overthrow" to be played out (by himself), a gesture we have seen at work in the address of both Protagoras and Pittacus by Socrates. See Martin Heidegger, *Nietzsche: Volume I and IV*. Trans. F. Capuzzi (New York: Harper and Row, 1982); *Nietzsche I/II* (Neske: Pfullingen, 1961); *On Time and Being*, trans. J. Stambaugh (New York: Harper and Row, 1972); "Plato's Doctrine of the Truth," trans. J. Barlow, in *Philosophy in the Twentieth Century III*, ed. W. Barrett and H. D. Aiken (New York: Random House, 1963); *Platons Lehre von der Wahrheit* (Bern: Francke, 1947).

PART II

Parables of exteriority: materiality in "classic" American texts

3

Too legit to quit: the dubious genealogies of pragmatism

This is the way one should understand the Lacanian thesis according to which Good is only the mask of radical, absolute Evil, the mask of "indecent obsessions" by *das Ding*, the atrocious, obscene Thing. Behind Good, there is a radical Evil: Good is "another name for an Evil" that does not have a particular, "pathological" status. Insofar as it obsesses us in an indecent way, insofar as it functions as a traumatic, strange body that disturbs the ordinary course of things, *das Ding* makes it possible for us to untie ourselves, to free ourselves from our "pathological" attachment to particularly worldly objects. The "Good" is only a way of maintaining a distance toward this evil Thing, a distance that makes it bearable.

Slavoj Zizek, *Looking Awry*

What I would like to ask in this essay is whether what we today call "neo-pragmatism" cannot be seen less as an extension of high American pragmatism than a contemporary ideology that evades the very materiality (of language, of the sign) that *it* has implied from the start (at least, that is, since Emerson and Peirce, if not Protagoras).[1] Or differently put: whether the role that neo-pragmatism has played in contemporary critical politics, and more particularly that of the late 80s in a general turn from "theory" into historicism, cultural studies and the politics of identity, has not involved an *ideological blind*? This is certainly all the more difficult to ask when that ideology (I use the term in its post-marxist sense) appears under the *label* of "the" most nascent American tradition, but that's one of the points I want to make: that the oddly *nationalist* rhetoric that has set "neo-pragmatism" against *theory* (which is also a code for the alien, the non-human, the "French") is not only contradictory − particularly where multiculturalism is at issue, as in Cornel West's *American Evasion of Philosophy* − but misses what might be called most "American," the place where American pragmatism in its root sense may be already a *post*-humanist

---

1 An earlier version of this paper was given at the "Pragmatism and the Politics of Culture" conference at the University of Tulsa, on March 27, 1993, and I have retained the format of that presentation.

project. That is also to say where pragmatism's contemporary theories (in Rorty, or West) involve, instead, regressive attempts to shore up an iconic humanism, a theology of the self, a space of interiority, that implicitly evades the *materiality* that has always been at stake in what we can call the American break, one which recalls that the term *pragma* is equatable in Greek with a "thing" (or what we might name *gall*, recalling Zizek's recent use of late Lacanian idiom, *the Thing*). At stake, in short, is whether the critical politics mobilizing neo-pragmatism against "theory" entails a misreading of its own pedigree, a fairly mystified attempt to return to a space of the subject or self that pragmatism was implicitly designed to empty or exceed, and hence, whether what it ends by evading is not, in a sense, America itself.

Largely begun or at least re-installed by Richard Rorty's *Consequences of Pragmatism* (1982), American neo-pragmatism itself has served a fairly pragmatic role.[2] As a sympathetic and vaguely nationalist rallying point before the diverse aporias and (literally) foreign agents of post-structuralism (or "deconstruction"), it not surprisingly translated at times into a renunciation of "theory" as such (as in *Critical Inquiry*'s "Against Theory" debates). A particularly interesting chapter in the "return to history" of the 80s, was that neo-pragmatism at one time or another claimed diversely original American critics ranging from Rorty to Fish, Harold Bloom to Lentricchia, and Walter Benn Michaels, subsequently refashioned (and appropriated) by Cornel West to consolidate an ascendant multi-culturalist vision of leftist critique (at which point Bloom and Fish fade in relevance). The original philosophical mandate of pragmatism was to present an alternate to systematic philosophy, the Enlightenment, foundationalism, totalizing metaphysics, transcendental positivisms, essentialism, and totemic empiricism. Critical neo-pragmatism seemed to refashion this in its own way: it was to return the American critical community from methodology and rote textualism to something, well, pragmatic, situationist, individualist, historical, interventionist. What was less clear was what might be being *evaded* here, or how and whether anti-theoreticism did not play, just a bit, to the lower end of American anti-intellectualism, or to a deeper anxiety of identity?

2 The primary works in this discussion will be Richard Rorty, *Contingency, Irony, and Solidarity* (Cambridge University Press, 1989), and *The Consequences of Pragmatism* (Minneapolis: University of Minnesota Press, 1982); and Cornel West. *The American Evasion of Philosophy: A Genealogy of Pragmatism* (Madison: University of Wisconsin Press, 1989).

First Rorty, who was so instrumental in reviving the idiom of pragmatism, and who seems in a way to provide Cornel West with the occasion to form a new narrative — a new "genealogy" if you will, keeping in mind that this term, in West's exceptional book, *The American Evasion of Philosophy: A Genealogy of Pragmatism* (1989), is *not* used in a Nietzschean or Foucauldian sense. That is, what West calls "*a* genealogy of pragmatism" going back to Emerson is not offered as a critical narration aware of its fictional status and designed to undo a historical knot in the present — on the contrary, it is a "genealogy" in the routine, unphilosophic sense of providing a pure, and in this case entirely male, deed of origin and legitimation: here, for the cultural left assuming the tattered mantel of the academic *center*.[3] One of the questions I want to ask, then, is how this happens — through what moves, or why? How, that is, pragmatism moves from being the foreclosure of History (Emerson) to a potential historicism, from a resistance to all essentialisms and symbolic law to a theologically inflected program in which the individual seems absorbed by a communitarian voice (I am alluding the West's powerful prosopopeia, "prophetic pragmatism"), a site claiming purity of descent before the names of the fathers (those hanging on the branches of the tree on the cover of West's book). This, I suggest, is the truly interesting *story* — the genealogy of a genealogy — and, to be properly historical, it may not be unrelated to the critical ideologies of the 80s, and to some of their most notorious impasses: the shift, as it were, from a politics of difference to a politics of identity, the return to a pan-*mimeticism* that, despite the desires of the left, seems to have continually strengthened the neo-conservative right going into the 90s, and the site (increasingly apparent) wherein something like New Historicism appears more and more as a Reaganite phenomenon. One is reminded, say, of how the left and traditionalist right joined to abject

---

3 In the present genealogy continuity is asserted, much as Brook Thomas links neo-pragmatism to leftist New Historicism and legitimizes both as a continuation of tradition. Brook Thomas, "The New Historicism and Other Old-Fashioned Topics," in *The New Historicism*, ed. H. Aram Veeser (New York: Routledge, 1989), 197: "The move ... from poststructuralism or postmodernism to pragmatism ... should caution us that rather than offer a new way of relating to the cultural past, the turn to pragmatism reaffirms the liberal tradition of American progressivism and its sense of temporality, a tradition from which the new historicism has never really broken." Here continuity and "the liberal tradition" are retrieved, much as West would impose a sane and sober culture of organic intellectuals in a left-protestant polis at worst perplexed by its institutional power.

deconstruction in the name of the return of the intentional subject of history, only to see the re-empowered traditionalist turn against the former and lump it with deconstruction (as occurs in the multiculturalism debates). What is really suppressed may be that this *other* pragmatism (or Americanism) had, starting with Poe *and* Emerson, tried to close out the romantic model of *interiority* itself, which both Rorty and West labor to keep open. Accordingly, neo-pragmatism can be read as a reaction against what could be called pragmatism's *own* logic.

I will return to these issues, but for now we must note the obvious, that every genealogy begins, as it were, with a fiction or crime (as Balzac says about every great fortune). What I would like to do is at least indicate where other "genealogies" of pragmatism can be constructed, for example where an other *reading* of Emerson can certainly be produced. One in which, say, the essay "Experience" would be properly seen as announcing the foreclosure of that category (as the title ironically implies), the subject of "experience" him or herself dispossessed by the *materiality* of signs; or, for that matter, as if in a parody of all genealogies, go back to "father" Protagoras, whose famous dictum on the *metron* – that is "Man is the measure of all things ...," often cited as a founding text (however contradictorily) of relativism, humanism, and pragmatism – may be read as a *performative* text in which the category of "man (*anthropos*)" is decentered, dismantled, and dissolved by a term, measure, which inscribes this non-subject in an activity of sheer semiosis and differencing not unlike, say, Peirce.[4] The problem is that even suggesting this indicates what Rorty and West *begin* by wanting to "evade" in the act of preserving or restoring against "theory" a subjective space that may not, as we see with Protagoras, have been there to begin with. But I promised you a story, if only a short one, and I return, again, to Rorty. I would only add that if this story is not straight, as you see, not linear, it may be because the term "pragmatism" involves a certain circular density (a theoretical concept that would evade theory) and a circulation-effect: that is, like Poe's

---

4 The term "materiality of language" is used to denote the possibility of a more radical "materiality" that precedes the humanist model of meaning (meaning as property or interiority). It will be linked, momentarily, to the term *pragma* which itself occurs at the etymological heart of "pragmatism." Accordingly, "materiality" alludes to a dimension of language that precedes figuration, as it is possible to read the Protagorean *metron* itself as doing.

letter or the phallus, it not only chooses and interpellates its momentary claimant, but is a name that will be contested as conferring a certain power, at least until it migrates again.

Rorty's exceptional role here is interesting since, unlike West, for whom American pragmatism seems a closed family affair, it is for him *double*. That is, "pragmatism" *already* has two branches, two variant logics, of which one will be that of the *humanist*, the American, and hence the home-team (and who could identify *against* this!), and the other, truly *other*, that of the continent, of "theory," the dialectical school associated with the *un*human, itself therefore external: "Bloom is a pragmatist in the manner of James, whereas Foucault is a pragmatist in the manner of Nietzsche. Pragmatism appears in James and Bloom as an identification with the struggles of finite men. In Foucault and Nietzsche it appears as a contempt for one's own finitude, as a search for some mighty, inhuman force to which one can yield up one's identity" (158). You see the point: here it is the American way that forms a certain *us* (the human), while the binarized other – alien, unhuman, theoretical – forms a *them*: not pragmatism and theory, but an untheoretical pragmatism and a theoretical pragmatism, as it were. It is not surprising that a sub-agenda becomes clear, that of maintaining a certain *interior*, a certain *self* or American "identity" (perhaps what is always, in advance of itself, in question: perhaps whose very definition is to be in question permanently), against this *exterior*. Yet, oddly, this is done by the reinvention of a split between a "private" and "public" space, for which we may read interior versus exterior. What may be odd, here, is that in making the first the domain of the "ironist," as Rorty has it, he effectively locks in with that presumed interiority the very beast he had meant to preserve it from – at least, that is, if the domain of irony is that of the self dispersed by the material or external properties of language. Nonetheless, Rorty also uses this category (the "private") in a *double* fashion, as when it is meant to neutralize, say, Derrida, to cut off his text from the "public" space of history. Thus he says of *The Post Card*: "The later Derrida privatizes his philosophical thinking ... There is no moral to these fantasies, nor any public (pedagogic or political) use to be made of them ... He privatizes the sublime" (125). Yet Rorty's compromise is configured increasingly in oddly ethical or defensive terms: "The *compromise* advocated ... amounts to saying: *Privatize* the Nietzschean-Sartrean-Foucauldian attempt at authenticity and purity, in order to prevent yourself from slipping into a political attitude which will lead you to think that there is some social goal more important than avoiding cruelty" (65). What is effected by Rorty's "compartmentalization of the self" is a dubious sequestering, the linking of an ideology of the self to a sort of life-extension machine based on the neutralization of inside and out, the avoidance of "cruelty," i.e. efficacy, rupture, voiding, intervention, and erasure.

The avoidance of cruelty, here, sounds very much like the avoidance of exteriority itself. The problem, to return to my earlier suggestion, is that in creating two *pragmatisms* – the human (or humanist), self-situated, and uncruel *vs.* the materialist, post-humanist, for which the *self* is an effect – and then choosing the first as "ours," as *American*, Rorty may in fact be choosing the wrong one, that least in accord with a performative reading of the American tradition (which, if you will forgive me, can be seen as, shall we say, decidedly Nietzschean, and in rupture with historicism and the experiential self). He may choose, that is, the pragmatism that is least *ours*. The question remains, why?[5]

But here things get inverted again, because one can plainly see why Rorty's return to the "private" had aroused the resistance of the politically engaged. It is here that Cornel West intervenes. Or at least, in a sense; because a problem inhabits West's discourse as well: the very moment, we might say, that he rewrites Rorty's *private* space as that of the public, historical, and political mode of pragmatism – when West would seem to nudge Rorty's *flanneurism* toward the outside – well, something different occurs. West, who erases the *two* pragmatisms to reconstitute the paternal purity and descent of a single (male) line (represented by the tree resting over a book on his cover (though what sort of "tree" – that is, a natural or organic line – stems from a *tome*?)), and who, in turning back to the world, ends by making yet a greater turn *back* toward a theologized self, only now communitarian: he returns further toward interiority ("prophetic

---

5 For a nuanced appreciation and critique of Rorty's argumentation see James McCumber, "Reconnecting Rorty: The Situation of Discourse in Richard Rorty's *Contingency, Irony, and Solidarity*," *Diacritics* 20, 2 (Summer 1990), 2–20. Here, after noting the questionable "redescriptions" Rorty makes of Hegel, Heidegger, and Derrida, he notes that "it is as if the absence of any account of the re- in redescription absolves Rorty from sustained encounter with the texts he discusses" (10). For a more incisive critique of Rorty's account of relativism see Barbara Herrnstein Smith, *Contingencies of Value: Alternate Perspectives for Critical Theory* (Cambridge, Mass.: Harvard University Press, 1989), particularly "Matters of Consequence," 150–87.

pragmatism is a child of Protestant Christianity wedded to left romanticism" [227]).

The problem here, and it is with neo-pragmatism in general as a critical ideology, is that the very discourse that advertises a turn toward a more radical materiality or *pragma* (or, as West says early on, if only for a moment, the "materiality of language" [4]), ends by doing the opposite: evading not (or not only) philosophy as epistemology — as if, once again, getting "practical," eluding *mere* theory — but by evading, in a sense, a primary moment in pragmatism itself, indeed, in America itself. What might be called a strain that aims to evacuate the regressive, "private" self or identity here returned to *as if* against the claims of an alien "theory."[6] But there is more: this plays out one of the critical blindnesses of the late 80s in which a certain *turn* from the rhetoric of the text toward the political culminated (and have we grasped this quite?) with the more neo-conservative national and nationalist climate opening the 90s. It may be that one problem of the left, its "crisis," involved an essential error in viewing the political as the equivalent of an ideology of representation or *mimesis*. One might ask where, instead, a more pragmatic pragmatism that is at once American *and* "theoretical," may see intervention as a matter of changing our very modes of *mimesis* themselves: a pragmatism which again sees epistemology as the very site of the political … But to continue:

If in West's book pragmatism becomes programmatic and theological, and in the hortatory voice of "prophetic pragmatism" (which I will call *PP*, for brevity) abstract, idealistic, and just a bit autocratic (as I will note), West sees this as an evasion of evasion, as when we hear of "the complex relations between tragedy and revolution, tradition and progress" that "(p)rophetic pragmatism refuses to sidestep" (226–7). If this leads to *PP*'s reclamation of a productive future, its adversaries include "postmodernism" and the "faddish cynicism and fashionable conservatism rampant in the intelligentsia and general populace" (239) — that is, of course, the relativists, atheists, and post-structural nihilists (as in West's mock-Bourdieuian dismissal of a Derrida whose "relentless skepticism … may be symptomatic of the

---

6 One possibility is rethinking the term *pragma* as what Ned Lukacher, in writing on Shakespeare, simply calls "stuff" or "anamorphic stuff." He notes this as a site of history: "It opens the space of the aesthetic as a strategic defense against power's appropriation of the stuff of language" ("Anamorphic Stuff," 890).

relative political impotence of marginal peoples," such as "an Algerian Jew in a French Catholic (and anti-Semitic) society" (236) – so much for Derrida). Yet if West is "disturbed by the transformation of highly intelligent liberal intellectuals into tendentious neo-conservatives owing to crude ethnic identity-based allegiances" (7), there is evidence that West's rhetoric at least flirts with this fold or trap too. There is the question, for example, of what is excluded by *PP*'s very *inclusivity*, its exhaustive drive to *in*corporate. Whether "prophetic pragmatism" is a movement or a position personified to argue West's vision, the incantatory repetition of the felicitous alliteration cannot but gain, it would seem, authority as it accelerates. For example, when we hear that, "For prophetic pragmatism only the early Hook and Niebuhr – their work in the early thirties – maintain the desirable balance" (226) between Emerson's optimistic theodicy and the tragic Trilling, one must suppose that no *solitary* pragmatist, or *prophet*, might disagree, or have a different reading of Emerson, or even stand outside the *surveillance* of a politically sanctioned community – the very thing pragmatism was designed to enable. In one sense, *PP* comes to exclude the site "pragmatism" was first invented to open.

West (or *PP*) thus admonishes Foucault in a way that displays not only West's utopian hopes but also his ostensible blindness: "by failing to articulate and elaborate ideals of democracy, equality, and freedom, Foucault provides solely negative conceptions of critique and resistance. He rightly suspects the self-authorizing and self-privileging aims of 'universal' intellectuals who put forward such ideals [like West?] yet he mistakenly holds that *any attempt* to posit these ideals as guides to political action and social reconstruction must fall prey to new modes of subjection and disciplinary control" (226). Does he? Here is the collective and familiar warning and retreat of certain forms of American intellectualism (theistic, ethicist, "marxist," self-privileging) from the "relentless skepticism" of the continental model, calling for a time out, the need to recoup – somewhat like Detroit before the soulless mimetic victory of Japan. Yet West recurrently does "fall prey" to just what Foucault described, making his restriction itself prophylactic.

"Prophetic pragmatism" evinces, I suggested, certain autocratic tendencies. It is, first of all, a call for a "sane, sober, and sophisticated intellectual life in America and for regeneration of social forces empowering the disadvantaged, degraded, and deject" (239) – all admirable aims, though this *assumes that the identity of these terms is not problematic or even contested* (who decides, say, what constitutes an "insane" pragmatism or one lacking "sobriety"?). *PP* increasingly is invoked as a panoptical, even a desiring subject with a strangely impersonal command: one hears again and again what *PP refuses, judges or wants. It* comes to sound, we might even say, like a kind of "sane" hysteric (the "interplay between tragic thought and romantic impulse, inescapable evils and transformable evils makes prophetic pragmatism seem schizophrenic" [229]). While at times West slows the drive of his vision in order to accommodate errant members ("Of course, he or she *need be* neither religious nor linked to religious institutions. Trade unions, community groups, and political formations also suffice" [234]), *the good type of intellectual* – born or bred – emerges behind the always dangerous metaphorics of what is *organic*: "An organic intellectual, in contrast to traditional intellectuals ..., attempts to be entrenched in ... organizations, associations" (334). What becomes apparent is that West, like Rorty, formulates strategies to protect a culture of *interiority* not altogether distinguishable from a threatened semantic economy or religious humanism whose political credentials have never been altogether assured. What we might here want to call the ideology of this pragmatism seems less a natural outgrowth of a tradition than a determined, if entirely legitimate, usurpation of it. If West's swerve toward oratorical *totalization* behind folk idiom echoes Emerson, the latter's rhetorical doublings and erasures disappear as West ends with a flat program against what is called, simply, evil:

Prophetic pragmatism is a form of tragic thought in that it confronts candidly individual and collective experiences of evil in individuals and institutions – with little expectation of ridding the world of *all* evil. Yet it is a kind of romanticism in that it holds many experiences of evil to be neither inevitable nor necessary but rather the results of human agency, i.e., choices and actions ... It calls for utopian energies and tragic actions, energies and actions that yield permanent and perennial revolution, rebellious, and reformist strategies that oppose the status quo of our day. (228–9)

In the recent work of Slavoj Zizek a sort of postmodern theology emerges via Lacan in which the "good" is mounted as an ideological evasion of a radically exterior "evil" (Thing) that, nonetheless, inhabits and to some extent directs it: "Good," we hear, "is only the mask of radical, absolute Evil, the mask of 'indecent obsessions' by *das Ding*, the atrocious, obscene Thing." Recalling the link of the Greek word *pragma* to "thing," it is a model of ideology that may be useful in assessing the revival of *pragmatism*. Going back to Rorty, now, is it clear just how classically this ideology of neo-pragmatism is constructed: locate an outside (the other pragmatism, say, Nietzsche's and Foucault's), and reject it as alien, though what is being ejected, the pragma or evil "thing," materiality as such, in fact lies behind one's own (American) pragmatism (in Poe, in Emerson, in Peirce, and so on); then refashion what is called "our" pragmatism itself as that which, having ejected the alien or unhuman figures, can be restituted as a legitimized morality of the integral human subject and a seamless model for action to boot — then give it a pedigree?[7] The ethics that emerge from this conceive of an "evil" to be got rid of and a romantic humanism that is recentered in the subject's will. It is, again, also a strategy to reassert a romantic (and religious) cult of interiority. One danger here is a potential reversal in which the proclaimed ethicist's position rotates from being pragmatist in the longed for sense of the concrete, to being rather abstract or theoretical after all. For if this reversal does occur, then the abjected or so-called "formalist" position — let's say, the *exterior* site of Nietzsche for Rorty, Poe for Bloom, "post-structuralism," in general the un-American — emerges as an ethically transvaluative project and, as the name Poe suggests, as all along American.

In conclusion one could again suggest a different "genealogy," almost parodic, going back to Emerson, or for that matter Peirce, or better still, to that ur-father of pragmatism, Protagoras himself. Indeed in a sense, the chronology or genealogical chain would be somewhat irrelevant, since in each case the official reading of each seems to have

7 I use the term "ideology" in a post-marxist sense, as a means of accessing the systematic and at times chiasmic inversions whereby interiorizing systems of meaning appear constructed over the structural abjection as "external" or other of a term that resides at its putative (dispossessing or external) core. This simplified description removes the term from the language of "false" consciousness, and may be considered an extension of Althusser's work. Perhaps the most popular current recirculation of this term, if not the most rigorous, occurs in Zizek's work, where the political and aesthetic analysis of "ideological anamorphosis" occurs within an appropriation of the late Lacan's notion of the Thing alluded to above (see also Slavoj Zizek, *The Sublime Object of Ideology*). Zizek tends, however, to evade the problem of language's own "materiality" in ceaselessly evoking the phallophany or epiphany of "the Thing," and overlooks altogether where language itself — as inscription — routinely operates from the site of the Thing as such. A recirculation of the term might instead lead us in the direction of de Man's late conception of *aesthetic ideology*, where this occlusion is precisely avoided.

evaded this point. The doubleness of West's pragmatism (heard in the initials *PP*) answers a "crisis of the American left" through legitimizing a regressive drift to the right by way of its own theistic ethicism. For all of this, when West treats Peirce's "profound pragmatic revision of the Emersonian evasion of modern philosophy" (44), he cites the following four revisions of Cartesianism as paradigmatic:

(1) We have no power of introspection, but all knowledge of the internal world is derived by hypothetical reasoning from our knowledge of external facts.

(2) We have no power of intuition, but every cognition is determined logically by previous cognitions.

(3) We have no power of thinking without signs.

(4) We have no conception of the absolutely incognizable.

One may agree with West that these "conclusions map out the new terrain on which American pragmatism will reside" (45), without drawing the same conclusions as to what that terrain signifies. For what Peirce says, in brief, is that "consciousness" of the subject is an *effect* of material or *external* signs ("external facts"), and that it derives from a complex or commentative interaction with other, anterior texts. He says, moreover, that "outside" of this infinite semiosis there is no consciousness, no subject, no "man." The tradition West wants to return Peirce to, that of semantic interiority and religious humanism, is precisely the tradition from which Peirce breaks here, in this text, and which is interdicted by the *first* principle (though whether this is really "new terrain" is disputable). What is genuinely radical here, and what should *not* be "evaded," is not only that the model of all cognition is the interaction of external signs but that cognition could itself be viewed as a trope for something like reading, that consciousness is a *product* of just such a transaction. If the *second* principle outlines an intertextual or allegorical basis for cognition in which "*intuition*" does not figure ("every cognition is determined logically by previous cognitions"), the *third* and *fourth* principles are conclusive. Indeed, if Peirce recalls to contemporary ears here Wittgenstein, Lacan, or early Derrida, these principles trace the double trope of pragmatism back to Protagoras as well. I have already mentioned the oddness of Protagoras' master-text on the non-word *metron*, which comes to us through the distorting medium of Plato (whose relation to Protagoras' signature has yet to be traced). *Metron* suggests, in short, a certain radically material signifying function precedent to all figuration that has both an organizing and unnameable role.

In West's account, both the explicit attack against relativism and the recentering of the subject remind us of the other "father" of *pragmatism*, Protagoras, who was also the supposed father of rhetoric, humanism, and relativism – in short, interestingly for genealogical purposes, of (at least) both of Rorty's pragmatisms at the same time.[8] This is not the place to launch an alternate genealogy of pragmatism, but I will note one direction this could take.

As I suggested, the word *pragma* may be associated in Greek with "thing" or commodity, and may even be slang for a sexual transaction. In Plato, however, at least in the performative dimension of the *Protagoras*, the term appears through a series of displacements to be associated with letters as such and, even, with an early (some scholars say the earliest) hint of the Platonic *eidos* itself. That is, Socrates in this dialogue alters his usual harassing question – Is there such a thing as X (Justice, Virtue)? – and for that substitutes the question of whether X (Justice, Virtue) is a "thing (*pragma*)" (330c). The reason this otherwise minor shift is at all interesting has to do with the action of the dialogue, which proceeds in a seldom remarked free-fall through every representative speech *genre* and ends, at its center, in the reading by Socrates of Protagoras' reading of a poetic text (Simonides') itself reading another or an inscription (Pittacus' "pithy" saying), that is in turn a retort itself. The dialogue drifts from a mode of social dissimulation to a *mise en abyme* of reading. Moreover, in this reading scene the initials and hence letteral signatures of the represented speakers (Socrates and Protagoras) reappear oddly in the cited texts (as, in more ghostly fashion, must those of Plato *and* Socrates). This

8 Among the targets to be creatively revised is the presumed "relativism" or covert "formalism" of poststructuralism and its diverse replicants (the "faddish cynicism and fashionable conservatism rampant in the intelligentsia and general populace" [239]). This is explicit toward the end of the book, where Derrida is set aside, while "The Challenge of Michel Foucault" is briefly critiqued from a position articulated by Said ("Prophetic pragmatism objects to Foucault's project not because he has no historical sense but rather because it remains truncated by the unhelpful Kantian question he starts with," which "shuns the centrality and dynamic social practices structured and restructured over time and space" [224–5]). What becomes clearer is that behind the evocation of Emersonian self-reliance is a traditional Americanist claim for the subject, the soul, the individual, and a resurgent theology – what is good, what is evil – that flows from this.

raises the question of whether Plato is reading Protagoras through Socrates' reading of Protagoras reading Simonides' reading of Pittacus, or whether Socrates is reading Plato himself? This fact itself suggests that a certain problem of inscription may inhabit, for Plato, his own understanding of Protagoras, a problem that is also complexly dissimulated in the dialogues. As I have examined, something in the name Protagoras brings out, and conceals, these problematic conjunctures. By way of a reflexive doubling in (and of) the dialogue, the term *pragma* will appear associated not only with reading, but with the materiality of inscription, and it can be read as initiating a figural series of associations across Plato that extends beyond Socrates' discussion of the "primal letters" or *stoicheia* in the *Theaetetus*.[9] As noted, the largely doctrineless dialogue called *Protagoras* nonetheless constitutes a profoundly performative "reading" of Protagoras' text by Plato, one that haunts later dialogues. Since the *Protagoras* presents the only scene of Socrates rhetorically reading a (poetic) text, we might be tempted to say that in Plato the character Protagoras for some reason is associated with *reading*. As such, "father" Protagoras presents a curious model. It may be that Protagoras' "measure (*metron*)" is misread when heard as the by-word for a relativist *humanism*. On the one hand, it may be that Protagoras' dictum ("*Man* is the measure of all things ... ") does not so much mean to centralize "man" as a subjectivist figure, the individual as measure of "all things," but rather it supplants that subject with the predicate and non-word *metron* itself – a term of radical exteriority. It is, in fact, a post-humanist text. If this is the case, it would produce an alternate Protagoras than the one Plato had to caricature to conceal the reflexive, materialist, or *anti*-humanist moment. The trope of "man" may be implicitly dismantled as the limitless activity of the unnameable and material machine of infinite semiosis. *Protagoras*, here, can appear as a double text which undermines the "humanism" he is iconically taken to represent. *Metron* would thus name something that is without a name, a movement of marking differences that can itself be called prefigural – as in a series of marks, or sounds, or in the precession of speech genres and written texts to letters in the dialogue *Protagoras*. To cite

---

9 When the otherwise casually mentioned problem of inscription is given as an example of education by *memorization*, for instance, it leads to the example of making letteral outlines by stencil or copying, and the word for "traces outlines" is *hypogram* (326d).

Protagoras' *metron* – which we may hear, say, in the beating of "The Tell-Tale Heart" – is to point to what might generate, if retro-actively, the irreducible and unrepresentable trope of materiality. To contrast these two readings of the Sophist's famed dictum, both of which seem present in Plato (the first publicly, in Socrates' routine in the *Theaetetus*, the second performatively, in the *Protagoras*), we may say that the canonical or *mimetic* reading of the utterance assumes that "man" is a known quantity (the integral subject) who measures "all things" (those with and those without being) according to his/her centrality and perspective. The text is subversive as such, since it notes the relativity of cultural experience, yet it is also recuperable as a centered humanism (à la West or Rorty). The second reading, however, assumes the name of "man" is here *de*defined, a dissolved space-holder of the discoursing subject who, inscribed in and as language, is supplanted by the predicate, the *metron*, as a cutting, criticizing, or reading activity (Whitman might call it tallying) that is fundamentally external to and defining of "man." The first can appear subjectivist; the second seems much the opposite, but depends on the thematization of reading as differentiating (measuring), as a material activity preceding metaphor, or that "rhetoric" Protagoras was also said by some to have invented.

The point here should be condensed. Any grand "genealogy" of pragmatism is a complicated affair, caught and truncated in the infratextual abyss of Platonic positioning and the highly elusive figure of Protagoras to emerge through Plato. I say elusive, because this is precisely what Plato himself underlines by making Protagoras at once seem publicly open and utterly dissimulative when in battle with Socrates. In fact, Protagoras calls himself twice a "father" in the dialogue, as Emerson might, but in each case in a move (rhetorically transparent) to secure the audience's transference and foreclose Socrates' power. It involves a strategy to bind both his audience and Socrates by what he elsewhere calls a *proschema* (316d–e), a *screen* or pretext which permits him to assume innumerable *names* in his genealogical history stretching back to Homer, intended to legitimize inversely the non-word "sophist." Protagoras as character marks in Plato a dangerous space, one that can wreck the mimetic premise of dialogue itself by veering into letters (or the materiality of language and history) and can dissolve the pretext of an integral subject. His pretense to the authority of mock-paternity – which anticipates in all respects West's own – acknowledges the social value of generating a "genealogy," yet marks the impossibility of any Oedipal or familial order proceeding from a conceit of language as *pragma*. The renowned but often banally translated "Man is the measure ... " could more interestingly be tracked, perhaps, if we did not assume "Man" as the given narcissistic subject, but reflected "him" back into the parameters of "measure" itself. Such a text might no longer be called simply relativist *or* humanist, since it also constitutes a defacement of "man." "Measure" could now be rendered by a series, not of letters but of marks, knocks, or bars that are almost possible to render graphically (/ / / /). Precisely such a bar series can become the emblem not only of repetition and narrative, but of castration, materiality, anteriority, allegory, exteriority, semiotic "death," listing, the machinal, and the generative point of linguistic consciousness as such. Protagoras' *metron* may present, as Bloom suggests, the first pragmatic theorization of the sort of materialism cited from Peirce.[10]

To conclude, then, neo-pragmatism may not only be read as the choice of one pragmatism (American) over another (continental, Nietzschean, "theoretical"?), but as the evasion of a more fundamental pragmatism that is already American. If there is an American "pragmatism" that foregrounds these issues of linguistic materiality – and there is, it is called American literature – it might be objectionable from certain perspectives in West's program for appearing at points frankly post-modern or "nihilistic." It may be that what America needs in response to its various wounds – of, by, and inflicted on the left and the right – is not another Christo-moralist retrenchment, but rather and precisely *more pagans*, that is to say, more fetishist polytheists and ecstate-atheists among its critical ranks, more pirates disrupting the commercial trade-routes of sanctioned (including leftist) discourse, more linguistic trans-genderists, nihilist jesuits, fringe marxists, and amok micro-textualists. That is, more deterritorializing "formalists" and, all in all, more *pragmatic* interventions in the legal machinery of mimetic reproduction that represent the possibilities of

10 This last association is made by Bloom, who notes in his *Agon: Towards a Theory of Revisionism* (New York: Oxford University Press, 1982): "The crucial term in Protagoras is *metron*, 'mastery over something,' which for the purposes of literary criticism I would translate as 'poetic misprision' or 'strong misreading.' Untersteiner says of *metron* that by it Protagoras portrayed Man as 'master of experiences' precisely in order to overcome 'the logoi of opposition to each other,' which is to say that *metron* comes into play in order to master the tragic difficulties that both produce and are lyric poetry" (35).

materialist quest(ion)ing today. For if the critical community is not to regress to a *mimeticism* that is pre(post)modern (or pre-Protagorean), even under the *abstract* icon of a politics of the concrete, it may have to return to what it found rhetorically necessary, going into the 90s, to suppress, the pragma or stuff of language. How much has the mimetic conception of "the political" in the 80s contributed simultaneously to the anti-intellectual, neo-conservative cast of academic discourse opening the 90s? Another way of saying this would be that it is entirely possible to read the originary texts of pragmatism (from Protagoras, to Emerson, to Peirce), as precisely concerned with *epistemology*, only in a performative and linguistic way; that the split between the political and the epistemological (or textual, or theoretical) is misleading, is the blindspot of neo-pragmatism itself; and that, contrary to West's founding genealogical evasion, epistemology may be the very site of *the political* – as any rigorous analysis of aggressive nationalism suggests.

Is there an anti-mimetic politics at work within the structure of reading and resignifying itself? It is this other pragmatism that I want to suggest is at work, all along, in "classic" American writing, and that can be given a transvaluative import. The following essays try to explore, in different ways, how the materiality of language is deployed to exceed an always older model of meaning or the subject in the instances of Poe (sound), Whitman (voice), and Melville (letters) to alter the very terms of mimesis.

❖❖❖

4

Poe's *Foot d'Or*: ruinous rhyme and Nietzschean recurrence (sound)

❖❖❖

> The harbingers of modernism, Poe and Baudelaire, were the first technocrats of art.
>
> Theodor Adorno

In Poe's tale of entrapment and revenge, "The Cask of Amontillado," there is a fairly pointless aside that, on reflection, opens onto a central question about how we read Poe today – that is, as readers located between the traditional American abjection of Poe and the pivotal role he has played in post-structuralist theory.[1] As Montresor leads the object of his revenge, the drunken Fortunato, through the catacombs to his living entombment, he is asked by Fortunato to describe his family arms. The question is delicate since it testifies to Montresor's prestige on a point (like Poe's own general belittlement) he has reason to be resentful of. The answer, however, is odder still since the *arms* – in which aggressive and martial term it is hard not to hear a reference to body parts – consist of a severed foot. It is, however, not supporting anything else, but rather raised to the level of an emblem, large and golden: "A huge human foot d'or, in a field azure; the foot crushes a serpent rampant whose fangs are imbedded in the heel." What is odd, perhaps, is that a trope of materiality (feet) seems enshrined as its own self-destroying signified ("fangs ... in the heel"), a foot or leg itself cut off (like Cassio's leg) and raised to the status of a subject – a material signifier that also represents its own signified in a dangerously circular loop. It seems dangerous because it predicts the act of "crushing a serpent" (Fortunato?) as what will sacrifice the golden foot itself –

---

1 In "Deconstructive Poe(tics)," *Diacritics* (Fall, 1988), R. C. de Prospo complains that while Poe has become the special province of deconstructive readings, these have been assimilated to traditional Americanist perspectives (55). He suggests that the opposition is, in some sense, misleading and specular. He adds that the "one definitely original task that remains for deconstructionist critics of Poe to accomplish in the 'fresh' rereading of Poe's poetry" (50), which I pursue here. All citations of Poe texts will be from Edgar Allan Poe, *The Complete Tales and Poems* (New York: Vintage Books, 1975).

transform, that is, the signifying or mimetic order that Poe's text will engage. It will be the burden of this essay to suggest, nonetheless, that Poe smuggles into this an emblem of his own materialist poetics. Moreover: I will suggest that through this we are empowered to ask a series of questions infrequently asked of Poe's work. The first concerns what might be called a Nietzschean moment in Poe. I mean to ask where he uses the facticity of language to explicitly transvalue or even destroy the classical system of representation and mimesis which he inherits. Another is where he — American literature's "odd man out" — seems to undertake this destruction/transvaluation in the name of America itself. Before returning to the difficulties posed by Montresor's arms, I propose to lay out what I mean both by Poe's materiality and his transformation of mimesis itself through examining his treatment of sound.

1. Poe's pragmatism: notes on the jingle man

"I answered then truly that I knew them only from Poe's criticisms: cruel and spiteful things which I should be ashamed of enjoying as I once did."
"Whose criticisms?" asked Emerson.
"Poe's," I said again.
"Oh," he cried out, after a moment, as if he had returned from a far search for my meaning, "*you mean the jingle-man!*"   William Dean Howells

Among the most familiar of poems from one's earliest readings, "The Bells" often eludes serious commentary, as if it were just too obvious to need interpretation.[2] Yet what may pass for a kind of gothic nursery rhyme about bells, is perhaps the key to why any discussion of intertext in Poe risks a sort of free-fall. If we note, for instance, that the very concept of echolalia to which the poem is dedicated doubles as the trope of literary allusion — as if an aural echo, itself, reflects a citational echo — then we must ask why the text accelerates this concept to the point of *absorbing*, and then emptying, any discrete "meaning." It is as if Poe's paean to the technocracy of sheer sound over semantics mirrors an American refusal to be inscribed in

---

2 Even comprehensive commentaries on Poe's oeuvre, like David Halliburton's *Edgar Allan Poe: A Phenomenological View* (Princeton University Press, 1973), hereafter cited as *EAP*, or J. Gerald Kennedy's *Poe, Death, and the Life of Writing* (New Haven: Yale University Press, 1986), virtually omit all reference to "The Bells" — though, in Halliburton's case, it is arguably where Poe treats the engenderment of "phenomena" through language.

anteriority – or to let a future reader inscribe his writing in Poe. In "The Bells" we see a metatext whose *technical* turn into the metallic universe of sound not only empties the concatenations of sense it at first solicits, but further puts the concept of text production into question. The entire problem with finding a vantage point to read the poem, however, must be approached through the tendency of the tradition to abject Poe himself, to cast him out in the position of the empty "Thing" in whose work the symbolic fabric of meaning is jeopardized.

In discussing "text and intertext" in Poe, I will try to make three points. The first is that Poe's own writing may at times imply a willful foreclosure of what we like still to call *intertextuality* – that is, the networking of revision and allusion that normally assures a text's readability by inscribing it in a discursive series or tradition. To claim that this represents a calculated American aggression is but half the equation, since "The Bells" presents other problems. Among these is my second point, that what the work calls "runic rhyme" is not a throwaway phrase but denotes a superficially encrypted writing *by sound* that directly disturbs the machinal or mimetic reading of the text; one that gives aural concatenation the status of letters, like runes, and virtually installs (or reactivates) an alternate system of sense production that renders the conventions of the text as self-parodic institutions. My third point is that this materiality of sound suggests a certain *pragmatism* – that is, a reduction of language to its material status recalling the etymology of *pragma* as thing.[3] Poe's "pragmatism," which is so different from that attributed to an Emerson (at least superficially) and directly opposes the recent revival of neo-pragmatism as a critical alibi by liberal humanist critics, plays an unexpectedly Nietzschean role in the text.[4]

---

3 It is not arbitrary that the psychoanalytic reading of Poe invokes the Freudian – and Hegelian – conceit of *das Ding* in depicting the purloined letter as a non-symbolic or prefigurative "real." See Francois Peraldi in "A Note on Time in 'The Purloined Letter': Hegel, Poe, and Lacan," in *The Purloined Poe: Lacan, Derrida, and Psychoanalytic Reading* (Baltimore: Johns Hopkins University Press, 1988), 341.

4 Halliburton likens Poe's treatment of "things" to Marx's notion of reification, "the process through which man turns his labor, and in a sense himself, into a thing" (*EAP*, 247). He also attaches Poe's characters' "primitive, animistic anxiety" to the German tradition of the grotesque's *Tuecke des Objekts*, called "the fear that 'things' are 'out to get you.'" For Halliburton, Poe underlines the thing's "artificiality," "the alienated and alienating quality of the technological environment" (247).

Let me begin, though, by recalling the nature of the text's reliance on sound — moving through four stanzas or different metal bells, pretending to seasons or the ages of man yet subtly effecting a collapse of difference to a sheer dispossessing clang that suspends even that narrative pretext. The emblem of this is how the refrain ("Bells, Bells, Bells," and so on) moves from jingling celebration through sheer repetition to emptying sound. What begins as "tinkling" becomes "jangling" and "wrangling," while all too conventional rhymes are jarringly exposed, chained to the metonymy of harsh echo. The increasing ringing eventually moves toward a point where the personification of both sound and voice seems foreclosed.

If the canonical status of "The Bells" is odd — at once utterly familiar and yet largely unread — it mirrors Poe's frequent treatment by the "high" literary tradition, at once in and yet kept out of the canon.[5] Yet nothing seems clearer, now, than that "The Bells" performs *a violent critique of mimesis and the logos as such*. It reveals the technocracy of sound as the very engine of textual production. Not only is repetition itself shown to establish verbal sense or identity, but it proceeds to dismember words into syllables through rhyme and, finally, turn each into a clang (of) itself. *Bells* is a term quintessentially onomatopoetic, yet it also collapses the mimetic function of language as the word becomes a "thing" itself, void, a sound become its own reference. This aural acceleration begins by multiplying and interlacing sense with echo itself, a term itself troping textual citation or allusion. If the text proceeds from the promise of clarity (Silver Bells) and union (Golden Bells) to the brazen alarum bells of the third stanza, in the fourth all intertextual capacity of allusion seems reversed, sucked up, absorbed, as "man" is depicted as a virtual prosopopeia of sound. By absorbing past as well as any future readings, "The Bells" appears as a sonar black hole among texts, a metapoem that must be given distance or be trivialized and simply set aside. Another way to put this is that Poe's poetic machine *exposes* the technology of textual production through its dependency on the materiality of sound. Hyperbolically if not in fact, it contains in its clownish refrain every

---

5 Shoshana Felman draws attention to the contradictory status of Poe's "case history" by asking whether his official rejection may indicate a collective repression as well: "The fact that it so much matters to proclaim that Poe does not matter is but evidence of the extent to which Poe's poetry is, in effect, a poetry that matters" ("On Reading Poetry," in *Edgar Allan Poe*, ed. Harold Bloom [New York: Chelsea House, 1985], 137).

laborious and multiply impacted pun Joyce can inscribe in the composition of *Finnegans Wake*. In this leap into techno-culture by asserting the metallic dominion of sound over sense, Poe closes out (again) the subjective model of expression on which the humanist institution of "literature" depends.

If the poem knells — one will say, yet again, if in advance — the death of literature by soliciting and then undercutting any intertextual foothold, making that a thing, it nonetheless suggests something of Poe's own American exceptionalism, and here the spectre of pragmatism returns.

I turn to the third stanza, that of the "brazen" or bronze alarum bells, depicted as a warning of invasion. It is in this stanza that the bells no longer "dwell" or announce a future, no longer "*fore*tell," yet trying to speak, to exist in the "now," they are rendered mute, and the very personification that depicts them as "angry" itself recedes. The problem is that what is invading as if from *outside* is the bells themselves which do the warning, the material linguistic element — what, anticipating a bit, I will call the *pragma* — which generates linguistic "consciousness" and its forgetful illusion of having some interiority, some recess, or crypt apart from that clang of language. This seems the import of the vision near the end of the Babel-like human bell-tower (with "rust within their throats" [956]). As though anticipating the canon he would routinely be exiled from, "The Bells" exiles itself from reading by preceding and naming the construction of all poetic sense dependent on the controlled or chance con-catenation of false analogies. In doing so the poem threatens to expose the technological basis of any semantic system or text. Reducing the "old world" tradition, when the end of the poem at least suggests a reversal or transition in the affirming dance of the mad King who "tolls." With its recurrence of fragmented rhymes from earlier parts of the text — recalling what rap music calls sampling — it suggests an affirming Nietzschean turn to the text's semantic nihilism that is rarely discussed. For in essence, Poe is exploring the material basis of signification. We might say that the emptying of the interior is viewed not tragically, but with technocratic abandon as if the intent were to wear down the policing role of "anxiety." What it leaves behind as debris is a conception of mind as an *intertextual* effect based on personification and repression. The text's acceleration of sound, which, again, puts it in touch with the later works of Joyce, renders antiquated a basically modernist vision before that "happens." Such is Poe.

Now, in making these remarks I have jumped the gun a bit, having left the text itself behind — what, after all, is still *just* a gothic nursery rhyme about, well, bells. Metal bells. And must be, and for good reason.

We may now read this problem through Poe's recurrent abjection — since it never was a *rejection* — by the "high" canon. Indeed, this gesture was recently reiterated by Harold Bloom, our foremost guardian of the intertextual.[6] For while dismissing Poe's vulgarity on grounds of taste (his poetry is called "of a badness not to be believed"), Bloom notes: "If we read closely, Poe's ultimate trope is 'absorption,' and we are where we always are in Poe, amid ultimate fantasies of introjection ... That makes Poe the most cannibalistic of authors" (3). Yet what a writer *cannibalizes*, as Bloom knows, is less bodies than anterior script, and the metaphorics we have come to associate with "psychosis" in Poe's case may now be rewritten.[7] What troubles Bloom, we might say, is less the *literalness* of psychosis before his own clearly *neurotic* model of meaning, one based on discrete repression, repetition, and return, than the possibility that *the economic model of repression does not apply*. Indeed, that the binary assumption itself — of psychosis versus neurosis, say, or Poe versus Emerson, or a negative American strain versus the affirming pragmatist — might fall apart.[8] Bloom pretends one must choose between them: "If you

---

6 Harold Bloom's amusing litany of imprecations against Poe moves quickly beyond "the scandal of what might be called 'French Poe,' perhaps as much a Gallic mystification as 'French Freud'." For Bloom, Poe's "palpable vulgarity" raises "perpetually the issue of whether literary merit and canonical status necessarily go together. I can think of no other writer, down to this moment, at once so inevitable and so dubious" ("Introduction" to *Edgar Allan Poe*, 4). Bloom's exuberant Poe bashing redoubles and, in the process, unhinges the traditional devaluation.

7 A different way to put this is that what the psychoanalytic model indicates with the label psychosis is what is unaccountable by a certain historicizable model of representation itself, of which "repression" and one form of mimesis are policing — and politicized — terms (a perspective not limited to that developed by Deleuze's *Anti-Oedipus*).

8 "Repression" represses not only a repressed content or, after that, an awareness of repression itself; it represses (that is, forgets) that it is itself a construct. What does the concept of repression repress? In fact, Bloom's founding of an American sublime on a vast "repression" appears as a defense before a more puzzling absence of repression that may be peculiarly American. In *Poetry and Repression* (1976), Bloom begins by celebrating as a poetics of repression what he is compelled to depict as a proto-psychosis or "refusal" irrecoverable by a neurotic

dislike Emerson, you probably will like Poe. Emerson fathered pragmatism. Poe fathered precisely nothing, which is the way he would have wanted it." Why, again, does American neo-pragmatism as a critical ideology, particularly as projected onto Emerson, seem imperilled by Poe? Even in Cornel West's *The American Evasion of Philosophy*, "pragmatism" ends up, again, as the umbrella term for an evasive academic humanism, however reoriented with political conscience. What if Poe's own pragmatism — that is, his reduction to a materiality of language and the *techne* as such, void of subjectivity or romanticism — teaches us how best to read Emerson today, certainly in an essay like "Experience"? For there Emerson forecloses the concept of "experience" — the ironic point of its title — by never getting beyond a reflexive problem of reading signs, as marked by the inability to mourn the death of the son, Waldo.[9]

We are forced to ask again: what allows us to read the word bell itself as Poe's reduction to the "stuff" of language, its prefigural materiality, its *pragma* — before the inscription of sense? Bells oscillate between name and "thing," simulacrum and brute sound, signifier and signifier-as-signified in an anamorphic loop. How do we read, however, the hieroglyphs of sound called runic rhyme? The poem opens familiarly:

> Hear the sledges with the bells —
> Silver bells!
> What a world of merriment their melody foretells!
> How they tinkle, tinkle, tinkle,
> In the frosty air of night!
> While the stars that oversprinkle
> All the heavens seem to twinkle
> With a crystalline delight;
> Keeping time, time, time,
> In a sort of Runic rhyme,
> To the tintinnabulation that so musically wells

model: "Emerson therefore founds his Sublime upon a refusal of history, particularly literary history" (254).

9 This returns us to the point in the essay where what is mourned is the absence of mourning itself (in this case, for Emerson's son, Waldo). One can contrast this reading with a recent piece by Sharon Cameron, "Representing Grief: Emerson's 'Experience'," *Representations* 15 (Summer, 1986), where she addresses as literal the question of the death of Waldo, though the text's lament is for the blockage of mourning itself. Through the rhetoric of mourning for mourning, what Emerson conceals is the lost category of "experience."

> From the Bells, bells, bells, bells,
>   Bells, bells, bells —
> From the jingling and the tinkling of The Bells.   (954)

If the poem asks what the different metals signify (silver, gold, bronze, and lead), it notes the imposition of sense over the *same* "sound" (bell), where difference as hysterical multiplicity can collapse to a "muffled monotone." The *keeping* of "time" suggests that temporality is linguistically produced through phenomenal differences that the bells mark, yet also erase. Runic rhymes dismember and reorder the conventional words into sound elements, recombining through chance concatenations to yield a kind of microverbal soundscript written across the text's surface. For example, the repetition of the syllable "in" in the first stanza in "ti*n*kle," "twi*n*kle," "overspri*n*kle," or even doubled in "ti*ntin*nabulation" demonstrates where repetition seeks to impose *interiority* fictively on the metallic stuff of sound relation, what precisely bars that as such. Similarly, in this context, "crystalline *de*light" would seem to name a translucent disaster, a light that is the foreclosure of light, like a black sun inhabiting or preceding the dismembered syllables' assumption as the agents or fabricators of sense.

Runes are thus also *ruins*, figures destroying the mimetic surface of the text yet also involving archaeological or intertextual traces. It is in the third stanza that the linguistic functions of *fore*telling ("their melody foretells") and recollecting collapse, as the asserted "now" itself cannot be achieved in the text's increasingly dubious present. I will suggest that here Poe's cannibalistic *intertextual* logic is best exemplified, if only because it leaves the trace of an encounter. Let us say that in the unachieved "now" of the text ("Now — now to sit or never") we see Poe's American "introjection" of a High Romantic sublime, parodically citing and reversing Wordsworth in a radical absence of transcendence. Rather than the supra-temporality conjured in Book v of *The Prelude*, say, where the poet projects a naturalistic apocalypse as "now" that masks the linguistic collapse of *pre-* and *re-* terms, Poe parodically discloses this collapse as an American sublime in the absence of any "Now," a self-disarticulating *non-present* without any transcendence, before or after.[10] The famed inwardness of

---

10 Poe's non-present negatively rewrites Wordsworth's strategy in Book v of *The Prelude*. In "Missed Crossing: Wordsworth's Apocalypses," *Modern Language Notes* (December, 1984), Andrzej Warminski explicates that scene as "a totalization ... of what one could call the *pre-* and *re-* moments — prospective and

"Tintern Abbey," say, has been reduced to mere "tintinnabulation," dispossessed by the exteriority of language itself – what Baudrillard calls the *ec*-stasy of communication (from itself). The third stanza's "startled *ear* of night," as a dismembered ear (or mouth) that "fully knows" (and "distinctly *tells*"), becomes the fictive seat of cognition and measure, the prosopopeia ("startled") of a personification that gives a face – or at least part of one, an ear – to absence ("night"). At this moment "bells" – now a non-word and non-name – precedes all figuration and briefly becomes a representation of representation, the linguistic hyperreal or *pragma*, maliciously dismembering the "ear god" of High Romanticism. The very element on which the human voice depends, sound, *ex*poses it as a nearly pre-human effect in a babelesque vision ("the people – ah, the people – / They that dwell up in the steeple" [956]). Language teeters on the brink of becoming *white* noise as linguistic consciousness precedes even the binaries of gender or species "neither man nor woman ... beast nor human," living or dead. If language appears momentarily as something non-human, so does the human; if the tower-image suggests the effect of hearing someone speak a wholly alien tongue, it is to reveal one's own speech as such.

Yet for all this gloomy posturing, there is nothing truly morose about the work. Indeed, the mad king affirms the repetitive dance of random lines, recycled verbal debris, and beyond the final reversals Poe's text seems poised at a transvaluation of linguistic thinking, pointing beyond the reduction to the linguistic *pragma* that makes the poem either the most dangerous of texts or, as is more generally thought, the silliest.

We can sympathize with Bloom's no doubt knowing dismissal of Poe. Who, after all, really wants to have to *read* "The Bells" – or who, now, ever, can stop doing so? We see, though, that the "badness" of the verse is indeed "not to be believed" (to quote Bloom). If it is not read, that may be because it itself actively reads any poem relying on random aural concatenations for its sense, that is, every poem, in every language. If the letters E-A-R almost reproduce the initials E. A. P., Poe may be said to seek his runic signature in the ear, much as the "mad ex*post*ulation" of the third stanza involves an *ex*ternal positing of sense on the acoustic stuff of language in which Poe's own *name* is

retrospective, proleptic and recollective, etc... synthesized in a 'living Presence,' a living present, one could say" (99).

echoed. Rather than the loose writing of which Poe is often accused, we find in the trope of runic rhymes a complex or mason-like precision of writing at work less in the word than in the *pre*semantic unit: in puns, inscriptions, echoes, and cross-signatures. "The Bells" is the one text whose clang has no intertextual echo, since it is nothing but that. In attempting to reduce "literature" to a technological artifact, Poe forecloses any view of literature as a reserve of interiority. The death that "The Bells" knells may be of this institution or its historical ideology as such — a view that, at least, returns to Poe a proper historical agenda.

2. The "Cask" of America

I at once looked upon the figure of the animal as a kind of punning or hieroglyphic signature. I say signature; because its position upon the vellum suggested this idea. The death's head at the corner diagonally opposite, had, in the same manner, the air of a stamp, or seal. But I was sorely put out by the absence of all else — of the body to my imagined instrument — of the text for my context. *The Gold-Bug*

"The Bells" informs our opening questions in several decisive ways. Where are we authorized, now, to use what Poe calls "runic rhyme" as a decisive principle of reading? Where does the Nietzschean rupture of narrative time in this poem inform our ability to address narrative elsewhere in Poe?

It is not hard to find bells in "The Cask of Amontillado," though their use is initially unclear. They rest atop Fortunato's head (as his "conical cap and bells"), and we hear of them only once at the end, when he refuses to give Montresor the satisfaction of a reply when he has come to himself, chained and entombed: "'Fortunato!' — No answer. I called again — 'Fortunato!' — No answer still. I thrust a torch through the remaining aperture and let it fall within. There came forth in return only a jingling of *the bells*. My heart grew sick — it was the dampness of the catacombs that made it so" (279; my emphasis). While Montresor interprets his own anacoluthon for us ("— it was the dampness"), it marks a repression, since what it in fact suggests, given the assertion of hermeneutic control that the plot turns around, is a reversal in the drift of power between the two. Instead of a voice, cringing or otherwise, in which Montresor can delight in the other's enchainment, his very consciousness of being as good as already dead, of being dead, Montresor receives as echo only a jingling of bells. That sound tears down any possible recognition, as if Fortunato were all along entrapping Montresor in turn, if in an undefinable way. If so, what or who is Fortunato in this text? Why does the text – to frame this differently – demand a metatextual performance in which the stakes are the transformation of textual laws themselves? What is at stake?

"The Cask" never receives the attention given to major (or even routinely cited) tales. It is short, accomplished, yet with few loose ends or enigmas. The narrator – Montresor, we later learn – recounts the narrative to some unspecified "you" of his revenge against a nobleman, Fortunato, who we hear injured and, finally, insulted the narrator, though in what respect is not said. This gap in the text, indeed its "origin," must be filled or overlooked by the reader. While the narrated account is so immediate that it at first seems to have just occurred, we learn at the end that a "half century" has passed, that the tale has been, perhaps, endlessly *repeating* itself, that the narration itself is about that repetition – strangely echoed in the second word of the tale ("thousand"). Thus this pretext of Renaissance revenge conceals yet another transaction, seemingly internal to Poe's own writing project and specifically in his relation to anteriority itself – to that which instigates *revenge*. We can address this other text primarily through *runic rhymes*, a mode of reading licensed in "The Bells." Here one can read the tale as a performative and metatextual *act* in which Poe brings an entire historical model of meaning to the point of destruction together with the narrator who himself deploys it. Yet in doing so, that model seems to persist through the narrative of its own cancellation.

Poe's "Cask" often seems to be passed around, then, circled or returned to, picked up and set down, yet seldom emptied or drunk from, and for good reason. Set before the tale, after all, the title itself names a container that is itself a fiction in the fiction (Montresor's promised Amontillado which we never encounter), a content that does not get presented. Moreover, it will be used as a fiction – like the story – for *other* ends, or as a lure, a seduction to entrapment. The title of the text, in effect, announces another story than the one that it names, while that one, the Poe tale we expect, never appears. Thus the focus may be on the act of narration, a metatextual event for which the missing "insult" is a clue. Yet D. H. Lawrence chooses this text to illustrate his understanding of Poe. In doing so, he comments on the "lust of Montresor ... to devour utterly the soul of Fortunato ... Perhaps, in the attempt, the victor breaks the bonds of his own identity, and collapses into nothingness, or the infinite" (*Studies*, 97).

J. Gerald Kennedy pushes this vaguely moralized reading even further, returning to the passage we just cited on the jingling bells, and deciding what it signifies: "The victim's silence affects (Montresor) as no verbal reply could, for it signifies the silence of mortality and foretokens his own death ... The victim of revenge is invariably the self" (*Poe*, 104). While Kennedy builds a moral into the text that heroicizes the self, each reading suggests a sort of *circular* or self-cancelling logic to the enterprise, and we may revise that by asking whether the iconography of the "self" itself — shorthand for a representational system of meaning — is not the intended victim of the narrative. The lack of reference for the act of revenge (injuries, insult) appears theorized by the text itself as a general structure of repetition and *ressentiment* on which any system that equates meaning with appropriation may depend. This fact brings us back to what I called the Nietzschean problematic in Poe: "The *thousand injuries* of Fortunato I had borne as I best could, but when he ventured upon *insult* I vowed revenge" (274). Why after all do the seemingly innumerable injuries culminate in a single insult, a verbal gesture, and what is implied by the repetition of the opening syllable (*in*) itself? What depends here on runic rhymes to read? What (narcissistic?) wound would the text correct?

To open the work to a reading of its puns is, first of all, to hear in the name *Fortunato* reference to fortune, or for that matter chance, and we may then ask, what it means for Montresor to want to entomb or fix a personified figure of *chance*? Chance here may be thought as the material or external element capable of intervening in (and in-augurating) any system like a text or the narrative of a life that involves a more or less randomly generated series of events. Chance returns us to the function of sound itself in "The Bells," or to the concatenations of sense, *tyche*, anteriority, or the "Real" as what is radically exterior. The injuries and insult of chance could represent, then, a wound that — however we choose to read it — provokes the retro-projective attempt at control and *re*dress. If thought as *ressentiment* or repetition of an incursion attempts to assert its own power by again controlling or responding to that which negatively engendered it (the absent referents of the opening), we see how the text at its very opening seems to undertake a circular project: to be revenged against Fortunato, in a strange sense, which is also to fix or overpower the random and chance itself, is also to reflexively control or remove what gave rise to the possibility of consciousness, the wounded "I" that itself speaks — to overcome citationality or language by itself. It recalls the science-fiction trope of reaching into the past to correct (but then perhaps alter or erase) the present. If this does not illuminate the image of the foot d'or on Montresor's arms, at least it suggests how to address certain enigmas of the writing. In this scenario, to avenge oneself on a figure of chance – or on *figuration* itself, and with it, the weight of all past writings that impinge on the writer – may be to turn against what gives rise to the text itself, "me," what is *mon*, the "I" of Montresor. What writer, after all, has not ruined innumerable sentences by pursuing the seductions of a chance sound pattern, a random association of sense? Yet if the very meaning of words relies on their repetition, and that of sounds, as we explored, then what is also resented is repetition itself. This casts a curious light on the final revelation that the event happened half a century ago, and has been retold and retold ever since, as if the price of foreclosing repetition is to repeat that gesture of voiding mastery over and over again, as the loss of what Kennedy called "the self." Yet there is another problem to the rules of this game, which is that of the writing: one may abstractly *resent* the chance conditions of one's birth (one is poor, ugly, maimed), yet to overcome or fix chance is dubious since, even if successful, as in gambling, that too may be due to chance – *il y a et il n'y a pas le hasard*, as Mallarmé says in *Igitur* with this text, no doubt, in mind. We may be misreading Montresor's plot as a straightforward will to mastery over chance since his ultimate stakes may be considerably more complex, anamorphic, or duplicitous. Fortunato's narrative entombment may be staged by Montresor or Poe's narrative to overcome the *re*sentment of Fortunato/Chance as well, the dependency of the entire system on this familiar problematic. It raises the question of whether we cannot read mastery rather as the overcoming of mastery, of meaning as a system of property altogether. Is the very logic of *Meinung* that we hear echoed in the name Montresor, then, what is in fact being sacrificed – and now we can add, with Montresor – by the machinery of the tale?

"Chance" takes on a different meaning in the name Montresor. Here *tresor* may itself be translated as treasure, or fortune, or, again, chance, and hence Montresor may be unexpectedly heard as my-treasure or my-fortune, and hence as *my-chance*. Yet whose *mon* is in question, whose chances? Is it Poe's "chances" at stake in the tale – how he will or will not get the text itself right, or prove acceptable to the canon (always a problem), or how the text succeeds in the calculated mastery of verbal concatenations? Or is there a more general problem to be heard in the syllable *mon* itself related to the founding of verbal meaning in consciousness by appropriating, incorporating, making *mine*. Differently put, this may itself be described as the systematic interiorizations by the "I" that, once again, construct meaning, or *Meinung*. However the "*thousand* injuries of Fortunato" may anticipate Poe's subsequent critical fortunes, here chance might not only represent the materiality of sound, or the (narcissistic) wound inflicted by the writer's dependency on *anterior* texts (say, for Poe, the text of Shelley). It is important to examine, then, what may be called the "runic rhymes" of the opening paragraph, and I underline some elements that seem marked or highlighted by repetitions, making them points of convergence of sense:

The thousand *in*juries of Fortunato I had *borne* as I best could, but when he *ven*tured upon *in*sult I vowed re*ven*ge. You, who so well know the nature of my soul, will not sup*pose*, however, that I gave utterance to a threat. *At length* I would be avenged; this was a point *definitive*ly settled — but the very *definitive*ness with which it was *re*solved *pre*cluded the idea of risk. I must not only *pun*ish but *pun*ish with im*pun*ity. A wrong is un*redr*essed when *retr*ibution overtakes the *redr*esser. It is equally un*redr*essed when the *aven*ger fails to make himself *felt* as such to him who has done the wrong. (274)

I will summarize what has been said so far. The "*thousand* injuries of Fortunato" implies that the agent of wounding may not be this or that specific offense, but sheer repetition itself. This is demonstrated by the syllable "*in*" — "*injuries*" and "*insult*" — which suggests that the mind/*Mon* conceived as *in*teriority is itself the technical product of this effect, of material language or *ressentiment*. Thus, the opening tropes birth in a funny way ("I had *borne* as best I could"), a being borne of and by "I." Yet the paragraph also seems wild with runes of other sorts, in particular the prefixes *pre-* and *re-* between which the absent present of the text drifts. Moreover, read according to the text's theorization of runic rhymes one sentence resonates particularly. The line, "I must not only *pun*ish but *pun*ish with im*pun*ity," can be said to authorize not only a reading of *punning* inscriptions as agents of the text but indicates such to be less benign than themselves violating, indeed, punitive. If I now go on to suggest that the tale is about reading, that is not to rehearse boring reflexive moves we can apply to any text but specifically to ask where, in Poe, *one* system of meaning — the mimetic, appropriative, and hermeneutic system represented by Montresor — may be here brought to a critical impasse, turned against itself, or pushed to project another in which different values may be at stake historically. When Montresor adds, "*At length I would be avenged; this was a point definitively settled* – but the very definitiveness with which it was resolved precluded the idea of risk,*"* more runic puns seem illustrated: "length" may not yield both logos and *legs* (the material carriers of sense like puns themselves, of which more later), but "point" can imply the site of cognitive contact (a sort of *pun*ta), the place where two metonymic chains of signifiers touch and appear generated, while de*finit(e)*ively implies a negation of finitude itself that is at stake in the performance of the tale.[11] If the narrator's "revenge" on Fortunato may be read, then, as the impossible desire of consciousness to surpass its emergence as *ressentiment*, or its dependence on repetition ("thousand"), that appears as the text's apparent attempt to exceed figurative language itself – to entomb that with and as Fortunato himself. This final translation of chance as figuration introduces us to a different dimension of the word play altogether.

When Fortunato is met in "the supreme madness of carnival" we recall that carnival time is generally presented as one of suspension and reversibility, or what Bakhtin calls time "without before or after." Fortunato wears a multi-colored costume: "The man wore motley. He had on a tight-fitting parti-striped dress, and his head was surmounted by the conical cap and bells. I was so pleased to see him that I thought I should never have done wringing his hand" (274). This "motley" figure (echoing the French *mot*) is not only contrasted to the literalist narrator's black *roquelaire*. Fortunato as a figure of figure does not coincide with what he signifies as such, a cognitive disjuncture that the text marks in his appearance as jester. Yet if the motley costume is one of color or trope, the *"coni*cal cap and *bells"* inversely notes the ambiguity of a *cog*nition associated with presemantic bells, heard again in the phrase, "(w)ringing his hand." The alternating bars of "parti-striped dress" suggest, in contrast to figuration, then, the reduction to whatever alternating marks, bars, or differential intervals – like the Raven's knocking – give rise to trope or to perception ("pleased to *see* him"). When Montresor notes of the two that in "the *matter* of old wines he was sincere. In this respect I did not differ from him materially," it is this *materiality* that is suggested.

---

11 At the end, Fortunato is "fettered" like an *inverse* Prometheus – he is called "the chained form" – though, instead of stealing fire and language, he has these returned to him in a scene of decreation.

But it is here that the whole set-up is given a different twist, for we must recall that the *Mon* of Montresor is itself heard elsewhere too, that is, of course, in the title. Given this play of rhymes, what the proper name *Amontillado* seems to connote is not only an absent vat of sherry — what Hitchcock would call the text's McGuffin — but the implications of "cask" itself in every sense, including those of container, and the cognates that lead through chance and falling.[12] Yet the story could not be called, say, "The Cask of Malaga." In "Amontillado," then, we can hear the negation of the *Mon(t)*- system announced discretely if firmly in Montresor's own name. This promised negation announced by the title itself seems suddenly to involve the plot of the tale and to coincide with the (never to arrive) wine, the absent contents, and the failure of the fiction to be other than a ghostly promise of something it cannot deliver. Rather than being a skit about (failed) mastery or even the deadly routine of appropriation and absorption that every system of meaning demands, I earlier suggested that the tale may instead represent the ritual sacrifice of the entire system of representation and naming that Poe inherits and puts into question, an entire machine of interpretation emblematically presented in the proper name and "I" of the narrator. The *A*- of Amontillado can now also be heard at once asserting as *and* dismantling an assertion of being itself by the first person — (I) AM/A- Mon. This returns us to the entombment scene. Unlike "The Bells," which may be said to empty out all citational allusion by its accelerated echolalia, the entombment of Fortunato depicts incorporation or absorption. Here the absent sherry must be given yet another verbal fold, because the name both posits and negates in letteral play not only the *mon* of internalization (what is "mine"), but the implicit echo of a *Mo(u)nt*. Associated with echoes and the past, this would either be, for Poe, Shelley's Mont Blanc or Mt. Sinai. In either case, the *Mo(u)nt* in question would be a textual figure. Mount Sinai would of course name the site at which occurs the giving of the Law, while Shelley's Mont Blanc recalls a textual scene in which perceptual consciousness is allegorically spawned through criss-

---

12 The word *cask* implies not only a container as case or casket, of course, but a tomb, as in the French *tomber*, hence to fall, which is also the German *Fall* as "case" — including among its etymological cognates "chance." Indeed, wine and mine may appear as an inverted letteral system in which the chance form of a letter becomes a pivotal semantic moment.

crossing echoes and erasures projected before a "natural" sublime presence. Poe's a-privative form, however, seems to supplant *any* natural image, such as Mont Blanc, with the sheer runic play of names or language, rewriting the natural pretext of the sublime mountain used by Shelley into what occurs within the material crags of dissonant words. What begins as the promise of incorporation and meaning in the narrator's plotting (*Mon*) proceeds to undo itself and every subjectivizing logic available to it (*Amon*). In a way, the reading of Lawrence could even be affirmed, though the "self" which he claims in the story is obliterated would not be that of some character or psychology but rather an entire conception of the subject or self itself. Moreover, that "loss" would here be given a positive value, as of something bound to the past and to be, at a cost, dissolved, the system of *ressentiment* turned knowingly against itself. If the gesture seems Nietzschean, it must now be added that the entire plot seems stamped as a distinctly American project.

As Poe shifts from description to inscription, he precedes Shelley's pseudo-origin of perception by transposing the criss-crossing echoes of the mountain's vales into linguistic terms, the criss-cross of runic rhyme. The reference to "borne" and to "nature" ("nature of my soul") in the first two lines transfers the ridge of Mont Blanc to a chance point of linguistic origin – what is called Fortunato's "*weak point*" ("He had a weak point – this Fortunato – although in other regards he was a man to be respected and even feared"). This can be heard quite simply as a Lacanian *point de capiton* that would congeal and erase figurative series.[13] If we pursue a further twist of the cask and case of "Amontillado" – and we are invited to do so by its status as a proper name – it might break down into a *combinatoire* of runic figures that include, at first, Am, Mon, Mont, A/mon(t), yet finally, too, the *series* of bars or intervals ("parti-striped") that all but appear preletteral slashes in "T-I-ll." This precedes any generated word as the marking of sheer difference by an alternating bar series might: / / / /. It dismembers the name in a way that will *not* allow it to be quite re-membered, since it exceeds any possible mimetic recuperation. To

---

13 Herman Rapaport, in "Staging: Mont Blanc" (in *Displacement*, ed. Mark Krupnick [Bloomington: Indiana University Press, 1983]), formulates the concept of the ridge in Shelley's text: "The arete (ridge, mount, peak, spine, cross-point) may come to be seen as a perpetual shifting, an eternal return to the same as different, an obsession where desire is fixed or pinned down, and precisely there where one has a suspension" (66).

read the "cask of 'Amontillado'" as if the wine-name involved a cryptonomous function allows us to locate, tentatively, the proper name "America" scattered in this letteral spread, a signature which is anything but essentializing.[14]

If one way to read Montresor's performance is as an aborted Nietzschean gesture, a (failed) overcoming of *ressentiment* by itself, it appears as a doomed self-cancellation which, in turn, must re-enforce that system without escape. According to such a reading, the *Mon(t)* suggests now both names (*noms*) and mind itself. The mind's dependency on citation makes language one figure of exteriority on which the injured and insulted "I" thoroughly depends. In a spectacular manner, it is the very superficiality of the tale that licenses an intricate metanarrative on what makes its own writing (im)*possible* ("Amontillado? A pipe? Impossible! And in the middle of carnival!"). Montresor's noting "half of a century" had passed suggests less an inability to *escape* temporalization ("*definitively*") than an inability to get back *into* time or finitude from a position that can only be endlessly re-narrated and circles back to enfold the opening sentence.[15] Rather than an engaging tale of vengeance, the story appears to ritually undo and reinscribe itself in a representational dilemma it does not have the means to exceed − except in producing itself as its own remainder. Yet rather than being sloppy or haphazard as writing, we see that Poe's microverbal phrasing down to the letter reflects, again, the brick-laying precision of a *mason* − which is the metaphor used by Montresor, as it might be for the technically engineered writing syllable for syllable or brick for brick in the plot to wall-up and surpass figuration itself, to get at the Real. Before entering the final vault, for instance, Montresor makes an awful pun that seems typical of

14 This recalls how Poe elsewhere puts such titles to use, as in the last line of *The Fall of the House of Usher*. Not only does the title, like the word "cask," echo with cognates of "fall" ("Usher" suggests the Hebrew term for *chance*), but in the text's concluding passage − "While I gazed, this fissure rapidly widened ... and the deep and dank tarn at my feet closed sullenly and silently over the fragments of the 'House of Usher'" (157) − what is clearly cited and reinscribed as a subject of the language is the tale's own "fragments," which feeds the just concluded text back into the title in a reflexive loop.

15 This moment is suggested by the mirror-like standstill of the *re-* prefix itself: "Against the new masonry I *re-e*rected the old rampart of bones." Such a specular standstill recalls that in the name Ed/g/Ar, where the *ar* − earlier heard in Montresor's "*ar*ms" − echoes the resonant R(e)- while the *-ed* suffix suggests the problem of the past tense.

everything garish and open to aesthetic repudiation in Poe (who does "punish with impunity"). The exchange has essentially to do with signs and, as such, has a peculiar subtext. Fortunato asks Montresor for "a sign" that he is indeed a *mason,* meaning in this case a member of the Masonic order. It seems a childishly crude skit: "'You? Impossible! A mason?' 'A mason,' I replied. 'A sign,' he said, 'a sign.' 'It is this,' I answered, producing beneath the folds of my *roquelaire* a trowel" (277). Montresor's troping of *mason* ("the brotherhood") yields a meaning *so* literal that it breaks all frames of metaphoric reference to produce a *thing,* here a blunt trowel. Like Fortunato, we remain blind in dismissing it as a cheap pun ("You jest"), since the trowel becomes an emblem here both of Poe's word-laying on the presyllabic level and of a psychotic drive for the "thing." Montresor's *m*(as)*o*nry seems an aptly technocratic way of representing the web of runic rhymes that contrive to fix the play of meanings. The technique is again demonstrated when Fortunato notes that Montresor has "been imposed on," in which a play on the positing and imposing of sense on the stuff of language emerges as a subject of the fiction all along. This inscribes Poe's signature in a place which dramatizes the reader's construction of the narrative, since the echo of Poe's name in cognates of *pos*iting itself appears not only in the act of being impo(s)ed on. Instead, one can speak of an act of depo(s)ing at work, as occurs within the performance itself. The play and import of Poe's *mon/nom* appears confirmed in diverse variants and cognates strewn across the text, including "sup*pose*," "im*pose*," and "im*pos*ture" (Italians "practice imposture," "I will not impose upon your good nature," "You have been imposed upon"), yet also "*pos*itively," "re*pose*," and "im*pos*sible."[16]

---

16 In the catacombs the narrative moves through a sort of white writing where the difference of black and white appears suspended – what is called, in a scriptive metaphor, "the fabric" of "the white web-work which gleams" of "*nitre,*" the last being a white night or white blackness. There are several occasions where, failing to be successfully *posited,* language occurs at the border of a dissolution. The fettering of what is called the "chained form" of Fortunato takes place in a "*recess*" also called an interval, a sort of non-place where the act of fixation occurs ("merely the interval between two of the colossal supports"). This pattern of chronicling a prefigurative moment represented by the catacombs throws light on Montresor's mock redoubling of Fortunato's own "screams," re-echoing those emitted from "the figure within." So far as origins are concerned, the scene, showing the futility of Fortunato's crying aloud where there are no ears to hear, seems to mime a reverse origination of speech itself: "A succession of loud and

These passages suggest a broken circular logic. If the text opens by seeking vengeance on what in fact engenders it, Poe's own poetic gambit appears summarized in one central image. It is that which I opened with and now return to, Montresor's family *arms*. Arms, as limbs, are regularly grasped in this text ("I made bold to seize Fortunato by an arm above the elbow," "again offering him my arm. He leaned upon it heavily"), yet the family "arms" that Fortunato links explicitly to *forgetting* ("I forget your arms") project another dismembered extremity, a foot, and this image itself involves an anamorphic logic that seems both to highlight the function of materiality in Poe's conception of the sign and to erase what it signifies. Indeed, one may even hear in the word *arms* an echo of the "R(e)" of repetition itself. Montresor's reply is, once again: "A huge human foot d'or, in a field azure; the foot crushes a serpent rampant whose fangs are imbedded in the heel." If one difficulty in reading the emblem lies in its circular or anamorphic nature — that it depicts itself as crushing a serpent whose fang in turn destroys it — another lies in the idea of a foot that is itself cut off from any body, severed or *detached* as a representation. If the image generally reflects Montresor's self destroying plot, it also depicts the gamble of Poe's own treatment of material language. In presenting it as severed, the text raises the "foot" of signification to the status of a subject or signified itself, a *foot d'or*, though in becoming the "thing" represented, it sabotages the very structure of meaning it presents — the fangs embedded in the heel while being crushed. To read Montresor's arms we must recognize that the foot, "huge" and severed, is the referring-referent itself now without any body to carry — a figure of what precedes figurative meaning, a lower or material order: sound, letters, cryptonyms, intertexts, and hypograms. The foot is representing and represented *itself* — a "thing" and sheer emblem simultaneously, doxa in the place of idea, body for head, *gold* and not a paper currency

shrill screams, bursting suddenly from the throat of the chained form, seemed to thrust me violently back. For a brief moment I hesitated, I trembled ... I reapproached the wall. I replied to the yells of him who clamoured. I reechoed them, I aided, I surpassed them in volume and in strength. I did this and the clamourer grew still." (365–6) The "solid fabric" of the catacombs is, like the "web-work," a texture of writing. Poe's skit suggests the reversal of a text like that of Wordsworth's boy of Winander episode in *The Prelude*, where the mimic origin of speech is linked to a figural death of the subject. Rather than the boy of Winander's mimic hoots, Montresor reverses the origin of sound and word in a doubling designed to still the "figure within."

representing another reserve, the apotheosis of the linguistic pragma or sound-effect of "The Bells."[17]

Like the "Amontillado" that overtakes the narrator's own name, the "arms" suggest a figural system that *appears* to be self-cancelling. If the destroying circularity implies a technological rigor to Poe's practice, one of the things as if cancelled in this (self) sacrificing ritual of Montresor (or Poe), which sacrifices the sacrificer along with the system – or would if he were not caught re-narrating the event *in*definitely – may be the mimetic order of the sign itself.

Read in a performative mode, "The Cask of Amontillado" undoes the inherited system of narrative meaning and takes that undoing as the implied plot of the narrative. More curiously, it presents this as a peculiarly American moment which can only be itself repeated, in which Fortunato can also be read as a figure of the past, citation, the old world that American writing would erase ("the matter of old wines"). If in wandering amidst the anagrammatic interstices of the non-word Amontillado we make out the proper name "America" itself, this should not be surprising from the author of "The Gold-Bug." But like any ghost that cannot achieve phenomenal presence, even the signature of "America" has no essential identity to claim but instead marks the space of a historical evacuation. While the "am" of both America and Amontillado, for example, might be read to echo a subject's hyperbolic claim to being, even the biblical fiat ("I am that I am"), each veers into a negating moment or trap (A-Mon(t)). If Montresor can be said to narrate the dilemma of American writing, it can be read in two ways. On the one hand, it would erase an impinging past at the risk of erasing itself; yet on the other hand, Montresor's own will to incorporate, to entomb, or to make "mine" only mimes normal interpretive practices with its apparent valorization of the self, the private, and the interior of the catacombs. The trouble is that the tale, in Montresor's name (literally), only seems to sacrifice itself in order to explode the model of interiority altogether, since what may be most disturbing here is that the voice of narration turns

17 Keeping the relevance of Shelley in mind, the association of prefigurative sound with measure, feet or tread is developed in Paul de Man's reading of *The Triumph of Life* ("Shelley Disfigured"): "The 'tread' of the dancer...is no longer melodious, but reduces music to the mere measure of repeated articulations. It singles out from music the accentual or tonal punctuation which is also present in spoken diction" (*The Rhetoric of Romanticism* [New York: Columbia University Press, 1984], 113).

up again and again in the same spot – only as a ghost. The text oscillates, then, between these two (cancelled) positions, not as merely possible readings, but as specular ones that cannot (not) escape the other's dooming embrace. This seems to be why, however much American writing can be seen to take as its project the transformation of an older order of sense dependent on metaphors of interiority and to celebrate the exteriority of what Whitman allegorically calls the "outdoors," Americanists seem to recuperate that defensively as though that betrayed an expressive economy of the self. Poe seems to theorize the materiality of language as the basis for a transformation that cannot (not) be confirmed because it cannot (not) survive its own success, but which also cannot stop since it is also already there. When Poe substitutes for the "natural" image of Mont Blanc the letteral play of runic names he rewrites High Romanticism pragmatically – that is, as a materialist – from an American nihilist position that presupposes nothing ("You ... will not suppose"), a gesture that is clearly as liberating as it is (im)pos(s)ible.[18]

Addressed as symbolic praxis, Poe's "Amontillado" checkmates one economy of meaning – the logic of the *Mon* – which is also that which routinely regards Poe's work as an alien, obscene, or external phenomenon, as we saw with Bloom. Indeed, the ambivalent treatment of Poe by the Americanist high canon resembles a classic ideological construct, a value cluster defensively built upon what it abjects, and abjecting what it is already built upon. The circle that seems broken is not that of Zarathustra, but it does link Poe to a shift in the structure of the sign itself that is still being played out.

18 The signature of America lurking in the promised Amontillado yields a second echo cluster. Once dissolved into its parts it can hardly be re-membered, though, since after the hyperbolic (I) *Am-* one encounters a *combinatoire* of *runes*: (A)mer(e), (no) "mother" as mat(t)er ("I did not differ from him *materially*"), yet also (a) *marr*ing as origination, as well as a specular sea (mer(e), mar(k)). The play within the determining non-name "America" would bear greater scrutiny elsewhere, particularly as it inscribes not only in the "I's" auto-citational claim to being (AM), as in the promised "Amontillado," but a punning inscription of a problematic genesis (mere, marking, and mat(t)er). Traditionally, the figure of the land as mother appears at stake in American letters, as in Annette Kolodny's *The Lay of the Land* (Chapel Hill: University of North Carolina Press, 1975). Yet it is not the idle personification of the land as mother, but its negation in a scene staking out the positing of the subject ("am"), where a mer(e) is (no) a/mer(e), a-mar(k) leaves the signature of "America" in a site perpetually obliterating its past.

❖❖❖

5

Only the dead know Brooklyn
ferry (voice)

❖❖❖

It is a priceless historical joke that the one poet we accept as the National Bard should lack all the accredited national virtues ... Whitman speaks for the national ethos, the divine average, the *En Masse*, but he is actually a solitary, a secretive watcher ... It is all a comedy of errors, and if one sometimes feels that Whitman's critics serve him right, one may also indulge the feeling that Whitman serves America right.   Irving Howe

Tu le connais, lecteur, ce monstre delicat,
– Hypocrite lecteur, – mon semblable, mon frere!   Baudelaire, *Au Lecteur*

I want to ask after the possibility of an "evil" Whitman, a Whitman who, in the sense of *mal* used sometimes by Baudelaire, is more alert to the violent implications of rhetorical strategy than we tend to allow, considering his repeated denial of interest in literary technique or style.[1] After all, when we hear him saying almost as much in a remarkably convoluted address in "Crossing Brooklyn Ferry" ("Nor is it you alone who know what it is to be evil, / I am he who knew what it was to be evil, / I too knitted the old knot of contrareity, / Blabb'd, blush'd, resented, lied, stole, grudg'd" [196]), is it only, being in the past tense, as further confessional proof of his care? In many respects, a certain familiar "Whitman" remains a distracting cultural icon – that is, the image circulated of a writing, author, or idea attached to what Benjamin calls its "afterlife," the iconic mode in which a production is circulated as commodity – and, as such, a site where ideological analysis, cultural criticism, and close reading may profitably join up.[2] Invested in, identified with, transferred as

---

1 This lack has recently begun to be addressed, as occurs to some extent in Tennie Nathanson's *Whitman's Presence: Body, Voice, and Writing in Leaves of Grass* (New York University Press, 1992), particularly chapter 5 ("Writing and Representation") and 6 ("Inscriptions").

2 The situation gave some merit to a remark by Irving Howe in a piece on Whitman criticism in the 50s: "Whitman has not been very fortunate in his critics – and, one sometimes feels like blurting out, it serves him right! ... As a result of his need

educational codes, such icons (the "Walter," say, mocked yet left unshaken by D. H. Lawrence) play organizational roles independent of analysis, become cultural referentials installed as implicit guardians against alternate readings. Yet what happens to Whitman's "voice" if it is thought not through transparency – which always suggests, or promises, a transparency of language itself – but the reverse, through Whitman's decidedly knowing reflection on and manipulation of the material dimension of language itself which he pretends to dismiss?[3] Throughout this essay, I will use the term materialist to suggest where Whitman can be read, contrary to custom, as a text fully aware of its status as a certain technological achievement – even to the point of making that technology a figure of what his own text is performing in the trope of Brooklyn Ferry. Aside from presenting us now with an unusually double text (or talk), this suggests Whitman's awareness of the *negative* power wielded by naming and by addressing the other (reader) in a hortatory manner – what I will call, temporarily, Whitman's *inscription* of the reader. It is the effects of such inscription, I will argue, that substantially complicate and revise any pretended immediacy, transparency or presence, and for that matter, the very integrity and even intention of the voice itself. Despite the proverbial "presence" Whitman projects, there has been comparatively little theoretical attention given to him until recently, as if his assertion of transparency were granted at the price of interest, or as if he were simply the most easy figure to sacrifice to the controls of the Americanist ideology of the self.

For contemporary readers, however, there may be a tendency to simply assume Whitman's claim to "transparency" is itself another

---

to think of himself in a variety of prophetic roles, Whitman became a victim of his own legend rather than a subject for critical apprehension" ("Walt Whitman: 'Garrulous to the very last'," in *Modern Literary Criticism*, ed. I. Howe [New York: Grove Press, 1958], 419). Howe is canny in reviewing the terms of this problem then: "All this has made it extremely difficult to get at Whitman the poet and almost impossible to get at him directly: too many traps and barriers of our culture stand in the way. We have no choice but to begin with his critics, about whom Whitman once said – and here he was truly a prophet – 'I will certainly elude you'" (419–20).

3 My use of "material" here will allude primarily to a facticity inherent in *language* that blocks all transparency. It nonetheless echoes a remark by William Dean Howells' that Whitman's writing represents "not poetry but the materials of poetry" (cited in Kerry Larson, *Whitman's Drama of Consensus* [University of Chicago Press, 1988], 10).

stratagem, and if so the question becomes how successful, and to what end? Where in routinely constructing "Whitman," do we overlook a rupture in the address itself, one irreducible to explanations available through some dissenting tradition relying on an image of the anti-social Whitman?[4] I will ask, instead, where Whitman's inscription of the reader can display not only a highly sophisticated formalist and metatextual dimension, but where that might appear to be "dialogic" not in the sense of a communal bonding, but in that blunter and crueler sense of a battle for mastery with an unremarked yet structurally necessary vampiric moment, which the pretense of "transparency" obscures. It is this which Whitman increasingly struggles to recuperate through projected intimacy. I will suggest that it is the suppression of this rupture, more than any presence of voice as such, that lends Whitman's text its feeling of radical alterity.

Given its unique inclusion of the reader, we might call Whitman's

---

4 A critical tradition of questioning Whitman's transparency certainly exists, starting with Lawrence's mocking the pretense to presence as another of his cunning "post-mortem effects" ("Walt's great poems are really huge fat tomb-plants, great rank graveyard growths" [*Studies in Classic American Literature* (New York: Viking, 1961), 165]). Nonetheless, this tradition is sometimes restricted by taking the form of a psychological note on anti-social traits. This is the case in Quentin Anderson's questioning whether Whitman is not "psychotic" in his relation to words and their values in *The Imperial Self* (New York: Columbia University Press, 1971). Probes of this "other" Whitman, of course, occur throughout the critical literature, but are frequently overshadowed by the demands of focusing on the psychological or historical subject. Important studies as different as David Cavitch's *My Soul and I* (Boston: Beacon, 1985), Ezra Greenspan's *Walt Whitman and the American Reader* (Cambridge University Press, 1990), or M. Wynn Thomas' Marxian *The Lunar Light of Whitman's Poetry* (Cambridge: Harvard University Press, 1987) return, at critical points, to rhetorical questions. These are more particularly developed in Kerry Larson's *Whitman's Drama of Consensus* (1988), using a reader-response idiom, and in James Perrin Warren's *Walt Whitman's Language Experiment* (University Park: Penn State University Press, 1990), which addresses Whitman's "appealing to the mediating power of language" (171), and recently in both Tenney Nathanson's *Whitman's Presence: Body, Voice, and Writing in Leaves of Grass* (1992) and Mark Bauerlein's *Whitman and the American Idiom* (Baton Rouge: LSU Press, 1992). Important and vital recent work in the area of politics and sexuality in Whitman include M. Jimmie Killingsworth's *Whitman's Poetry of the Body: Sexuality, Politics, and the Text* (Chapel Hill: University of North Carolina Press, 1989) and Betsy Erkkila, *Whitman the Political Poet* (Oxford University Press, 1989). A recent critical collection edited by Robert K. Martin, *The Continuing Presence of Walt Whitman* (Iowa University Press, 1992), suggests where he is currently revitalized as an icon of gay studies, an appropriation that must appear linked to the tradition here being critiqued.

lyric "dialogic" in a way not evoked by any typical Bakhtinian model – for he suggests a dialogism *without an inter-subjective component*.[5] Bakhtin, after all, excluded the "lyric" from any dialogic or social discourse, though perhaps for reasons that are generally unrecognized. If by dialogic we do *not* mean the hermeneutic give and take of communication, but rather strategic incorporation and defacement of another's word from a rhetorical position of power, it may be that Whitman's lyric is all too dialogic when it inscribes the "You" as a figure of the text.[6] That is, by involving the reader in the construction of the speaker at its source, the prosopopeia of the speaker puts both the vatic "I" and the reader at risk together. If so, Bakhtin may eschew the lyric because, at a point preceding mimesis, the most violently erasing and colonizing moments of language are too uncontrollably in play. This invariable battle for mastery would seem the furthest removed from what we understand as Walt's reassuring and affectionate voice; it is the point of this chapter to suggest the opposite. I will explore this primarily in "Crossing Brooklyn Ferry," a text which represents Whitman at his otherwise most generous, vatic, personally concerned, and inclusive; a text in which we appear so much embraced as to be anticipated and affirmed across time.[7] My point will not be to propose yet another "reading," or to argue that it is better, but to ask where a radical self-division preceding and in the voice which we actively suppress rewrites the vatic ferryman as a sort of scriptive, and knowing, Charon. The one notable shift I will make, however, is to read the "ferry" itself as a figure of metaphoric transport or language, which alters significantly how we read what (or who) is being crossed.

5 My approach may be considered a counter-statement to Donald Pease's attempts to update the problem of "voice" and subjectivity in "Blake, Crane, Whitman, and Modernism: a Poetics of Pure Possibility," *PMLA*, 96, 1 (January, 1981).

6 Larson is particularly shrewd in noting of "Crossing" that "the logic of its vision dictates that the conventional contract between reader and author be not simply recast but formally dissolved" (9), thus addressing where the text "splintered into two styles of address ... where in one moment the text represents an open space for invitation and integration in the next it becomes a zone of prohibition and outright exclusion" (20). Similarly, Bauerlein marks "Crossing" as "the poem most clearly about reading" (106).

7 As Quentin Anderson notes: "The dimensions of the problem of talking sense about Whitman show up with greater clarity in 'Crossing Brooklyn Ferry' than in any other poem" (165).

I.

Whitman's claim to transparency and the eschewal of "literary" technique has, naturally, influenced how he has been read – as he intended. This was present, even, in his substitution of a graphic reproduction of his face in place of the author's name on the first edition of *Leaves of Grass*, a face so open, it is assumed, that the name is displaced by it, by the apparent presence of what precedes language and transcends signature. To substitute a face for a name is an intriguing use of graphics, yet rather than suggesting the openness of being face to face one could also read the gesture as one of subliminal control and seduction, particularly if the act of giving a face can also conceal its more originary absence. One may measure the extent of that absence by the very need to give a face instead of a name.[8] That this "openness" is a figure of *control* may be endorsed by Whitman's obsessive early attention to his own reception by readers, specifically by his having written *in advance* even of publication certain "anonymous" reviews of his book (reviews, as it were, of "Myself" by myself as another). These reviews confirm Whitman's familiar icon, yet also create by fiat an imaginary community of already in place readers, among whom the coming reader could then assume his or her place.[9] In these, typically, the rhetoric of asserted "health" and other value terms is so extreme that its logic should be noted, as when he is willing to risk: "If health were not his distinguishing attribute this poet would be the very harlot of persons." If the radical "health" claimed for such a violently imposed and invasive "voice" with its claims to immediacy were even vaguely flawed or suspect – that is, if there were anything unhealthy, fractured, dissimulative, unopen in it – the entire gambit would be faulted, the voice would be a "harlot." For Whitman, this health was defined as a theoretical program that

---

8 See Cynthia Chase, "Giving a Face to a Name," in *Decomposing Figures* (Baltimore: Johns Hopkins University Press, 1986), 82–113.

9 These reviews focus not on the text but, again, the corporeal icon: "large, proud, affectionate, eating, drinking, and breeding, his costume many and free, his face sunburnt and bearded, his posture strong and erect, his voice bringing hope and prophecy to the generous races young and old ... talking like a man unaware that there was ever hitherto such a production as a book, or such a being as a writer ... If health were not his distinguishing attribute this poet would be the very harlot of persons. Right and left he flings his arms, drawing men and women with undeniable love to his close embrace" (cited in Zweig, *Walt Whitman: The Making of a Poet* [New York: Basic Books, 1984], 4).

entailed a rejection of artfulness, technique, or "literary" writing, a purging of both textual self-division and intertextuality, present in the ideal of transparency.[10] Typically, one hears remarks from an entire tradition of Whitman readers like that of biographer Paul Zweig: "This is the special claim Whitman makes upon his readers: the claim of intimate presence, as if the poem ... were not a text but an embrace" (11). Yet when we read in another early notebook of Whitman's that the "place of the orator and his hearers is truly an agonistic arena," we are apprised that what seems an embrace must also be calculated; a move in an *agon* of seduction and defacement to which the creator of "Walt" is alert. How does he deal with the fact that to include another, especially a reader — that is, to turn up from the act of text production to eyeball the reader and include him or her as another figure of the text — may be an act of aggression, power, or erasure?

To address this more clearly we might ask where, if at all, Whitman abandons the pretense of transparency, or equality, or even inclusion? Where might he address, for that matter, the materiality of signs and language, the *techne* which he announces no interest in? Where does he theorize not communion but the community's own inability to read to begin with (or read him) — a logic which permanently splits his own "voice" and demands of it only further dissimulation and doubling? In a typical passage from the *Preface* to *Leaves of Grass*, he seems to do all of this, not only obliquely, but through a series of dissonances and ellipses. Here, Whitman's own awareness of the material problem of his own language emerges with utter clarity, yet it does so in and through a series of ellipses indicating the allegorical nature of this "public" address. Whitman in this instance is speaking of the poet's relation to those things he would, supposedly, merge with:

The greatest poet hardly knows pettiness or triviality. If he breathes into any thing that was before thought small it dilates with the grandeur and life of the universe. He is a seer .... he is individual ... he is complete in himself .... *the others are as good as he*, only he sees it and they do not. He is not one of the chorus .... he does not stop for any regulation ... he is the president of

10 Even his early notebooks dictate a method of non-literary composition: "Make no quotations and no reference to any other writers ... Rules for composition — A perfectly transparent, plate-glassy style, artless, with no ornaments, or attempts at ornament, for their own sake" (*Making*, 8) — a sort of radical rejection of *intertextual* commerce or anything not transparent, a literary construct that abolishes the "literary," the reflexive, or what draws attention to language.

regulation. What the eyesight does to the rest he does to the rest. Who knows the curious mystery of the eyesight? The other senses corroborate themselves, but this is removed from any proof but its own and *foreruns* the identities of the spiritual world. A single glance of it mocks all the investigations of man and all the instruments and books of the earth and all reasoning ...

The land and the sea, the animals and the fishes, the sky of heaven and the orbs, the forests, mountains and rivers, are not small themes ... but folks *expect of the poet to indicate* more than the beauty and dignity which always attach to dumb real objects .... they expect him to *indicate the path between* reality and their souls. Men and women perceive the beauty *well enough.. probably* as well as he. The passionate tenacity of hunters, woodmen, early risers, cultivators of gardens and orchards and fields, the love of healthy women for the manly form, sea-faring persons, drivers of horses, the passion for light and the open air, *all is an old varied sign* of the unfailing *perception* of beauty and of a residence of the poetic *in outdoor* people. They can *never* be assisted by poets to perceive ... some may but they never can. (492–3; my emphasis)

What is meant by a seer, or by *seeing* here – that which marks the poet's *difference* – and why is the statement linked to ellipses? Ellipses, after all, involve grammatical marks that nonetheless register a *rhetorical* break of sorts, and Whitman uses them here with curious variations as though marking different types of rupture (two, three, or four periods). What can indicate a lapse *or* excess may also, for instance, suggest a stammering emendation that doubles back over and supplants a preceding utterance ("... he is the president of regulation"), or by marking discontinuity, it can also cover a calculated omission ("..*probably* as well as he"). While in a writer like Celine ellipses mark a hyperbolic disruption of the "I," with Whitman it seems too often passed off as mere exuberance. It deserves another look.

The text seems almost to stutter, and specifically in those places which most closely elaborate the doubled relation of the poet to a reader (whose primary lack may involve mutely knowing this rupture). Whitman seems, for instance, to celebrate the poet's power only then to insist on his effaced equality or confluence with the masses. Moreover, there seems a fairly radical discontinuity between the framing eyesight and those who are *seen* by it, which opens another discontinuity (almost anamorphic) between the reader's expectation and the poet's word (which takes that expectation implicitly into account). The text theorizes and tries to occlude a gap between the poet's stated function and his reception. Yet as we hear Shelley's "legislator" intertextually invoked in the background ("the president of regulation"), the celebration of the poet's sameness to the crowd is contradicted by the assertion of his hieratic *difference* ("*pre*sident"). Whitman, as bard, calls the poet a "seer" — that is, a figure of vision that is also one of perception, of what imperceptibly links the eye or visibility itself to reading or tallying differences, to charting traces, to making *lists*. The poet is the one who can see and sight must be rewritten as a figure for reading. He adds, however, should the reader draw back: "the others are *as good as he*, only he sees it and they do not." Whitman's likening of the poet to eyesight constitutes a substantial difference, since it turns knowing as seeing into a power that *perpetually separates*. The assertion here that "the others" are "as good as he" seems weakly compensatory, a screen. This difference that is unmarked can only complicate or even imperil the relation, since by including "the others" which it addresses, it sees (for) them too as objects. The question, again, is not who takes transparency seriously (it is itself pretty transparent), but how the claim functions, and what it dissimulates.

This text on the eye is more complex and dubious still. If the eyesight of the seer clearly echoes Emerson's transparent eye-ball, it is nonetheless described in subtly different terms. And in fact it is quite different, perhaps even a reversal of the former's sense, since it is said to have reference *back* to nothing other than itself and, hence, being reflexive, is anything but transparent. It is, rather, a sort of in between figure and agent, not unlike language. This enigma is called "the curious mystery of the eyesight," and we are told that while all other senses "corroborate" themselves by reference *it* alone is "removed from any proof but its own." This eyesight, then, is not what some critics, borrowing from Lacan, call the constitutive "gaze." Rather, it seems if anything to designate a narcissistic and reflexive structure, one that is *not* mimetic like other senses but, in fact, precedes and generates ("*fore*runs") the "spiritual world." Its "single glance" can destroy ("mocks all"), like a catastrophe. Yet for further comment we are led to the next paragraph, where Whitman shifts abruptly to the *relation* of the many (invariably, potential readers) to the poet, and to their (anticipated) expectations of him. Since the text makes clear that he must *anticipate* these anticipations of himself — which in effect foreclose communication, given his difference — he invariably speaks in a kind of double-talk, which is to say, elliptically. The "curious mystery" seems to be that this reflexive "eyesight" does not signify only itself, but also visibility, marking, the outdoors, books, and "all reasoning"; that it simulates a *material* yet pre-representational moment of language – the very opposite of language as a transparent medium (for this is always what the question of any transparency refers to). Indeed, it may turn out that what Whitman means by the "outdoors" refers to this exteriority of non-transparent signs, one that resolutely bars a notion of interiority the traditional readings of Whitman's self or voice celebrate.

Whitman's rhetoric of inclusion effaces at this point a gaping rift, since the poet must contend with a claim that is a virtual guarantee of his being misread: "folks *expect* the poet to *indicate* more than the beauty and dignity which always attach to dumb real objects .... they *expect* him to *indicate* the path *between* reality and their souls. Men and women perceive the beauty *well enough.. probably* as well as he" (my emphasis). If the first ellipses (four periods) prepares for what could be called a *fold* in the commentary, the second (suddenly an abrupt *two* periods) covers an anacoluthon, a break in sense suggesting an unconvincing backpedal. What folks *expect* involves the manner in which the poet calculates their inevitable misreading of what he sees and relates, even if he cannot deliver "more" than, say, lists – or if the "path *between* reality and their souls," which lies in words like a ferry shuttling between shores, has a double edge or proves to be uncrossable. On the one hand, such a "between" involves claims to fluidity and vatic communion that conceal his difference; on the other, the passage speaks of *indicating* (that is, mutely pointing at) what lies "between" but may not literally pass from point to point, a caesura, precisely what is impossibly indicated by the ellipses. No, not even indicated, but so massively marked that it becomes as if *in*visible and the space over which another voice is etched or projected. In a sense, such a "between" is precisely what is not transparent and, in the tradition of Democritus and Lucretius that Whitman relies on, it *is* the simulacrum or eidolon. Rather than indicating a void to be traversed, it represents primarily the facticity of what can be called a reflexive and material sign function, the "eyesight," or "I"-site. Does the poet translate one or others across in the transports of *meta-phorein*, of *Ueber-setzung*, or does his vatic role lie in concealing the inability not only to do this, or to prevent them from being caught up in a suspended transport or a caesura, but to be even read by the others given *their* expectations? Is part of the knowledge that the poet recuperates and projects as secret power in fact that of this inability, inadequacy, or rhetorical blockage?

It is telling that this passage from the *Preface* moves from this impasse toward the celebrated types of outdoor health as if that could be continuous: "The passionate tenacity of hunters, woodmen, early risers." The problem is that, while celebrated, these figures seem covertly *reduced* in their differences, and indeed, there is a foretaste of such reduction as we hear that "all is an *old varied sign* of the unfailing *perception* of beauty." Beware of "Walt's" praise. What is called "the residence of the poetic *in* outdoors people" reproduces the anamorphic space or logic of what was called eyesight, that is, of being inside an outside ("*in out*doors people"). The problem is that the logic implied by the "old varied sign" again could suggest the foreclosure of access to this very readership. This seems noted, in fact, though they are all the while technically praised: "They can never be assisted by poets to perceive ... some may but they never can." Clearly, this has to be read two ways. To be placed or even praised on a list is ambiguous, since it can always read like a hit list — as, here, a list of social types the poet is *not* and cannot help to see. What seems to be a compliment cloaks the reverse, the naming of those unable to read the poet's words ("some may but they never can"), unable to (be assisted to) *perceive*. This, then, presents another double logic that the ellipses open up. The very best of those appealed to are stood apart from and reduced to an "old varied" list, "outdoors people," themselves the subject of and yet also virtually barred from reading, even though they are offered as models of health and presence for those other privative, unhealthy "folks" who are the remaining readers, those who (mistakenly?) "expect" the poet to indicate something — that is, to point to or at, or actually *cross* over, some path.

The path that Whitman's "folks" (and numerous critics) want indicated is a crossing, then, a communication or communion between permanently separated parties like reality and the soul, or self and other. In a sense, crossing over or "between" as a movement of transport double-crosses the notion of getting across, much as language does the act of communication, or the eyesight does seeing. The "outdoors" exists to be subtly rewritten, since it addresses less a landscape or place than the "curious mystery" of a reflexive and material figure, an "old varied *sign*" that links the pretense of immediacy to what is old, anamorphic, predetermined, split, and foreclusive. At the moment that Adamic naming is supposed to greet a new world, another gear in Whitman's lists casts everything, as sign, as all the more old, and as an acknowledged variation or repetition. If the figure of an embrace or communion is inadequate to frame Whitman's discourse, what is staged conceals a uniquely aggressive scene that must be read *more closely* still.

2.

The revision of the earlier version of the poem, "Sun-Down Poem" (1856), into "Crossing Brooklyn Ferry" (1860) involves a crossing of sorts already, occurring *in* the title to begin with. From naming a temporal event that is repeatable (sun-down), it moves toward indicating a process (cross*ing*) in which that solar event, and its temporality, appear less certain. In the earlier title, the word "poem" implies inversely that the poem has *no* name or title, that it is as if tacked on (call this what it describes, say, "sun-down poem"). It appears as the makeshift trace of the absence of name, which could even be heard somewhat more grandly as somehow tracing the sun-down *of* poems, or the rhetorical contract of poetic address. The subsequent title is also problematic, at least descriptively, since the "crossing" named is not physically *of* Brooklyn Ferry itself, as the grammar allows, but occurs technically *on* the ferry itself – thus drawing attention to the vehicle itself as subject (it might read, say, as "Crossing (the East River on) Brooklyn Ferry"). Though this is an otherwise casual enough synecdoche, its effect is to double the import of the title by making it a reading of the first version. On the one hand, we might say that the second title supplants the first, except that since that also denoted the absence of a title, the revised version erases, in one sense, an erasure of titles and of poetry ("Sun-Down Poem") – much as Whitman claims to obliterate the book or mere literature. Whitman supplants that title with the figure of (a) crossing, of crossing over, or crossing out (as one might in a textual revision). This little dance may seem a distraction, yet it has the effect of drawing us back to some of the less visible stakes at issue. With the first title still in mind, where does the text constitute some sort of going down or *going under*? And of what – a style, a sun, a poetic identity, a history? What catastrophe is revised or concealed in the opening invocation? The revised title involves, then, what might be again called a metatextual dimension, one that overlays or rereads the earlier text and becomes a commentary simultaneously on its technology:

that is, the poem excels at the very formalist poetics the poet unendingly denies. The revision does not merely complicate Whitman's claim to fluidity, but focuses on a "crossing" whose transports could either hasten or suspend the sun's decline, and this is done by addressing the technology of trans*fer* itself, the material "*ferry*" being crossed with or in.[11] Indeed, rather than the transparent poem we are promised, and which "Crossing Brooklyn Ferry" is held to epitomize, the work can seem the foremost treatment in any canon of the metatextual relation of (future) reading to the temporal *event* of inscription. One could consider it both a formalist and postmodern *tour de force*.

This retitling of the earlier text seems anything but casual. One may say, in fact, that a non-title that celebrates a going-under (which, perhaps, we might hear now in a Nietzschean sense) is replaced by a "crossing" which becomes itself the subject. If the scene of this crossing is the ferry, that vehicle of transfers and transference suggests the brute facticity of Whitman's poem (in *ferry*, as implied, we may hear the carrying-across of meta*phor*). Any transport "between" shores or realities, such as folk expect to have indicated for them by the poet, is supplanted by another. The text literally declares itself a sort of time-machine producing an anamorphic time-loop (or, as Nathanson calls it, a "Moebius strip") in whose address the reader's future present will appear caught ("It avails not, time nor place — distance avails not, / I am with you"), since in being positioned by the voice of anteriority, seen, "known," or placed by its side in the crossing, the reader is also rendered dead in advance of life.[12] Clearly, the text's argument does not depend on the continued existence of a

---

11 In *Disseminating Whitman: Revision and Corporeality in Leaves of Grass* (Cambridge: Harvard University Press, 1991), Michael Moon offers a sophisticated account of rhetorical positioning that nonetheless depends on a somewhat pre-critical notion of the "gaze" and its "Oedipal" machinery. Moon marks a shift from the fluid and affirming Whitman of "Sun-Down Poem" ("a collective or composite self designed to accommodate the reader as well as the author, to bring them into affectionate contact with one another") to one "not designed to represent untroubled 'fluidity'" (88), yet he cannot abandon the umbilical premise of a "Whitman" to be identified (with) as fundamentally "affectionate."

12 Nathanson's remark on the non-referential present of the text opens a "postmodern" Whitman and quells the sort of literal reading we still find: "like those dangerous representations which spawn subsequent productions that refer back to them rather than to 'things themselves,' 'Crossing Brooklyn Ferry,' which generates the present as the Moebius strip or eternal moment the poem's apostrophes name 'now,' is an ideally self-perpetuating structure" (260).

certain time-bound technology, here the ferry-boat to Brooklyn, which Philip Fisher cites as the proof of Whitman's ahistoricity and false claims to transcendence.[13]

Among the prospects the poem covertly raises is that of a restless quest to usurp future time by importing into it (knowing it will be "present" during the reading) the absent present of the voice. This it will attempt by asserting the privileges of temporal priority, of having been and being *here*, in life and the poem, first, and once that claim is tabled – which is nurturing yet also attacking and depleting – it must anticipate the counter-strategies. What had been routinely seen as avuncular care and generosity becomes, implicitly, something of a lethal chess-game. From the first line, rather than being invited to witness a ritualized crossing – say, simply celebrating the crowds and sunset – the second person reader is folded into the text and, as positioned, implicitly rendered *sub*ordinate. For while addressed "face to face," *as if* an equal to the figure we will call the bard, what the reader less often notes is that the speaker can be said to arise in the text in some sense face*less* himself.[14] He – literally, "I" – virtually precedes

13 In "Democratic Social Space: Whitman, Melville and the Promise of American Transparency," in "America Reconstructed, 1840–1940," Special Issue, *Representations* 24 (Fall, 1988), Philip Fisher castigates Whitman's ahistorical claims to transparency in "Crossing Brooklyn Ferry," where the readers seem situated in the technology (ferry) that will soon be outmoded, like the transcendent synchronicity we critics have moved beyond with our Foucaultian awareness of the historicity of "experience." For Fisher nothing in Whitman "stands so remote from our own thinking as his extension of transparency over time." He thus undoes Whitman's assertion of "unity" as the "transparency and cellular identity that he assumes between himself and all of his countrymen ... the form of continuity for national identity through time" (68). Yet assuming Whitman's own claims to immediacy, Fisher reads the poem almost as a documentary rather than a linguistic performance: "He imagines himself to be having an inevitable, natural, and therefore timeless experience" (69). However useful as an intervention, Fisher seems to want it both ways: *experience* would be historically conditioned (the product of signs) yet also a figure of unmediated subjectivity. Since in fact there is no longer any Brooklyn Ferry, history gives the lie to Whitman's most literal claims (that *you* will also be on this ferry, crossing the here and now). Accordingly, in claiming a transparent "meaning" of the poem-as-document, Fisher makes of Whitman a specular figure, misread (that is, as non-figural), and critiqued for Fisher's *own* sin of transparent historicizing.

14 Moon is drawn to the problem of "facing," or of rendering face*less* (defacing) that the text seems caught up in ("I would interpret the faceless crowds as a sign" (*Dissimulating Whitman*, 106), "while omitting to 'face' his fellow passengers," "the text's avoidance of 'facing' the crowds," "the speaker's not 'facing' the ferryboat crowd," "his 'unfaced' contemporaries, and his uncannily 'faced' or at

the entire mimetic field he implicitly, yet without assurance, invokes, a fiat lux or sun-rise which is, in fact, already old, recurrent, a sun-down poem. By opening with the Narcissus-like turn toward the water, waters "beneath" his feet, in order to receive a "face" as a reflection, the site also precedes voice and face, mimesis and identity. It turns towards a logic of signifying which, in the language of the body, lies under what might be called the material order of the feet. Whose, after all, is the second "face," the "you," if the poet's own reflection appears to yield the personified river's face itself? The address, for reasons that must conceal a critical anxiety of sorts, becomes one of Whitman's protracted attempts to anatomize the very vehicle – the meta-ferry, or material writing – upon which he both lushly depends and stands on and would extinguish, like the sun, like the formal apparatus of mere literature, into *lists*, lists which, seemingly transparent, can nonetheless display a sadistic, *in*scriptive component not altogether divorced from Whitman's own eroticism. Whitman's use of *listing* presents an important theoretical topos, since, appearing to both (re)name directly in the act of presenting, it is also potentially void semantically and veers into sheer formalization, and quanti-fication. Whitman's *listing* itself undermines the "transparency" it is thought to illustrate. A seemingly Adamic act, it also implies a substitutability that erodes difference, a paratactic disjuncture recalling Whitman's use of *series* of periods in an ellipsis. In fact, listing is a bizarre protocol of the classical sublime, evoking the catalogues of names and deeds in the Bible or Homer. The danger of disaster that Longinus attaches to the sublime is indeed threatening, for listing may collapse into an act that is numerically endless, where the sublime cancels itself by falling into mere banality. Whitman's attempt to exceed mere literature with a vatic act of unmediated listing – sometimes called "tallying" – undermines itself since words them-selves become thematized. As a word, *list* seems situated at an etymological crossroads, where the attributes of borders or hems, of a ship's listing (near disaster) and of sheer *accounting* double against materially aesthetic figures of reflection and desire (luster and lust), hence perception or reading, as in the ear's listening. It suggests also a *marking* that recalls the act of *measure*, tallying, or cutting. What might be called a scriptive or *technological* premise of Whitman's

least 'gazed on' posterity"), yet the "extended gaze" is interrogated as a "vehicle for desire" in which the poet's "affectionate presence" and fluidity are maintained.

language emerges here. In fact, what Philip Fisher recoils from when deriding the figure of "transparency" may be less the ahistorical claim, than a certain erasure that underlies the performance. If to list recalls the Elizabethan lust of the eye, or desire, and hence to luster, it also suggests a *reflection* binding perception to the exterior world — as in the use of *Schein* in German Idealism. What Whitman calls the "outdoors" becomes, as measure, potentially a figure not for the transparency of the outer world but for the materiality of signs as well, visibility as *reading* differences, marks, and tallies.

In a text whose first title implied solar extinction, the relation to the reader may be assumed more than merely "affectionate." Yet after the title — "Crossing Brooklyn Ferry" — the text opens:

1.

Flood-tide *below me*! I see *you* face to face!
Clouds of the west — sun there half an hour high — *I see you also face to face.*

Crowds of men and women attired in the *usual costumes*, how curious you
are to me!
On the ferry-boats the *hundreds and hundreds that cross*, returning home,
are *more curious to me than you suppose*,
And *you* that shall cross from shore to shore years hence are more to me,
and *more* in my meditations, than you might suppose.

2.

The impalpable sustenance of me from all things at all hours of the day,
The simple, compact, *well-join'd scheme, myself disintegrated, every one*
disintegrated yet part of the scheme,
The similitudes of the past and those of the future,
The glories strung *like beads on my smallest sights and hearing*, on the walk
in the street and the passage over the river,
The current rushing so swiftly and swimming with me far away,
The others that are to follow me, the ties between me and them,
The certainty of others, the life, love, sight, hearing of others.

(194; my emphasis)

Despite the elegiac tenor that draws us in like participants, of the text's opening three "you's," we should note, the first two seem not even human. What we witness, instead, is the vatic "I" in the complex act of positing radical personifications which, in turn, indicate or conceal the voice's own tentative, unformed, personified status. In the case of the flood-tide "*below* me" and the clouds, the *facial* presence is at the least suspect, and anthropomorphic, while (the) "I" proceeds to situate the human inversely in (or as) the precarious site of a *failed* personification. The audacity and quasi-biblical tone of "face to face" may be but one measure of the Narcissus-like speaker's uncertainty — indeed, is there a *voice* at all yet? — rising above fractured and engulfing flood-tides of signifying relations. Relations that may in fact retain or return to the eye no one "face," but crowds that will in fact come to seem increasingly *un*human, readers whose temporal placements are insecure and whose future life the text situates as already predicted, and enjoyed in advance by the ghost-voice, dead.[15] The "I" is also seeking its mirrored face or image as if before it knows what that is. In what may be called a wild prosopopeia, then, Whitman depicts a dispersive scene from which no narcissistic voice can simply disentangle itself or arise — emerging instead, by a fiat that is also a literary citation, in the collective debris of an imperilled *pre*mimetic voice, one dissolving the outlines of distance, temporal identity, memory, and features. That the curious "face to face" claimed for the "Flood-tide below me!" may now be difficult itself to affirm is emphasized by the fact that the "flood-tide" — that is, the East River — is hardly mirror-like to begin with, less Narcissus' pond than a tidal basin whose reversible currents may return no single image from its rough, briny green waters (even without its current pollution). What opens as a violent claim that names the threatening chaos of potentially engulfing anterior signifying chains ("Flood-tide below me!"), covers a just as radical lack or defacement. The "face" is *im*posed, as is the "you," while the potentially blasphemous biblical allusion of facial co-presence conceals a rift through which the poet may stand apart from the specularity he encourages in the reader — exhausted, no doubt, by the labors of birthing simulacra.

That the text opens with a failure of self-constitution appears to be confirmed in the address of the "Clouds of the west." These, as coverings, seem to be hailed *over* the displaced and descending sun, screening the one figure of presence not addressed and, in fact, going down. Rather than emerging as plenitude the bard's voice proceeds

---

15 Of the address of Whitman's future readers, Moon suggests that "the text foresees them becoming sufficiently 'other' from the poet and from his contemporaries that they (posterity) can complete the circuit of desirous gazing which his contemporaries cannot" (*DW*, 109). Since the crossing is symmetrical ("it circulates the reader back and forth between the points of desirously gazing and of being gazed at desirously" [110]), the recuperative machine of "Oedipal culture" allows figures like desire and castration to account for all spill-over or excess.

over a lack registered in the first title of the poem. Moreover, the *also* of "I see you *also* face to face" situates the clouds as figures of repetition and dissimulation rather than of origin. One result is that the astonishing claim of personification holds the ghostly "I" suspended, a *faux* prosopopeia of itself (what we would otherwise call a mask). It may be that the "sun-down" comments on the historical demise and pathos of the very "I" being ritually staged, as if again, by the text, that "I" momentarily said to be "*dis*integrated." (Indeed, perhaps the voice's only means of assuring that there is a sun — that it is not, say, a black sun — is by attending its death, completing the (impossible to complete) crossing.) At all events, what emerges can be called a *double* face, a highly marked rhetorical duplicity or two-facedness that cannot possibly receive its own image back. Thus the "sun" is depicted in words that suggest, inversely, a *rising* or dawn ("half an hour *high*"), taking the sun out of the natural order and into a semiotic one of potential temporal reversibility and dis-*orient*ation: east/west, early/late, past/future. Yet the text does not proceed unimpeded to either of the two reading options that are most typically asserted, that focusing on the transcendent affirmations of union across time *or*, inversely, on Whitman's purportedly antisocial nature. What is interesting is how incompatible the two directions are, and what each may want to evade — a trans-temporal "crossing" might be confirmed that is more vampiric than "anti-social." Rather than being transparent the poem is the site of radical eclipse, of sun-down, of a "voice" absent to itself. It is unsurprising, then, that the next address collects men and women into a group, nameless and faceless, on the verge of becoming lists, so many costumed cyborgs.[16]

I should perhaps point out, here, that I am not asserting that this is *the* only reading of the text, only that it is necessarily *virtual* as well, an excess that inhabits and inversely empowers readings which persist in its rhetorical occlusion. This evil twin of "Walt," so to speak, is nonetheless fully aware of these maneuvers. If the next address first places the reader safely by the gazing side of the speaker (who seems superior by virtue of his ability to see), the "*Crowds* of men and women" are not left inert. The "crowds" — which reiterates the

16 As noted, Quentin Anderson reads Whitman as "psychotic" in his relation to the word and its values. Rather than identify Whitman's voice as an overflowing "presence," psychosis suggests an endless and multiplex positional construct ("myself disintegrated, every one disintegrated"). One of the imports of Whitman's text, then, is its drive to deface.

"Clouds" – are, in effect, not addressed blankly or with affection; rather, they are transposed or crossed *back* into the lower position, that of the "flood-tide" suspended or "disintegrated" nearly into the inanimate flux. The "I" that would be perceived as full or disseminating is, like the sun, striving from a simulant or clouded position for the pretext of self to be staged – in which "agonistic arena" various players of the poem are inscribed. The act of giving associated with the sun appears in this belated and beclouded eclipse to be reversed, like the ebb-tide, into what Harold Bloom has called a contraction.[17] For to be transposed "below me" – with the tide and the crowds now – is a dubious position indeed, technically one of enslavement yet also of what the speaker is materially dependent upon for his linguistic *footing*. Yet this lower position is also empowered since it alone can return *my* face – or provide it – just as the reader may be regarding the text itself as such a flood tide. After this point, the text can be read as a maze-like construction, which brings us to the future – that is, always also the present, or present-absent – reader.

In question here is the fourth "you" ("*you* that shall cross ... years hence"), that is treated with exhilarating intimacy. For the voice not to be scrupulously "healthy," though, raises the equally exhilarating possibility of betrayal or being double-crossed. Positioned alongside the speaker at first in looking at the *other* crowds, he or she may also be transposed *back* to the "crowds" and the tide's first position, literally beneath "I's" feet. That the act of reading has become sheer transaction, bartering or crossing positions, or domination, is indicated by Whitman's turn to address that in the work. Thus the trans-temporal claims appear less an affirmation of transcendence than a means of reflecting on the relationships that sustain the poet's footing where there is, literally, no ground. Whitman opposes an ungovernable flood of simulacra (signs) by asserting a colonizing intimacy with the reader, a reader who, according to the *Preface* at least, may be as foreclosed from actually reading Whitman as the "crowds" herded onto the ferry, their "present" parasited.

The "well-join'd scheme" ("myself disintegrated, every one

---

17 Harold Bloom in *Poetry and Repression* remarks a radical duplicity: "Whitman says 'I celebrate myself' and he cunningly means: 'I contract and withdraw while asserting that I expand'" (249), yet turns back to the elegiac mode and restores narrative closure ("The tally notches a restored Narcissism and the return of the mode of erotic self-sufficiency" [195]).

disintegrated") that replicates the flood-tide can be a web as well, impossible to rehabilitate by a theory of eidolons. "Scheme" is also a classical term for figure (*schema*), and disintegration would seem here to name where material signifiers can undermine or precede the transports of metaphor. Inscription for Whitman (the first section of *Leaves of Grass* is titled "Inscriptions") can denote the act of verbally situating the other within the relational power of one's text, both a giving of place and evacuating subordination to the empowered voice, that voice contracted, as poet, to the role of seer. It involves an act at once erotic and, in a way, deadly. Whitman's crossing may assert less trans-temporal union – a weak, literal, or mimetic reading – than an archly reflexive meditation on and manipulation of the temporality of the text itself. No doubt, a scene of *in*scription may also be at stake in the way the poet lines up and variously positions "crowds" in "the usual *costumes*," into which the future "you" (that is, *you*) may be inversely transposed by the backdrift Whitman opens. It is one thing, after all, to stand by the bard's side contemplating the sun-set, and quite another to be located, deprived of voice, among the costumed hordes ferried unaware to "death," or having their representational "death" taken for granted, without promise even of arriving. (Indeed, one of the problems now seems less the bard's persistence across time, than the inability to die, to know death.) Thus this thematized trans-temporality is not a union across time; rather, both points in time are vacated and antagonistically intertwined in the contingent synchronicity of the writing and reading – for Whitman presents himself as reader, and time-travelling reader, in the poem. The point then is, to repeat, not Whitman's narcissism or antisocial nature. Where every affirmation must involve a strategic shift of footing and every inscription a negation, the poet's rhetoric cannot be contained by any one reversal or crossing. One may understand why, from the first, it was important for Whitman to assert a mode of reception for his work, to advertise, and review himself in a certain way, around value terms like "health," since here, in a sense, "Whitman" becomes as voice the invading, nurturing, or destroying other, the (Lacanian) "Thing" conceived as empowered exterior. The "antisocial" distancing implied by "*usual* costumes" momentarily melts the observed riders into groups *lacking* individuality, copies without originals, repetitions of old varied signs.

It is not arbitrary that the poem, then, as with the biblical allusion that opens it, should be suffused with an *intertextual* ethos. For instance, the "glories strung like beads on my smallest sights and hearings" covertly cites Emerson's "train of moods like a string of beads ... many-colored lenses" from "Experience," a line implying the priority of tropes over perception. Like intertextuality, the troping of the reader moves into a reversible zone of signification predicated on relations of revision and defacement. By the power dynamics of these relations, in short, we may read the performance less through the "usual costume" of Whitman's vatic equality or the "affectionate" stance we are encouraged to "fuse" with, than as an "agonistic arena." By invoking the future reader, the privileged priority of the poet is advanced – he ("I") can see "you" while you cannot see him, he was there first, he knows you in advance (which, in fact, reverses the obvious: you can read him, you know him, you are anonymous). Here the reader is also *anteriored* by inscription, even potentially placed in the faceless, costumed crowd of foreclosed readers/riders, positions crossed, any future "present" also vacated and parasited. The reader is asked, according to a now structural logic Whitman's voice exploits, to contemplate (or occlude, and in the process redouble) his or her position as *pre*-living, the inverse side of temporal continuity and union. This itself produces that double consciousness of his own death that the reader abjects in recommitting to the blithe voice of the bard – sealing the already corrupted or ideological production behind a more comforting Whitman. This does not make Whitman bad or dishonest, but simply a smart and, strictly speaking, materialist poet. It also shows a technological wizardry seldom granted him, and named in and as the "ferry." If Whitman's agon involves strategies of entrapment and seduction, the transparency of his text evaporates and we find rhetorical techniques more in line with the relation of Poe's Dupin to the Minister D.

When the bard says "you that shall cross ... are *more* to me, and *more* in my meditations, than you might suppose," a contract with the future – or "present" – reader is proposed and broken. Yet it is one of power expressed as withheld and undeclared knowledge ("more ... than you suppose"), of excess masking deficiency, and that which is withheld must reflect the relations we are discussing. This claim positions the reader "below" as potentially eroticized as when Whitman speaks, as it were, from behind. "More curious" and "more in my meditations" serve a double purpose, then, since by not naming the excess produced through inscribing "you" in the text as future reader, "I" decenters (the) "you" and makes *it* (now a third person) a textual figure while (it/you is) reading. He guides, that is, your self-reading by pretending to conceal the open fact of your pleasure in this cross-over, and that "you" has potentially assumed the vacated — and always vacant — "seer" position as well. Whitman remains in these moves positional, elusive, and masterful, that is, aware that he *simultaneously* traverses a sort of trans-temporal death-machine, the ferrying technology of his text or voice as lethal excess. The excess, again, appears to be one of withheld or unnamed knowledge, of seeing while being unseen, as in the teasing reference to what "you might suppose" (another *sub*-posit(ion)ing). If the reader is displaced, it is not because a transcendent union failed or the ferry-technology ceased (one can still go to Staten Island, more or less). Here the ferry names the text's numerous "crossings" and double-crossings. One might even rewrite the title itself as something like, "Crossing(s) and double-crossings involved in reading the materiality of metaphoric transports and the contracts staged when these are simultaneously preceded as mere crossings, together with subsequent performative reflections on the temporal dislocation and violence of inscription, ... " which would be relatively uneconomical. When the always present (self-absent) future reader sees him or herself with the bard seeing him or herself as "future," the present of reading shifts to a past non-present of the "I" that is, now, a simulacrum (of) itself, while the text proceeds to actively *colonize* and anteriorize (render dead or, rather, undead) its readers' temporal horizon. The reader, in one sense, is empowered by the text not to the degree that he or she trusts in Whitman's pronouncements, but because he or she passes into being his or her own dead.[18] Rather than taking this double-cross as a mournful sign of betrayal by an avuncular icon, one can take it as a mark of Whitman's dionysian honesty, his willing tutelage of the active reader who may have become inattentive to the stakes of this game, reading, or to "life," the one who becomes accustomed to the usual costumes or pretense that there are no stakes in reading.

The "crossing" is never completed, never arrives, which may not be its point. Among other things, the criss-crossing in the "well-join'd scheme" that precedes names has the capacity to erase, like the

---

18 We see that Moon's symmetrical "circuit of desirous gazing" may be inadequate to account for torsions in which there seems to be no symmetry. The figure of "the gaze," with its intimations of fusion and possession, cannot account for the dispossessing power of the "curious mystery" of reading, and remains the reader's necessary invention and protection.

forgetting that the classically invoked river Styx or Lethe implies. The close reader in this account may enter Theseus-like a maze by accepting the bond(age) of transport and inscription, yet the monstrous "I" of Minotaur Walt, as if exposing the underlying psychosis, can even afford to taunt bluntly in section five, "What is it then *between* us?" That is, in the triple sense of: What (if anything) bridges the separation of years in reading that you, now, seem suspended by, or prevents you from dropping? What (if anything) assures the "affectionate" reading you proverbially and stupidly seek? What (if any) machine or technical device lies "between" us in this questioning (signs, language, the ferry)? In section seven he presses against us, as if physically, and asserts an *ex*timacy that subsists in concealed (sexual) knowledge and the equation of the priority of anteriority with standing behind one: "Closer yet I approach you, / What though you have of me now, I had as much of you — I laid my stores in advance, / I consider'd long and seriously of you before you were born?" Maybe; in any event, the vampirism of this voice is uncanny. The reader, willing or not, has been "had" in advance in multiple senses, even reduced to a generated eidolon or linguistic subject position fully predicted by the text as amok time-machine. One could argue that some interest resides not only in the claim of priority that traps the reader in this time loop, but in a further reversal it implies. This latter occurs through crossing the roles of visible and invisible in a scene of power: "Who knows, for all the distance, but I am as good as looking at you now, for all you cannot see me?" Such inscription, invariably aggressive and like the ebb and flow of a basin, must alternate between inclusion and vampirically draining the future of itself as its sole means of perpetuation.

Nor must Whitman wait until he is dead to enjoy the rhetorical privilege asserted, since he is always already dead and hence, not. What a rhetorical connoisseur must admire in Whitman is not the ahistorical idealism of the trans-temporal claim which Fisher critiques, but the radical materialism of the performance, the sheer sophistication of the metatextual moves, indeed, its historical audacity in critically reflecting on the disfiguring powers of his text.[19] Side by side with the

19 According to Fisher, Whitman's "American ... aesthetics of abstraction" appears
   in fact as "an aesthetics of the subtraction of differences" compared to our
   knowledge of specificity informed by Hegel, Foucault, or de Certeau. Fisher's
   critique emerges in reading "The Sleepers," where he notes that the "negation

more or less "affectionate" and embracing Whitman, I would argue, this *other* privative text and persona is always present, an evil twin more or, frequently, less disclosed. By inscribing the reader, Whitman circulates him in advance as a ghosted other in the text, trapped in the eroticized spatial relationships and temporal loop of the deathless dead, which may imply the near self-cancellation of a textual logic that consumes its future (readers). But this is also to say that the poet, crossing us back and forth between life and death and recrossing the Lethe-like vapors of forgetting, presents an act of mourning engraved by the extinguishing sun. Dis-integrated into this scheme, "crossing" migrates through implying sheer transport, metalepsis or temporal exchange, double-crossing and, finally, crossing out, though in no particular narrative order.

In fact the allusion to Lethe is and is not successfully made, since what would be "crossed" is not literally a river, not something that flows in one direction or from a source. It may be that the poem does not deliver to "death" but to the more problematic space of being unable to die, unable to go *down*, or even to forget the perpetual "crossing" named. The East River is not a river and does not flow to the sea. It is a tidal basin, a reversible simulacrum "river" in a repeated movement without end or direction. This Whitman notes: "Flow on river! flow with the flood-tide, and ebb with the ebb-tide!" The false name "river" appears now like the "I" itself, a metaphor cast over the very state of affairs that denies its identity. Whitman openly questions this duplicitous moment in section six:

"The best I had done seem'd to be blank and suspicious, / My great thoughts as I supposed them, were they not in reality meagre? / Nor is it you alone who know what it is to be evil, / I am he who knew what it was to be evil, / I too knitted the old knot of contrareity, / Blabb'd, blush'd, resented, lied, stole, grudg'd."

What the "evil" Whitman names may be the duplicity of his rhetorical power and will to power, where hierarchy is sheathed in the affirmation

---

not only of differences but of consciousness itself" (73) is the final product of Whitman's abstractions. Yet if Whitman's claims are taken literally, that is, as in no way figural or performative, Fisher's own notion of the concrete ends by repeating Whitman's model of supposedly transparent *lists* that are, in fact, "products" ("an array of everyday products such as Levi's, Model T Fords, and Monday Night Football"). What results, unobserved, may be a latter-day ideology of transparency, a (new) historicist notion of facts that Whitman, of course, avoids.

of communion, disfiguring aggression in vatic pose. And here again is the double logic of interpretation: does Whitman confess to be "evil" in an exculpatory manner (to be "good"), or is he describing his text fairly precisely at this site? The prospect of an "evil" Whitman only renders more interesting Whitman's powers of seduction, incorporation, and ambush – in, as the *Preface* notes, the structural impossibility of communion, fusion, or intimacy. As we hear in section eight: "What is more subtle than this which ties me to the woman or man that looks in my face?" (197). There is as much in the word "subtle" as there is in the word "ties." Yet "the man or woman" is no longer "you," and may be himself or herself without face as such, much as the old word-play on the Greek *sema* and *soma* that links semen and signs or semantics with the body and tomb turns the next question into one of a kind of rape or buggery – "Which fuses me into you now, and pours my *meaning* into you?" (197). Clearly, in this scenario and perhaps in general, the powers of possessing anteriority, of standing behind another temporally and positionally, assumes its own erotic exigency, one simultaneously proleptic and already accomplished. To read Whitman's "face to face" at face value is to miss its open logic of defacement, inscription, and, indeed, readerly ambush or rap(tur)e.

Why, after all, did Whitman so confidently predict eluding his critics, which is to say, also, "crowds" of readers? It may be he really meant not that by being too *literary*, critics would miss his prophetic import, but that by being too familiar, by presuming his intimacy at face value, they would miss his strategic mastery – a simple crossing. The "sun-down" crossed out from the earlier title thus makes the reader who does not engage the text agonistically "more curious ... than you suppose." What is indeed curious, is that the bard seems to say, that "you" would allow yourself to be led, unresisting, into the labyrinth of "my" system, that you do not prove a better "agonist," since if you are a passive reader nothing I promise or propose will matter anyway, and you are left with simulacra. It seems that the recurrent fantasy of some readers to be sexually possessed by Whitman may appear the case in a significantly more violating, metaphoric and, just perhaps, less consensual sense ("I had as much of you – I laid my stores in advance"). The question remains whether future readers of Whitman cross this threshold, which would have to come at the expense of an iconic approach that remains culturally invested. One can always say, of course, that it was not Whitman who launched this sort of linguistic violence, not him who spoke so psychotically, but his evil twin. Not "I," perhaps, but Myself? If Whitman has all along seemed a bit too avuncular for a poet, a bit too concerned for the inner self of the reader, a bit too vatic to be *true*, it may be because he is.

6

The letters of the law: "Bartleby" as hypogrammatic romance (letters)

****

> the slightest alteration in the relation between man and the signifier ...
> changes the whole course of history by modifying the moorings that anchor
> his being.   Lacan, *The Agency of the Letter*

> Bartleby was one of those beings of whom nothing is ascertainable except
> from the original sources, and in his case, those are very small. "Bartleby"

Melville's "Bartleby" — the ostensible tale of an insubordinate legal
scrivener's cessation of copying, and the employer-narrator's subsequent evacuation from his Law Offices — seems to ask how a text
can pose as an *event*, a historical occurrence that alters or modifies
signifying chains that pass through it. It does this not by choosing a
rhetoric of action or representation, however, but by narrating and
performing the dispossession of an entire mode of (re)production in
which, technically, the reader is him or herself located as well. For the
event of the narrative is the non-event of Bartleby's withdrawal from
the Law Offices of the nameless lawyer-narrator. If these offices can be
read as a scene of reading and writing, why does "Bartleby" proceed
to empty them — and what, in them, is meant by the Law? In a sense,
what makes "Bartleby" unique may be that it seems to be "about" the
cessation of writing (as copying), like a black-hole in the continuum of
literary history. But there is another question, more difficult to
negotiate: how do we follow Bartleby's trajectory outside of the Law
Offices of mimetic reproduction without altering our own model of
reading in the process? What are these offices which partake in a
bureaucratic, relentless sort of "law," if not Melville's truly appalling
and quite inert trope for the mimetic *logos* itself, a mechanical order
relying on copying, on mimesis? Why or how can the cyborg-like
copyist represent an intervention in this scenario? Why or how can
Bartleby be a figure of the poet or *writer*, let alone a great romancer
and originary genius like Melville — Bartleby, who is called, after all,
as far as possible from "that mettlesome poet Byron" (111)? It is

common to remark that after this text in his own scripto-biography, Melville ceased writing prose during the long lyrical hiatus ending only with "Billy Budd." What does it mean to depict writing itself as sheer copying, as recirculating citations? If we examine what are called the "premises" we note that it is defined as a scene of "*conveyance*," in this case of "legacies" and wills. This suggests an operation in which such things as anterior texts, citations, others' words, and contracts are *relayed* from a past into a proleptic or to-be-legitimized future. As Gregory Jay recently notes: "Bartleby's withdrawal from writing and his refusal to copy may be read as a willed disobedience to every prescription in his culture's 'general text'" (21).[1] If we accept this, the question becomes more tantalizing: what does it mean to dispossess the *mimetic* logos, the machine of production of mimetic writing, and its relentless ability to reproduce or legitimize itself? What draws attention to the fact that this law is itself a convention, a historical fiction, an imposition? We may hear in the lawyer's "premises" the representational, historical, logical, *and* aesthetic *pre*mises of this oddly bureaucratic logos all at once.

Is the challenge of following Bartleby's trajectory as readers to shift outside the mimetic or referential fictions of the Law Offices' scene of reproduction without production? What sort of reading does not remain mimetic, *within* the Law Offices it contrives to interpret? At what point does a reading of letters, even dead letters, present itself less as a willful spectacle of linguistic play than as a vehicle of transgression? Is there a time when the very placidity of letters rise up like surreal and overthrowing servants, called to a bacchanalia whose excess alters the semantic management of how sense is legitimized? Does the fact that letters precede mimesis make them an exception to its order? With these questions in mind I will not attempt another "interpretation," but will examine the offices themselves and the metaphors that constitute them. In fact, while "Bartleby" has attained

---

1 Gregory Jay, in *America the Scrivener: Deconstruction and the Subject of Literary History* (Ithaca: Cornell University Press, 1990) also suggests that: "Bartleby allegorizes a Derridean solicitation of the law, quite literally in the demands Bartleby makes on the lawyer/narrator. Bartleby occupies the very premises of the law, disobediently. He refuses the social contract, disbands the state by withdrawing his signature from its constitution" (22). The question is how, if this is only another possibility within the endless logic of the law itself, does he move outside the offices? The primary texts of Melville will be *Billy Budd and Other Tales* (New York: Signet, 1979), and *Moby-Dick; or, The Whale* (London: Penguin, 1981).

marked status with post-structuralist readers for its closing allusion to the Dead Letter Office and the use of this figure in Derrida's *The Post Card* (indeed, it figures throughout Blanchot's *The Writing of the Disaster*), there seems no consensus on the import of "dead letters" as such. What if, in the process of leaving the hermeneutic shelter of the Law Offices, we discovered something odd: specifically, that together with Bartleby's withdrawal, Melville displays a spiralling series of prefigural skits and micro-texts that operate outside any possible *mimetic* reading? What if we entered unaware into an anagrammatic pursuit of the "origin" of writing/consciousness, as Ahab does in his pursuit of the whale? But let me pursue this idea a bit further and suppose, that certain cryptonymic texts become accessible which, in different ways, have *no mimetic codes* (Saussure's original problem with anagrams), that they took place through highlighting what could be called "dead letters" or, more explicitly, cryptograms, or even what de Man called, in actively dovetailing both, *hypograms*? Then this epitome of formalistic play, of *mere* signifying play, could also constitute the material knife that cuts through the womb-like *wall* or enclosure of the old mimetic law. Perhaps the challenge of reading "Bartleby" constitutes this dare, to exceed the Law Offices, or to be reinscribed. According to this schema, the inter-subjective or humanist readings based on identification which the last line of the text seems to promote ("Ah, Bartleby! Ah, humanity!") could be among the most mechanically reproduced or, like the Law Offices themselves, non-human.

Which is not to say we ever really leave the offices. The cessation of copying may mean this: to interrupt the cultural recycling of a set of definitions (legacies), contractual identities, and meanings. Whenever we are moved to write yet again on "Bartleby," to add to its voluminous commentary, we suppress this question: what does it mean to "write" about not-writing, what could then be called not-literature? Hence, one thing that is of interest is whether the logic of the signature itself may operate inversely here, or destructively. Where, that is, does "Bartleby" perform what might be called an instance of disinscription, or removing one's signature from a legal and cultural contract?

Aside from an underdeveloped strain in Lacan and studies in cryptonomy derived from Abraham and Torok, we find little encouragement to letteral reading. Jean Baudrillard notes in "Symbolic Exchange and Death" that "Saussure's anagrams and Marcel Mauss's gift-exchange will appear, in the long term, as more radical hypotheses than those of Freud and Marx."[2] Asserting this priority over the master-narratives of modernist culture, or where an economy of inscription — like that of the gift — precedes interpretation, Baudrillard presupposes a subversive relation between microverbal structures and even social economy, between capital and semantic reserves, or as "Bartleby" says, credit and credibility. The metaphoric economy that dominates the Law Offices is interesting in this respect, since it at first links *interiorization* to figures of eating, and the latter in turn to writing. Called "a vagrant" — derived from *walken*, "to wander" — and a "wanderer who refuses to budge," Bartleby undoes the antitheses of sender-receiver, home-office, author-reader, movement-stasis, or sel-ler-buyer posited by the lawyer's declared profession of "con-veyancer": "Now my original business — that of a conveyancer or title-hunter, and drawer-up of recondite documents of all sorts — was considerably increased by receiving the Master's office" (110). That is, when we meet the narrator, the already *revoked* Master of Chancery or mastery of the chance concatenations of verbal signifiers that the imposition of sense entails.[3]

De Man's rewriting of Saussure's anagram into the term hypogram raises the possibility of examining the Law Offices itself as a sort of logos-machine (Deleuze's term in writing of Proust), one that functions under various strains up to a point in which Bartleby emerges as its own excess.[4] As we noted in discussing Plato, it translates not only as

---

2 Jean Baudrillard, "Symbolic Exchange and Death," trans. C. Levin, in *Selected Writings*, ed. M. Poster (Stanford University Press, 1988), 118.

3 Maurice Blanchot refers to Bartleby repeatedly in *The Writing of the Disaster* (trans. Anne Smock [Lincoln: Nebraska University Press, 1986]): "In 'Bartleby,' the enigma comes from 'pure' writing, which can only be that of a copyist (rewriting). The enigma comes from the passivity into which this activity (writing) disappears" (145).

4 De Man's complete passage comments on Starobinski's *Les mots sous les mots: les anagrammes de Ferdinand Saussure*: "Saussure notes and seems to be disturbed by the meaning of *hypographein* as 'signature,' but he also mentions a 'more special, though more widespread meaning as 'to underscore by means of makeup the features of a face (*souligner au moyen du fard les traits du visage*)' (31). This usage is not incompatible with his own adoption of the term which, by analogy, 'underscores a name, a word, by trying to repeat its syllables, and thus giving it another, artificial, mode of being added, so to speak, to the original mode of being of the word.' *Hypographein* is close in this meaning to *prosopon*, mask or face. Hypogram is close to *prosopopeia*, the trope of apostrophe. This is indeed compatible with Saussure's use of 'hypogram,' provided one assumes, once again,

under-writing (infratext or *sub*text) but as prosopopeia, and, finally, as *signature*. The term, like Bartleby, is uncanny, since it seems both an originating figure yet, emerging from inscription (*gram*), also *bars* the arrival of voice. The hypogram obeys a mad, in ways self-cancelling logic, implying a bar to being by the materiality that gives rise to its claim. My departure from both Saussure and de Man involves the acceleration of the figure in ways that will be apparent as a principle of intervention. In tracing the dispossession of the Law's "premises" I will move, somewhat parodically, through the three senses of hypogram: that of a potential *intertextual* bureaucracy for conveying and legitimizing past "originals"; that of preceding the legal emergence of the subject itself; and that of the itinerary of signature in this text. I will also ask where "Bartleby" must itself be read, today, as a hyperlinguistic rewriting of *Moby-Dick*, one transposing the overlarge romance of the sea and its pursuit into dry, utterly economic, even hyperlinguistic terms. Where is the earlier work's all important "whale" reproduced as the claustrophobic cipher called, in "The Story of Wall-Street," simply and unexpectedly a "wall," a term whose anagrammatic shift is effected yet again in the figure of the (l)*law* itself? How do we get from the representational dilemma of the hyperbolic "white whale" to the linguistic breakdown of Bartleby or what that text calls, outside the office, a "white wall"?

I have tried to suggest some considerations that impact on the reading of his work. In a sense, these extend the possibilities of reading in two directions – the first, in some sense beyond the mimetic terms by which we habitually read literary narratives (character, identification, inter-subjectivity), and second, toward a microverbal level of writing we usually give supporting status to. What I propose may appear, however, a bit more extreme, as I would ask where the text itself performs – as it were, in Melville's name – the act of deleting signature itself from within a historico-legal contract of production, and why Melville's attention to the letter provides the agency through which that spell is exceeded or dissolved.

the stable existence of an original face that can be embellished, underscored, accentuated, or supplemented by the hypogram. But *prosopon-poein* means to give a face and therefore implies that the original face can be missing or nonexistent" (*RT*, 44). If Bartleby's recurrent phrase, "I prefer not," entails a prefix that proliferates madly in the text, *-fer* also echoes the *phorein* of metaphor or figurative transport, and we are directed to a site that precedes figuration itself.

I. Policing the interface: walls, whales, wills

I will begin elsewhere in Melville's work. When "Ishmael" opens *Moby-Dick* with a chapter called "Loomings," he first speaks of a *hyper*bolic attack of what he nonetheless calls "hypos," which we take to be fits of depression. It is curious, since one cannot quite separate these from the "sub-sub" librarian, carrying old grammars, mentioned in the preceding foretext. Ishmael notes that, "whenever my *hypos* get such an *upper* hand of me, that it requires a strong moral principle to prevent me from deliberately stepping into the street, and methodically knocking people's hats off – then, I account it *high time* to get to sea as soon as possible" (93; my emphasis). What indeed has the sea – as word, place, or semiotic space? – to do with Ishmael's low spirits, called *hypos*, which suggest a coming up from under, a sublime (*hypnos*) emergence linked to an excessive moment in turn called an "*upper* hand" or, even, the "high time" of the narrative? What, indeed, is a "high" time of narration? Such a sub-marine figure may for one thing, like a whale, emerge to randomly tear apart a sea-surface that resembles, also, the reflected play of linguistic associations. *Hypos* may thus recall on the linguistic and material level what de Man names as hypograms. In fact, as with other maritime writings (Conrad certainly comes to mind), it is not certain whether the "sea" is a referential term or if it is not best heard as a semiotic or tropological problem – as Jameson tends to read it in Conrad's case in *The Political Unconscious*.[5] If so, Ishmael's *hypos* suggest where the sea is itself at stake in Bartleby's offices (the Law Offices might be called the bureaucratization of the sea). As beginnings go, "Loomings" is itself preceded by two foretexts that focus exclusively on words and even syllables. In fact, *Moby-Dick* appears almost generated from those *citations* (called "Extracts") and etymological notes that seem, if anything, closer in spirit to Bartleby than to the oversized sea romance, especially as the Consumptive Usher and *sub-sub* librarian that guard the opening of *Moby-Dick* appear to be direct anticipations of Bartleby. What again, if anything, links *whales* and *walls* at the interface of representation? *Moby-Dick; or, The Whale* opens with the text called "Etymology (Supplied by a Late Consumptive Usher to a Grammar School)," where the Consumptive Usher – "threadbare in

---

5 In *The Political Unconscious* (Ithaca: Cornell University Press, 1981), hereafter cited as *PU*, Jameson calls Conrad's sea "the non-place of the sea" (213), "that unique place outside of place" (242). See my development of this in chapter 8.

coat, heart, body, and brain" – stands with "a queer handkerchief, mockingly embellished with all the gay flags of all the known nations," dusting "his old grammars." Such an embellished cloth *rings* over variations in grammar and pronunciation that apparently degenerate from the name *whale* to the sheer Erromangoan phonetic signifier ("PEHEE-NUEE-NUEE"). After this Tower of Babel motif the first of the many citations indicates that the meaning of the word *whale* (or the book named thus?) depends on what has almost no *phenomenal* presence, that is, on a letter, and a silent one at that, an H. Nonetheless it is said to "almost alone maketh up the signification of the word," and is the first in the writer's own name – Hackluyt (or Herman): "While you take in hand to school others, and to teach them by what name a whale-fish is to be called in our tongue, leaving out, through ignorance, the letter H, which almost alone maketh up the signification of the word, you deliver that which is not true" (75). That all signification depends on what has no sound indicates a site in words that, like the whale, underlies verbal surfaces. The word "Usher," as in Poe's tale, recalls the Hebrew term for chance, while *consumptive* itself opens a series that will traverse Melville's writing, networking consumption with cognition, confidence with ingestion. As suggested, though, this hapless usher not only anticipates the "sub-sub-librarian" of the next foretext, where the "Sub-Sub" – or Hypo-Hypo? – is advised to release his burden and to surface or go hyper (the chronicler: "Give it *up*, Sub-Subs!"). What we might call, without exaggeration, the attendant hypogrammarian stitches the text out of citations, extracts and letters. Indeed, if letters with hardly any phenomenal presence are given such signifying weight ("almost alone maketh up the signification"), what seems indicated about the whale is a linguistic or letteral problem that precedes the phenomenal (sea/see) surface of reading.

Two dictionary citations are then given that derive the word "whale" from the Danish "havalt" as "arched or vaulted" and the German "Wallen ... to roll, to wallow" (75). Whatever binds the Melvillean "Sub-Sub's" extracts to the *h*-less syllable or the word *wallow* leads through a sea-change to what was initially subtitled, "A Story of Wall-Street," then, where issues of copying, citation, narrative identity, and letters appear. It has not been the norm to remark what the inescapable verbal transposition from the hyperbolic white *whale* to the "white *wall*" of Bartleby's office – or from either to the word Law that reverses the figure in an unexpected specular fashion ((e)la(h)w). It does not go without saying perhaps, since, like the prephenomenal "h," it cannot quite be *said*. This, though it is said (or written), and that by Ahab: "How can the prisoner reach outside except by thrusting through the wall? To me, the white whale is that wall, shoved near to me. Sometimes I think there's naught beyond ..." (276). What happens when this wall that contains and structures the conveyance of legacies (anterior texts) is moved, essentially dispossessing a fictional *law* dependent on mimetic copies and originals? Of course, Bartleby ceases "copying" at a particular moment, and that is when he is asked by the narrator to *compare* his work to the originals ("meaning to place the four copies in the hands of my clerks, while I should read from the original" [112]).

The traffic of "Wall-Street" may easily encompass diverse interpretive modes. When we attempt to read Bartleby as a character or moral figure to be evaluated, for instance, our mimetic habits intervene to create a subject whose history, in fact, the narrator is himself unable to provide – readings that place us, again, in the Law Offices.[6] The "Story of Wall-Street" is persuasively read as everything from a tale of Christ-like renunciation and man's (in)humanity to an anatomy of alienation in capitalism.[7] As noted, if the text's final line seems to endorse the humanitarian reading for instance – the utterance "Ah, Bartleby! Ah, humanity!" – the problem is it remains firmly in the mimetic premises the pale scrivener seems to dispossess. Certain metaphoric economies seem to inhabit or sustain the Law Offices themselves. The system of walls and screens that thread throughout the tale appear to construct interiors, for instance, yet one of the

6 In a recent treatment of the text in *Versions of Pygmalion* (Cambridge, Mass.: Harvard University Press, 1991), J. Hillis Miller notes that interpretations of the work tend to fall into two camps that try to "account" for the unaccountable figure, by either rendering him as a species of "humanity" (following the final apostrophes), or a specimen of the effects of capitalism. Miller attempts to preserve Bartleby's status "as the neutral in-between that haunts all thinking and living by dialectical opposition" (174).

7 Certainly many critical accounts move in this direction, yet there is usually a turning back, into the domain of the Law Offices. In a chapter titled "'Bartleby, the Scrivener' and the Transformation of the Economy," in *American Romanticism and the Marketplace* (University of Chicago Press, 1985), Michael R. Gilmore makes the familiar connection of Wall-Street to the "financial hub of American capitalism, ... the center from which radiate the many walls dividing society and segregating its members" (132). The problem of "capital" may be primarily performed in the linguistic bartering of the writing. Gilmore's approach is very much a part of the Law Offices (as a mode of reading) it would critique.

problems is that every inside turns out to be a pocket of exteriority. *Interiority* – private space, subjective authority, safes, recesses, partitions – seems to be a necessary pretext and fiction of the law, beginning with the "safe" narrator's voice. If the text appears, in turn, to relentlessly empty out interiors as subjectivity and as private space, it does so through repeatedly and enigmatically linking *eating* to copying, or copying to writing. Like the Manhattan Tombs that are oddly open-air, the air-shaft of the office forms an exterior site *in*side the building, a sort of anamorphic or what may be called *disin*-vaginating pocket: "At one end they looked upon the white wall" – in which one hears, again, the *white whale* – "of the interior of a spacious skylight shaft, penetrating the building from top to bottom" (105). What "penetrates" is a "shaft" that is, nonetheless, itself an inverted space. The wall determines "life" to be an artistic or representational category ("deficient in what landscape painters call 'life'") in the absence of any nature – except that of a voiceless semiosis ("The nature of my *a*vocations"). If exteriors appear in turn to be contained ("the interval between this wall and mine not a little resembled a huge square cistern"), they also emerge from doubled interiors ("I had my key with me, but upon inserting it, I found it resisted by something inserted from the inside" [118]), or from floating pockets ("I groped into their recesses ... It was an old bandana handkerchief, heavy and knotted. I opened it, and saw it was a savings bank" [121]).

Eating appears essential to running the Law Offices and yet it itself breaks down or off with the "advent" of Bartleby. His copying is first depicted as a sort of devouring: "As if long famishing for something to copy, he seemed to gorge himself on my documents. There was no pause for digestion ... he wrote on silently, palely, mechanically" (111). Nippers, who represents an editorial function, can even be displayed in a mirrored reading as (s)*RE*-pp-*IN*, which binds a project of interiorization to sheer repetition or to its attempt as copy. Copying, we understand, would internalize an external world (or script) and *preserve* memory as representation and self, yet here it also subverts its own work. What appears as Bartleby's accelerated (auto)consumption in declining to consume mirrors the disgorgement of safes, pockets, or reserves throughout the text ("I re-entered, with my hand in my pocket – and – and my heart in my mouth" [133]). What links copying to eating or *internalization* functions like a Hegelian dialectic that has broken down or stopped, a machine of historical interiorization as memorization (*Erinnerung*) that, like Nippers, simply has "*in*digestion." Accordingly, what may seem barred in reading "Bartleby," and what many commentators struggle to put back in place, seems first to be a conception of subjectivity or private social space. Only if both writing and eating properly internalize (or consume) does the machinery of historical "life" proceed; but when they do not the text appears to *fall* through every great age of the law and of writing in history, from Rome to Greece to Hebraic allusions, back to the "Egyptian character" of the Manhattan Tombs. The text's own turn to thematize sheer sound, is marked by a reference to *ringing* or *rings* – a term encompassing sound yet also a principle of recurrence. One example where these come together is when a succession of *in* sounds are repeated as an insistent movement inward on the level of inscription: "There was a strange, *in*flamed, flurried, flighty recklessness of activity about (Turkey). He would be *in*cautious *in* dipp*in*g his p*en in*to his *in*kstand." The first edition's title, "A Story of Wall-Street," seems itself to punningly name a site of total consumption ((W)*all*-(Str)*eat*), much as it names the directionless transport or metaphoric traffic that appears to be occasioned once the rule of the Law Offices comes to a halt.

2. Sea-Marks

Then falling into a moment's revery, he again looked up toward the sun and murmured to himself: 'Thou sea-mark! thou high and mighty Pilot! thou tellest me truly where I *am* ... This instant thou must be eyeing him. These eyes of mine look into this very eye that is even now beholding him; aye, and into the eye that is even now equally beholding the objects on the unknown, thither side of thee, thou sun!' The Quadrant, *Moby-Dick*

The question of sound lingers, resounds, rings. Why, in what is called the text's "sequel," will a ring fall out of an envelope in a circular allusion to sound ("Dead letters! does it not *sound like* dead men? ... Sometimes from out the folded paper the pale clerk takes a *ring*" [140])? That is, a ring that falls from the folds of "dead letters" and what they "sound like" (John Jacob Astor's name has "a rounded and orbicular sound (that) rings like unto bullion" [104]). Such ringing seems linked to the term consumption itself in the cryptic reference to Sing-Sing made when the turnkey likens the scrivener to the gentleman forger "Monroe Edwards" ("Did you know Monroe Edwards? ... he died of consumption at Sing-Sing. So you weren't acquainted with Monroe?"). Here, already, the idea of signature is partitioned from itself, as the *forger* Monroe Edwards suggests a cryptogram in which the initials M. E. echo one's *own* name (me) as forged, repeating as mine (*Mon*-roe) a name always anterior*ed* (*Ed*-wards). If M. E. expires of *consumption* at "Sing-Sing," it is in a drive to internalize through repeating, one linking sound to the consumption *of* the would be consumer. Consumption here suggests being *consumed by*, yet also the impossibility of consuming, an anti-cathartic and *indigestible* economy whose anamorphic space eludes the law of circulation.[8]

In a text where the narrator claims his "original business" to be "that of a conveyancer and title hunter," a pursuit of the original *title* of the story may be germane. Yet when we compare the first and second publications we find an immediate shift away from the "original" – and this shift leads us to where letters and, surprisingly, gender interlace ominously. Here the original title of the tale published in *Putnam's Monthly Magazine* (1853), "Bartleby, the Scrivener," itself subtitled in italics, "A Story of Wall-Street" (like *Moby-Dick* and *The Confidence-Man*, it bears Melville's idiosyncratic *hyphen*), reappears in a second edition chastened, cut down, pared.[9] Melville simply gives the tale the name "Bartleby," as if the text itself had folded back on itself and assumed the attitude of its character, or as though the name had simply consumed the seemingly descriptive title. Aside from this, there seems to be only one other alteration in the text, though it is very curious. Almost unnoticed, Melville drops the proper name of the Tombs' "grubman," and with it one or two lines. In a work resoundingly male, this second original version cuts the only allusion to a woman in the text who is given a proper name, the grubman's wife, "Mrs. Cutlets," a name that punningly involves cutting and eating in one. The line – whose cut represents a scar in the second, better known edition, a crease in which the absent text is redoubled

---

8 Consumption – as with the Late Consumptive Usher – again breaks into its components, "con" (cognition, conning, confidence), as well as "sum" (accounting, being), syllables with parallel echoes in other words (constitution, assumption) in which the exchange of parts (or letters) takes on momentum.

9 One could do a study, no doubt, on Melville's bar-like use of the hyphen alone, as in "Wall-Street," "Moby-Dick," "dead-wall," or "point-blank." Moreover, if one regards the "sea" as one possible origin of sight or life, whether we hear that in the word "se(a)quel" or not, the mirroring of its narcissistic surface must allow for a mock-specularity staged as a site of reversed script ("s-REppIN"). In the text the closing reference to "dead letters" can be read as preceding both specular and figurative models.

– involves Bartleby's being invited to Mrs. Cutlets' for dinner: "May Mrs. Cutlets and I have the pleasure of your company to dinner, sir, in Mrs. Cutlets private room?" In being deleted, the line appears doubly marked, giving Mrs. Cutlets' private room a threatening and obscene resonance, transposing consumption to being consumed (now implying the male sex), with the (non)enclosure of walls linked, punningly, not only to meat but to letters. Whatever cuts in letters, the at first tranquil word *sea* itself appears echoed in the initial "C" of Mrs. Cutlets, and her absence suggests a site of endless paronomasia, while the "C" itself becomes a stand-in almost for a pocket, reserve, or vaginal space viewed, however, as a false interior. It is curious that the only maternal figure available and, as such, linked to the sea – *mer* or *mer(e)* – should not only be threatening (it is not clear if Mrs. Cutlets would dine with or on Bartleby), but should also suggest a cutting-off linked to letters ("Mrs. Cut*lets*") or the "dead letters" of the sequel. The deletion of this female name in the nominal order of the text creates a negative reserve possible to associate with the consuming maternal order familiar from *Pierre*, yet also with the openly letteral, as well as with the absent sea itself – that is, the mother, *mer* or *mer(e)*. At the text's opening, "I" presents himself as narrating what cannot be narrated:

I am a rather elderly man. The nature of my avocations for the last thirty years has brought me into more than ordinary contact with what would seem an interesting and somewhat singular set of men, of whom, as yet, nothing that I know of has ever been written – I mean the law-copyists, or scriveners ... But I waive the biographies of all other scriveners for a few passages in the life of Bartleby, who was a scrivener, the strangest I ever *saw or heard* of. While of other law-copyists I might write the complete life, of Bartleby nothing of that sort can be done. I believe that no materials exist for a full and satisfactory biography of this man. *It is an irreparable loss to literature.* Bartleby was one of those beings of whom nothing is ascertainable except from the original sources, and, in his case, those are *very small*. What my own astonished eyes *saw* of Bartleby, that is all I *know* of him, except, indeed, one vague report, which will appear in the *sequel*. (103; my emphasis)

Given the metaphoric value of the Law Offices themselves, the opening ("I am a *rather elderly* man") may be read as naming a belated moment in history itself. The "more than ordinary *con*tact" required to write about writers of whom nothing has been written focuses seeing, hearing, and touch – contact of the senses – on the immediate yet elusive presence of Bartleby ("what my own astonished eyes *saw* ... that is all I know"). The desire of the narrative for originary knowledge rewrites sight as *reading*, yet returns us to what are called the only "original sources" for Bartleby, themselves "very small," like letters, in what is oddly named "the sequel," the final cut off text at the end.[10]

The word sequel breaks down in strange ways, as the verbal components of the text imitate Bartleby's insubordination. It may also be heard as *se(a)-quel(le)* or suggest what reflexively (the French *se-*) both produces (the German *Quelle*, spring or source) and quells or extinguishes. Recalling the Babel motif opening *Moby-Dick*, what it generates yet also quells might in one sense be the sequence of figures depending on the specular sea itself, a putative origin of reflection, life, semiotic play – mother, *mer(e)*, or *mar*. Where "no *mater*ials" are said to exist, one may address a sheer semiosis preceding or producing materiality itself – or at least phenomenality. We are here in Mrs. Cutlets' private rooms, as it were, within the associations of the signifiers that underwrite the Law Offices. What is called "an irreparable loss to literature" forecasts a loss not only to, but of "literature," the possibility of which Melville was throughout his writing career intensely suspicious of and which Bartleby in one sense forecloses, as the cessation of writing in the text (and Melville) suggests.

In the "vague *report*" we can also read "*se*(a)-*quel(le)*" as an origin of seeing or reading. In suggesting these associations, or scrutinizing their law, I have in mind the text of the sequel itself, whose "dead letters" we may now read both as the inability of a communication to arrive and as alphabetical characters ("very small"). Melville's Ahab-like quest for the *Quelle* of the sea itself pursues the equivocation between "mar" as an act of marking or marring and *mer(e)* as a narcissistic (if maternal) surface (*se mirer*), one that disappears in what Ahab calls a "sea-mark." Bartleby's virtual insubordination within the bureaucracy parallels an insubordination of syllables and letters – slave functions of legal meaning – within the semantic order of the narrator. That these seem empowered is first seen in the interface between *wall* and *law*. Both *mer(e)* and wall, for instance, appear echoed in the French word for wall, (le) *mur*, which then gives way to

---

10 Melville draws the analogy between reading and (or as) perception explicitly in a parenthetical aside: "(The reader of nice perceptions, will here perceive that, it being morning, Turkey's answer is couched in tranquil terms, but Nippers' replies in ill-tempered ones. Or, to repeat a previous sentence, Nippers' mood was on duty, and Turkey's off)" (114).

the stammering echo that immediately precedes the sequel itself: "'Eh! – He's asleep, ain't he?' – 'With kings and counselors,' *murmured* I" (139–40). The murmuring of Bartleby's "dead-wall reverie" grows louder as the separating double wall, membrane, or screen shivers into anamorphic variants, each with a separate itinerary in the text: *mur*, *mer(e)*, *mar*. The absent Mrs. Cutlets seems to precede the sea or sight (reading) itself.

In the text, like a close reading gone awry, terms like the scrivener enact what the text calls "re-*bel*lion" ("sundry twinges of impotent rebellion" [135]), the ringing insubordination of material sound that overthrows semantic premises. One series of such substitutions empowers the insistently inscribed syllables *mer* or *mar*, which tend to organize phrases invoking the complex resonances of origin, sea, and marring indicated, like "*meridian*," "*mere*," "*mur*mur," "*Marius*," even "*mayoralty*."[11] Thus the sun and the sea join in a specular pattern to obliterate the space of "life": "Of a *Sunday, Wall* Street is as deserted as *Petra* ... (Bartleby is) *sole spect*ator of a *solitude* which he has seen all populous – a sort of innocent and transformed *Marius* brooding among the *ruins* of Carthage" (120; my emphasis). The sun (*sol*) appears as the vanquisher first of human metaphors, then of itself, while the spectator in the sentence – with the gaze of Marius – appears to obliterate whatever horizon it is cast on. The obliterating agent in this could be called the eye/I as such.

3. Before the law

If the notion of the hypogram addresses the transpositions of legacies from the past into a putative future, and this through the absent present of the Law Offices, the value of the term seems to rest in the prospect of locating an archimedean point before representation. Yet the sequel covertly deploys its second definition as prosopopeia, the very emergence of voice or face. Set apart from the block paragraph this line ("Ah, Bartleby! Ah, humanity!") might appear the sequel *of*

---

11 The reader's relationship to such micro-texts may be aptly called one of *speculation*, since the substitution of semantic and monetary tropes ("bills") circulates in the absence of a mimetic law once the copying is stopped. Interestingly, this term (*mar*) concludes "The Piazza," where the *place* named is related to the haunting of a face: "To and fro I walk the piazza deck, haunted by *Mari*anna's face, and many as real a story" (102). The *face of Marianna* is tied in the text to an intertextual idyll in which Melville's rewriting of figures like Spenser, Shakespeare, and Tennyson is covertly a subject.

the sequel, a double apostrophe invoking humanity itself. This line is routinely used to support the more familiar humanist readings of the moral education of the nameless narrator, yet it has a trap:

> The report was this: that Bartleby had been a subordinate clerk in the Dead Letter Office at Washington, from which he had been suddenly revoked by a change in the administration. When I think over this rumor, hardly can I express the emotions which seize me. Dead letters! does it not sound like dead men? Conceive a man by nature and misfortune prone to a pallid hopelessness ... Sometimes from out the folded paper a pale clerk takes a ring — the finger it was meant for, perhaps, molders in the grave; a bank note sent in swiftest charity — he whom it would relieve nor eats nor hungers any more ... On errands of life, these letters speed to death.
>   Ah, Bartleby! Ah, humanity! (140)

Rather than investing Bartleby with pathos, the apostrophe of "humanity" itself may strip the *human* virtually of definition. It repeats and replaces an unaccountable name, Bartleby, and it is presented as a personification itself.[12] What the narrator calls being "un*manned*" by Bartleby may imply an un*nam*ing as well ("not only disarmed me but unmanned me" [119]). Bartleby, in a certain sense, represents a post-humanist figure emerging from and emptying an epochal definition of "man" as subject. "Humanity" appears as a term personifying dead letters, *accelerated* letters that paradoxically "speed to death."

Literally a "turning aside," the figure of apostrophe locates *its* own origin in Greek law courts, as a strategy of persuasion in arguing a case. It derives from the device used when an advocate turned away from the jury to address (and personify) an absent *third* party, thing, or god. In fact, the lawyer-narrator alludes to this when he notes: "I am one of those unambitious lawyers who never addresses a jury or in any way draws down public applause" (104). Yet if we search for the emergence of face as a place of origin, it occurs in association with

12 "Life" is likened precisely to what the text terms speeding ("On errands of life, these letters speed to death"), in the sense of Paul Virilio's *Speed and Politics* (New York: Semiotext(e), 1986), where the interplay of *vif* and *vivre* in French would appear to be in play: "speed" would be read, as in the image of transport suggested by "Wall-Street," as the acceleration of figurative transfers and connections. These "errands," moreover, connect not only to Bartleby's errance or vagrancy but to a precession which the narrator announces in the sentence: "Ere introducing the scrivener as he first appeared to me it is fit I make some mention of myself." *Ere* — as heir, err, (h)ere — announces the notion of (reverse) succession that transferring legacies and titles implies.

a sort of solar poetics, at the heart of the Law Offices, at a time called
meridien.[13] The at first promising coincidence of (a) *face* with a sun
leads the reader to the *"English*man" Turkey and the copying routine
of the logos-machine:

In the morning, one might say, (Turkey's) face was of a fine florid hue, but
after twelve o'clock, meridian – his dinner hour – it blazed like a grate full of
Christmas coals; and continued blazing – but, as it were, with a gradual wane
– till six o'clock, p.m., or thereabouts; after which I saw no more of *the*
proprietor of the face, which, gaining its meridian with the sun, seemed to set
with it, to rise, culminate, and decline the following day, with the like
regularity and undiminished glory. (105; my emphasis)

It is not the "waning" of the *sun-face* that most disturbs the narrator,
but the time of full blazing "when Turkey displayed his fullest beams
from his red and radiant countenance." "*Count*enance" as face resumes
the numerical system of counting and conning, though what "I" fears
from this formalization is an excess ("altogether *too* energetic") that
results in "blots," darkenings, and erasures. As it turns out, "*the* face,"
which is itself without anchor, cannot be originary. Turkey's equation
with a site of inspiration proceeds not from the excess of the sun's
presence, but from a redoubled absence or blackness ("as if cannel coal
had been heaped on anthracite"). The face becomes a prop ("it") said
to have a "proprietor." What emerges is a black sun, or rather
innumerable black suns, copies without original, themselves marking
eclipse, consumed or eaten indifferently in the form of "ginger cakes"
("what was ginger? A hot, spicy thing"):

Copying law papers being a proverbially dry, husky sort of business, my two
scriveners were fain to moisten their mouths very often with Spitzenbergs to
be had at the numerous stalls nigh the Custom House and Post Office. Also,
they sent Ginger Nut very frequently for that peculiar cake – small, flat,
round, and very spicy – after which he had been named by them. (109)

This "round" cake is to be had only near the Post Office, yet one may
also translate Spitzenberg roughly as "mountain top." In the surreal
metaphorics of the Law Offices, the mountain top seems a Mount Sinai
where the Law would have been inscribed and given, yet these black

13 For the treatment of apostrophe as the incantatory genesis of *triadic* social
   discourse, see my discussion of V. N. Voloshinov's "Discourse in Life and
   Discourse in Art" in the first chapter of this book. In this model, as in that of the
   court-room, apostrophe is triadic in that the first person, or speaker, addresses the
   personified "hero" while the utterance is witnessed, but not addressed to, the
   listener ("jury").

suns appear to be consumed in a hyperlegalist *communion* ("Turkey would gobble up scores of these cakes as if they were wafers" [110]).[14] These commonplace terrors of consumption had always reigned as ritual in the Law Offices before the "advent of Bartleby." Here interiority is inversely consumed by a radical and relentless exteriorization.

The Platonic concept of the sun as paternal origin allows us to forget what makes us heliocentrists. Unlike Bartleby, who may be said to forget to forget, we forget that it is but one of innumerable stars, myriad "copies" in turn without original. Melville does not forget this, however, since he refers us back to a star predictably absent in this anti-Platonic work, yet tied to the system of sounds, properties, tenancy, patronage, and chance. For the narrator introduces himself in relation to the absence of this *patron*, the *late* John Jacob *Astor*, the largest landlord of tenement properties and realties in New York:

All who know me consider me an eminently *safe* man. The late John Jacob Astor, a person little given to poetic enthusiasm, had no hesitation in pronouncing my first grand point to be prudence, my next, method ... John Jacob Astor, a name which, I admit, I love to repeat, for it hath a rounded and orbicular sound to it, and rings like unto bullion. (104)

The name Astor, clearly, rings with the Greek term for star, *aster* (an "orbicular" figure). One may speak of a *dis*aster, now, perhaps in Blanchot's sense, and extend this at the outset to a place in which the writing itself can be said to dissolve the representational system simultaneously into names, or pieces of names and sound, that this narrator loves "to repeat." Such a disaster – the absence of a model, a mimesis without models, and the absence of any paternal figure – siphons the temporal pretext from a narrative that had at best a fragile one among its "premises." Melville appears to use throughout his writing and nowhere more than here, a technique of repetition ("rings like unto *bull*ion") not of the word to create a sequence of emphatic variants of meaning, but at first of the syllable (*in, con, mer*), then of the letter (c, m, l, for instance), to isolate and reverse the flow of semantic authority much as Bartleby does to the narrator. We may have to

14 A variant on "Spitzenbergs" receives mention in the "Extracts" text to *Moby-Dick*, there linked to the white whale ("he caught once a whale in Spitzbergen that was white all over" [82]). Here Turkey's "moistening a ginger cake between his lips and clapping it on to a mortgage for a seal" not only connects this indigestible consumption to a type of death (*mort*) but provokes odd reverberations in the term se(e/a)al(l).

reread Melville's narrative ideas, accordingly, not as being characters or subjects, but at certain points as emerging in the form of words or, in fact, non-words like "co(n)-," "mer-," "ba(r)-," "-in(g)," and so on, rather than the familiar grand themes. Such pieces of script are multiply encoded and seem, from such a perspective, to generate the narrative or descriptive texts that they appear in, virtual personifications whose priority seems evident in their recurrence. From a writing like "Bartleby" that can appear generated by prefixes (pre-, post-, re-, con-, and a(c)-), Melville proceeds later to write a work which depends more or less exclusively on the multiple values of the syllable *con-* (*The Confidence-Man*) – already present in "Bartleby" in a series of words including: contact, conveyance, constitution, consumption, confinement, among others.

If the name "I" loves to repeat itself "rings like unto *bull*ion," where do the bell-like repetitions of sound *simulate* a new currency? "Like" bullion suggests *bills* that do not represent a reserve but become the pretext of a bartering, semantic exchange – as if of gold.[15] When we read of the narrator's "*sun*dry twinges of impotent re*bell*ion" (135), then, Melville's solar poetics appears impotently dispersed in the material resistance of (aural) signifiers, the re-ringing of re-bellion. What seems risked is not the exchange between narrative capital or credibility ("Will it be credited? Ought I to acknowledge it?" [130]) but the *material*ity that sound itself entails ("I believe that *no materials exist* for a full and satisfactory biography"). Writing (in) Bartleby "prefers (not)" to copy or even function in the bureaucracy of the logos, in a mimetic logic, and this becomes the premise for an apparently relentless reduction to a *nil*-point that challenges the law and politics of mimesis itself, through what amounts to a strike.[16]

15 If one looks for an "account" in the realm of the characters, and turns, say, to the idea of *will*, the term seems to madly proliferate. There is a riddle associated with the word "will," used successively as a legal document concerned with heirs and legacies, or as poetic "will," desire, a punning cognate of "wall," the transposition of "bills" of currency or credit, or the legal logic of the scrivener's utterances.
16 In "Afformative, Strike," trans. D. Hollander, in *Cardozo Law Review* 13, 4 (December, 1991), Werner Hamacher's focus on the law's preservation may illuminate the political dimension of Bartleby's curious *labor strike*. Hamacher explores a moment in which the law as imposition begins to cancel its own principle, to become illegal: "By turning from positing to preserving law, (the law) must also turn against hostile forces of positing and thus indirectly against its own principle – the principle of positing itself. In order to remain what it is – violence of law imposition – law-imposing violence must become law-preserving,

4. Crossing the bar

Toward the end of the tale the narrator offers Bartleby a job as a "bartender" ("How would a bartender's business suit you? There is no trying of the eyesight in that?"). Here we encounter a final punning association of one who tends (to) or, let us say, touches – makes epistemologic contact with? – something called *bars*. Such bars, inhabiting the title character's name, may be read here in the barest possible way, as minimal marks of serial difference that precede even letters yet on which all perception, or reading, depends. "Tender" suggests both legal *tender* (currency, bills) and *tenanting* as such. Such a tend(er)ing of bars draws us toward Bartleby's "dead-wall reveries," where bars, walls, and letters appear to converge in a psychotic stance.

We have already seen that the word "bar" may be said to engender a material series on which language depends, yet as such it represents a proverbial bar to being itself – the irretrievable pun of Bartleby's name. Among the "letters" that speed between "life" and "death" is the letter "C" that is or seems allied to the sea. As the third letter, it also suggests a triadic or pyramidal system at once originary and deadly – like the triadic structure of apostrophe – particularly when used with the letter "A" (one) or any vowel (like "O") that suggests the number one or zero. The first person ("I") that the act of speech as apostrophe brings into being through its addressee (a third man) has

must turn against its original positing character, and, in this collision with itself, must disintegrate" (1134). Hamacher notes that for Benjamin the prospect of an intervention in history can be thought through a figure of depos(it)ing: "deposing for Benjamin is a historical event; yet it is one that puts an end to the cyclical history of legal institutions and that is not thoroughly determined by this history. Deposing is a political event, but one that shatters all the canonical determinations of the political – and all canonical determinations of the event ... Deposing is thus not encompassed by any negation, is not directed toward anything determinate – and therefore is not directed" (1140). To think Bartleby's "I prefer not" in this fashion is to posit a politics that is not *positively* determined, that even depends on its interventionary force on not being so directed. For Hamacher, the site for the "afformative" is a premimetic one in language itself ("Language in its mediality is pre-positional, preperformative – and, in this sense, afformative" [1143]). According to this reading, Benjamin's notion of the proletarian strike can be seen, as in "Bartleby," as an act that is a "nonaction": "In this respect, the proletarian strike is 'analogous' to the 'proper sphere of understanding' – language. Directed toward nothing, signifying nothing, not acting, the proletarian strike, as the 'task' of political critique envisioned by Benjamin, is the 'annihilation' of all legal violence ... and is, like divine violence, 'law-annihilating' – as opposed to mythical violence, which is 'law-imposing'" (1149).

a price, since it makes the speaker himself a represented "I" or third person in turn, in essence killing (or suiciding) the subject as speaker. In "Bartleby" such a self-cancelling origin ("The *nature* of my *a*vocations") seems depicted in the anecdote of "the unfortunate Adams and the still more unfortunate Colt" (129), a murder-suicide where *A*dam(s) also represents the idea of the *first* man (or "I") and Colt the triadic system. The name Adam(s) is reiterated later on the same page when the narrator speaks of "this old Adam of *re*sentment," and where the so-called first man now appears already as a repetition, a copy, an "old" figure of *ressentiment*. The same letteral system is apparent in references to "the bust of Cicero," where the foremost legal rhetorician and orator is assimilated to an explosive stone muteness ("bust").[17]

Of the "Egyptian character" of the Tombs, for instance, we hear that its "surrounding walls ... kept off all sound," though even here something *springs*, hyperbolically, as "a soft imprisoned turf grew *underfoot*." If we can once again read the problem of legibility itself into this law, of *legere* or reading, then the legacies, or legs of sense appear to be again in question. What may be *under*foot, or hypo, at this point? If the first two senses of hypogram – as infratextual commerce (the logos offices) and as a bar(r)ing of voice (apostrophe) – have been noted, it is the third meaning of *signature* that emerges here in a nonetheless unstable way. It is unstable since rather than dispersing itself anagrammatically, it struggles to dissolve or even erase itself from the contract that seemed in place.

"Bartleby's" system of conveyances – of wills, legacies, credit, or letters – compels us to seek the missing "face" elsewhere than in

17 So obsessive is this configuration in which the origin of the first person or speaker is located (and negated) in its own linguistic death, that the letteral combinations of "C" (three) and "O" or virtually any vowel (one) overrun the text (ca-, co-, ac-). Another such text might be when the narrator, "thunderstruck," cites the example of the Virginian killed by lightning who "remained leaning out there ... till someone touched him, when he fell," an irruption connected to touch that prepossesses life or speech. There is an elaborate description of Turkey's clothes which makes the analogy between his face and the used, Joseph-like coat the narrator donates to him. Each is linked to light ("sport such a lustrous face and a lustrous coat"), and both appear to be figures of figuration. Interestingly, Turkey will appear as virtually *touching* his coat ("as a rash, restive horse is said to feel his oats, so Turkey felt his coat"). The image not only suggests the literalism with which such tropes appear to be touched – treated in their materiality – but links feeling and cognition ("felt") with the contact at once casual and reductive of a signifying chain.

Turkey's black noon. In a text replete with supposed safes and reserves, we might even look for it hidden in some recess or safe even. Given the specular field of the writing, witnessed in the interfacing of "wall" and "law," one place might be where "I" notes of himself: "All who know me consider me an eminently *safe* man" (Melville's emphasis). When the reversal is factored out and translates wall *as* law or allows us to read "reverse" in the word "*re*serve," we can rewrite "safe" as "fac(s)e" as well, as if the narrator said, however oddly, "I am an eminently fac(s)e man." Instead of a Biblical presence that the reference to Spitzenbergs (as Mt. Sinai) suggests, the letters of the law (l-a-w) literally turn about a mocking law of "dead" letters, much as the specular reversal of "wall" for "law" also led to a definite *loss*. First, that of the "whale" altogether whose transposition as "wall" could not be returned from (a turn from descriptive to inscriptive language), since among other things what is lost is that silent H which was said to have almost signified all. In the next transposition, from wall to the law itself, we lost another letter, a perhaps silent "l," which like Bartleby appears "unaccountable" and not much worth troubling about, at least were it not a figure of excess and itself the letter and hence initial of (the) Law and Literature, Loss and "Life," of Legibility, Legacy, and Letter itself. What, now, can be said of one errant (Egyptian?) character, the L, the letter of letters, that actively worries the very interface of mimesis? This, even though it might return us to an originary *elle*, she, or *mer(e)*, hence to Mrs. C(utlets), to the sea.

We might read this lost letter "L" as lodged in the name Bart*l*eby, or as a figure, like the first person "I," that appears scriptively almost as a bar (/). We are reminded that one meaning of bar, of course, is the legal profession itself and what Merriam-Webster calls "the whole body of lawyers" — taken from the bar in court where a case is pleaded. That this wall at once unmans and unnames seems evident in the contract that allows "I" *itself* to do all the talking, and we are led, as it were, from the figure of Bartleby back to the first person behind the narration, the doubled voice of the law. There is no doubt that this figural series prepossesses numerous words in the text, like "will," or for that matter "bills," that appear as pictorial repetitions of bars (i-l-l = / / /) yet circulate as if legal semantic tender, counterfeit or *faux* words. The narrator, for example, suggests that Bartleby "travel through the country collecting *bills* for *mer*chants" (135), and variants must include not only its paronyms, bullion and rebellion, but other cognates ("Bartleby was *bill*eted upon me for some mysterious purpose" [130]). As it becomes marked as a non-word, "bill(s)" is accordingly (dis)inhabited by a series of bars that also suggests repetition and anteriority. "Will" similarly circulates both as what the lawyer conveys as legacies and as the volition that Bartleby at once exemplifies and iconically undermines by his (in)action. In such a series successive replicas refer back to differential predecessors they repeat and alter, and this becomes the signature of a materiality that precedes representation. Does Melville circle, here, what was elsewhere called the pragma, through dead letters, approaching even the Protagorean *metron* as a fundamental means of material reduction or transfiguration? When Nippers is spoken of as "*ill*-tempered," for example, Melville inscribes this series in and as the disruption of a temporality that the work's own regression to Roman, Greek, and Egyptian origins performs. This prefigural notation recurs later in Melville, where it is associated with origination or budding, that is, as if with nature, yet also with stuttering and murder, in "Billy Budd." In pursuing the "white whale" less in descriptive terms than inscriptive ones, Melville tracks the dead-wall revery itself to this letter "l," or bar, and its obliterating trajectory – the minimal requirement of signification, writing, consciousness, semiosis, and letters. Bills are thus linked to the exchange not only of tender, but reading itself: "Some days now passed during which, at leisure intervals, I looked a little into 'Edwards on the Will,' and 'Priestley on Necessity.' Under the circumstance, those books induced a salutary feeling. Gradually ... Bartleby was billeted upon me" (130). Reading is associated with "intervals," and the suffix *-ed* binds the triple "l" of "Will" to a resurgence of anterior traces (-ed), while the prefix *pre-* ("Priestley") precedes representation itself (in German *Not* translates as necessity). In the title story of *The Piazza Tales*, the piazza (or place) presents an intertextual venue in which the text freely cites Spenser through Tennyson. The word includes in itself the alphabet (Pi-az/za); and it is said that: "No fence was seen, no inclosure," yet "with this cottage the shaded streaks were richest in its front and about its entrance, where the grounds*ill*, and especially the door*sill*, had, through long *eld*, quietly settled down" (97).[18]

---

18 Bills give way to the problem of accounting, numbers, and *listing*. The narrator opens with an act of surveyance, familiar from Kafka or Hawthorne, that involves listing employees ("Ginger Nut, the third on my list"), while variants of the word list, as with the word 'prefer,' later proliferate ("Mere self-interest, then, if no

I now want to switch my focus to one last rung of refinement — and while I could apologize for where this leads, and its seeming irrelevance, I will defend it in advance as the logical extension, even acceleration, of this analysis so far. Basically, the overthrow of the law, its dispossession, alternates with its perpetual recovery or restitution, whether in the lawyer-narrator's voice or our own, and the trace of resistance to this has been located — at least in this inquiry — in dead (or all too living) letters. My question at this point (and there is some need to personalize this) is how to read Bartleby's refusal of voice, character, or signature as an act reflected in the text itself. What can it mean to "read" a text at the "point" where Melville's disinscription is enacted, and with it the legal province of voice or grammar?

Yet what's *in* a name? However much I would like, again, to stop here, this logic should be completed if the relentlessness of Melville's text is to be appreciated. In the opening fiat — "I am a rather *elderly* man" — the assertion "I am" passes into an assertion of age and belatedness (Astor is already dead, the Master of Chancery revoked). Following the law of what precedes the letter, we can rewrite it even as, say, "I am a rather elderly *nam*(e)," or again, in a subsequent paronomasia, "'I' am (or: *M*(elville)) a rather *L*-derly name." Here a cryptonym not dependent on unconscious content but as if inhabiting language itself dispossesses the semantic Law Offices by way of a logic irreconcilable to mimesis, copying, description. If letters dismember, they are dismembered in turn. For that is precisely what Melville is, a rather L-derly name (it has three L's in fact). And the first such occurrence, (M)*el*, itself can be playfully said to recur (altered) in a second repetition, (v)*ill*(e), transformed from a sound to a series,

better motive can be enlisted" [130]). The problem of accounting yields a sort of formalization that is the parodic double of the bureaucratic logos-machine. Listing itself is ambiguous, a mode of controlled accounting that unaccountably moves beyond grammar as sheer enumeration, utterly banal and potentially sublime for accelerating beyond containment. Etymologically it is rooted in the figure of enclosure *klaustro*-, echoing the text's obsession with claustrophobic walls, or tombs, though if unpacked it also contains the idea of boundaries or edges, near catastrophe (the listing of a ship), the reflection of light (sight or desire), and the list(en)ing of the ear — the entire anamorphic circulation of an aesthetic or material effect. Thus the ear itself is connected to the word lust or lustre, which in Elizabethan English implies both desire and the reflective shine or appearance that we hear in the German *Schein*, the term linked by Hegel to art's sensual manifestation of the idea. The word list appears to straddle the most formalistic and banal of notations and the most phenomenally originary at once, as was said of the word bar.

inscribing the numbers one (*el*) and three (*ill*) echoed in the allegory of Adams and Colt — the triadic signature of discourse's barring of the subject it generates (as witnessed, earlier in this book, in Voloshinov's discourse scenario).

My reading of the Law Offices shows it to be a site where "American exceptionalism" is rewritten as a pseudo-Adamic moment (an "*old* Adam of *re*sentment"), a clearing house of historical memory whose role as conveyancer to a tentative future must break down. Bartleby's guerilla "*act*" — as character or text — is to open the possibility of a radical freedom and entrapment by suspending the contractual relation of meaning and tradition, of citation and cultural production, through the refusal of mimesis.

What seems to be in question is a quest for the linguistic genesis of the first person — whatever "I, Bartleby," might mean. The opening sentence now implies a series of transpositions that precede predication and prohibit the sentence from ever quite arriving (or leaving).[19] It is here — what the text also calls "ere" (err/before/(e)re) — that the question of the sea, or maternity, seems to reappear. I resist laying out several transpositions that open up once we allow the name Melville to itself resolve into a series of bars (as even the "M" or "V" may appear), and in which the first syllable "el," which is echoed in the gendered *elle* present by deletion in the text, is as if repeated in the second "ille," which seems as a parody of French at least de-gendered and plural, the very city (*ville*) of which the election for mayoralty is mentioned in the story. The evacuation of Wall-Street enacted by the Marius-like scrivener seems momentarily projected by the dissolution of this name itself into so many walls, so many bars, so many letter L's. From within the play of this logic, the sentence may be heard again as the pseudo-tautological "'I' am 'L'...," or made to stammer fragments like "'I' am (M)...a bar," or "I am ... Bartleby." The utterance may further be generated within a *combinatoire* now displaying a mock-gendered inflection, involving the *mer/mar* system, as "'I' am (M) *elle* (she, *mer(e)*)." If the text's dry male law was at first enforced by the exile of any female trace, not only does that trace return here — identified, first, with the deleted Mrs. Cutlets — but it

19 Again, the predication of "man" in the first line ("I am a rather elderly man") is punningly connected to the servitude not only of names, but of hands, *le ma(i)n*, as well — the figure of writing or touching. Bartleby is called "handy," while the locale of the text is, of course, Manhattan.

also reappears with a rigorous dismantling of maternity and the sea. *Who* "speaks" the text if it is neither the lawyer, nor Bartleby, nor "Melville," but a function before which each name is defensively put in place? *Who* writes (in) "Bartleby" and who – or what machine – stops writing?[20] If the errant "L" may appear also as an *elle*, a she (sea/see) or *mer(e)*, indeed, as "mother," it (neuter) again echoes the deleted Mrs. Cut-lets. From "I am a rather elderly man" we have come to produce, through the encrypted paronomasia of the sea's reflected surface, something like "I am *elle*, she, (the) sea, *mer(e)*," or, "I am (my own) 'mother,' generating – as cutting off," or, "I am (or is) Mrs. Cutlets," which is perhaps also to say, "I" am (or is) what (also) produces (the) "I" (myself), that it (I) also bars, destroy(s), cut(s) like a serial machine. In this redaction, the original claim to *being* (I am) is rerouted to acknowledge its status as a murderous personification. Bartleby's "dead-*wall* reveries" reflect the revenant inter-substitutions of this wall, bar, slash, or L, the "sea-mark" of Ahab. The opening sentence can be seen, in this way, to erase the entire narrative of *Pierre*, to subsume, condense, and rewrite *Moby-Dick*, and to render *The Confidence-Man* its commentary. This, though it might be impossible to arrest that sentence from translating yet again, from limitlessly consuming more text, however illogically, as "I am (the) *mer(e)*, the sea (C), Mrs. Cutlets," or again, "'I' *am* 'L,'" specular *mer(e)*/*mar(r)*, a she that is *no* she, no mother, a sea that is no sea, A-*mer(e)*." Yet here lies potentially the scrambled name "America" itself, buried in the predicative "am" that opens the series, the asserted proper name America as the negation of this maternal mark, this sea-mark or *mer(e)*. Keeping in mind the echoing proliferation of such terms (*meridien*, *ma(yo)ralty*, *mere*, *Marius*), we see what could be called a momentary psychosis of the hypogram, operating like a phonograph in the self-cancelling signature of America itself, poised to break down the Law Offices actively. The sentence might finally mean to stutter: "I 'am'/American 'letters,'" a sentence Melville might well write at this moment. The logic of anagrams appears to break all modes of ciphering with mimetic reference or, like the letter "h," phenomenal presencing. Without model, original, or ground, an American romance

---

20 Aside from the name "Bartleby," registering a sort of bar-to-being, other names occur in this mode in literature, utilizing the same problematic: one thinks of Hawthorne's Bartram in "Ethan Brand," Henry James' May Bartram, Faulkner's Homer Barron, Hitchcock's Judy Barton, and so on.

appears to be rewritten as the most banal or walled in confinement, as sheer formalism, yet one that intervenes in the usual business of historical transfer and conveyance in the Law Offices.[21]

Rather than drawing us into mere letteral play, the proposed reading may have an interventionist role to play, much as Bartleby's own trajectory dispossesses the logos office that appears machinal, controlling, and inefficient.

Melville's explicit transposition of the maritime "whale" to the "white wall" of Wall Street's Law Offices triggers an American speculation on the materiality of language. When the Law Offices are vacated, there is no further circulation of received legacies, no further copies, no further citations, for the duration of the narrator's text. It would appear, at least according to the end(s) of writing Melville circulates within here and, apparently, "lived," that in "Bartleby" a linguistic redefinition of "man" is explored that, momentarily, necessitates an emptying of "premises." After the "advent of Bartleby," after writing or reading him, everything and nothing is the same, since "Bartleby" also names a radical interruption in which the institutional contract of semantic hegemonies can be suspended ("I prefer not"). If "Bartleby" rewrites *Moby-Dick* in hyperlinguistic terms, the hypogrammatic "romance" or quest seems more devastating than that of the white whale which, if anything, may be modeled on it. "Bartleby" continues to occupy a space between "literature" and its foreclosure. It suspends reproduction as usual, reading as usual. It cannot represent a mere "moment" in a chronological history such as a break in Melville's production. Rather, the end(s) of writing that it marks should be conceived as possible at any point in that production, in any production, challenging the legal conveyances in which the community of readers are inscribed. To achieve the meltdown of the logos itself, as it would seem, Melville must undo the very structure of the signature. That is, its always having also emerged, become conscious of itself, already on a contract, within a "constitution" and "law" presented as universal or other than historically contingent. If one is always inscribed in a set of cultural texts, it would seem, then, that "Bartleby" is an exercise in the

---

21 Read hieroglyphically or as "Egyptian character(s)," for example, in the name *Melville* itself the "M" and the "V" could well appear as joined lines or inverted triangles, that is, as vagrantly positioned "L's" as well, which would momentarily dissolve the name into a series of bars or strikes.

powers of *dis*inscription, of burning through a semantic and repetitive confine, or order. This occurs through the active dissolving of the logic of contracts, constitutions, and signatures as such. It is the signature of the dismantling of signature.

The problem posed by this reading is that noted in the discussion of Poe: that of how a text can move beyond the mimetic system of meaning that it appears constructed within but which it also apprehends as a closed historical regime. "Mimesis" would seem to always reproduce itself as a remainder, a stain that then (vampirically) reappropriates the field of signs, while at the same time bringing itself to a crisis reminiscent of Othello's impossible suicide.

PART III

Pre-posterous modernisms

❖❖

7

Conrad's fault (signature)

❖❖

To a teacher of languages there comes a time when the world is but a place of many words and man appears a mere talking animal not much more wonderful than a parrot.
Conrad, *Under Western Eyes*

Conrad's discourse – an overlay of psychoanalytically charged terms and ideological, public slogans – must be regarded as a foreign language that we have ourselves to learn in the absence of any dictionary or grammar, ourselves reconstructing its syntax and assembling hypotheses about its meanings of this or that item of vocabulary for which we ourselves have no contemporary equivalent.
Jameson, *The Political Unconscious*

that infernal tale of ships … Indeed, the nature of my writing runs the risk of being obscured by the nature of my material.
Conrad, a letter

Once we designate a historical period by the term *high modernism* and question the act of reading, we have placed both that category and its mimetic status in doubt. If high modernism may itself be a defensive retro-concept, what in the modernist text threatens, still, our itineraries of reading? To read Conrad now – this, clearly, becomes more remote (like an alien language, Jameson will say) the more we try to name a duplicity, chasm, or fault that inhabits the event of this writing. If Conrad is repeatedly represented as some sort of break, fold, or rupture in historical trajectories, this fault between his mimetic pretexts ("that infernal tale of ships") and the material and figural domain of language is uncertain. Thus Jameson speaks of "a shift between two distinct cultural spaces, that of 'high' culture and that of mass culture."[1] When Jim leaps from the *Patna* only to land in the skiff with miserable company, one way to read it is as the facticity of a Conradian sublime – an Icarean "leap" staged before the absence of a catastrophe, the catastrophe of that absence itself, which becomes the origin of narrative. While the image of Marlow waiting for his rivets

---

1 Fredric Jameson, *PU*, 207.

seems to give this problem concretion – to repair the joints, to fix a ship of metaphor itself – I will focus mostly on a later text, "The Secret Sharer," which takes such *duplicity* for its theme. My intention is to read a reflexive moment in Conrad that addresses not only his own "strangeness" to (his) language, but where that fault becomes the subject (and blockage) of his text. To do so, however, I will address a dynamic of signature that has not, to my knowledge, been probed with this writer.

In *The Political Unconscious*, Jameson speaks of Conrad's text as marking "a strategic fault line in the emergence of contemporary narrative" (207), one, however, that is "undecidable" and threatens to reverse the divided markers ("so archaic, so regressive and old-fashioned, as to be at one and the same time post-modern, and more modern than any of his contemporaries" [219]). Several figures must be rethought in any attempt to read Conrad today: the ship and sea as semiotic markers, the reflexive mix of high and low styles, the power of specific words or syllables, the signature itself – each resists the familiar itineraries of Conrad's thematics of history, colonialism, and moral design. Thus Jameson suggests that "Conrad's discourse ... must be regarded as a foreign language that we have ourselves to learn in the absence of any dictionary or grammar" (246). Among words or non-words that haunt his text, or disrupt its mimetic surface, might be *fault, joint, see* (sight), and a series of terms departing from the syllable *con-* itself.[2] Yet Conrad's effaced alienness within his mastered language, this unmarked doubling within the familiar terms, also seems a subject for the fiction occasionally. We may read the adoption of the signature "Conrad" with the advent of his authorship as coinciding with a fold or effacement – into English, say, from a place outside or other (nominally, Polish). Such a fold or crossing is also unmarked, since it coincides with (his) writing as such, though the instance of the adoptive writer colonizing a master tongue in reverse (Joyce, Nabokov) suggests more than a metaphoric paradigm. This is the deadly experience of the east European disaster survivor, Yanko Gooral, in Conrad's "Amy Foster." Washed ashore in England as the sole survivor of a "disaster," he bears an impenetrable difference

---

2 Edward Said remarks, for example, on "the eerie power in Conrad of minimal but hauntingly reverberating phrases like 'the horrori' or 'material interests': these work as a sort of still point, a verbal center glossed by the narrative and on which our attention turns and returns" (*The World, the Text, and the Critic* [Cambridge: Harvard University Press, 1983], 96), hereafter cited as *WTC*.

within his adopted English itself ("his difference, his strangeness"),[3] which proves untranslatable, and is finally lethally isolating, even when he speaks in that tongue ("The whispered sounds I caught by bending my ear to his lips puzzled me entirely ... utterly unlike anything one had ever heard" [176]). Yanko Gooral's linguistic incommunicability is extended to his learned English as an absolute pathos. As his alien tongue cannot be placed as French, German, Italian, or Spanish, the dilemma is absolute ("He keeps on saying something – I don't know what" [188], "She had not understood, though he may have thought he was speaking in English" [189]), and his dying words seemed "no longer in his own language" (190) without being in any other.[4] A parallel "strangeness," as it is called, inhabits the unnamed narrator and captain of "The Secret Sharer" (hereafter, I will use the signature *SS* both for economy and to insert the role of the letter itself in this scene). Though ostensibly the reverse of that of "Amy Foster," since "strangeness" is here attributed to the captain of the ship himself, the central speaker and narrator himself, it is a "strangeness" spoken of as being not only to his ship but to himself ("what I felt most was my being a stranger to the ship ... a stranger to myself").[5] If we read the ship to be mastered in the *SS* as a metatextual figure, too, of Conrad's own text, such a difference within his language may be nowhere more (un)marked than in this highly finished tale about staging a total *blind* to visibility, to interpretation itself, with the deceived crew representing its readers. What is encrypted – perhaps, with Leggatt – in the *SS*? The tale appears to be partly about a duplicity within that production as well – where "doubling" is both its apparent theme and a figure repeated so openly as to be used as itself a screen.

Unlike Jameson's fault line of history, Said locates a rift in terms that are intended to be psychological but appear linguistic. He speaks of Conrad's "duplicity of language," of a "chasm between words saying

---

3 Joseph Conrad, *The Portable Conrad* (New York: Viking, 1969), 187; hereafter cited as *PC*.

4 Said draws attention to the tale without probing the impossible paradigm it offers, since his aim is to close, in some measure, the fault or "rift" he addresses aesthetically ("the rift between a fully developed but, with regard to other people, only an intentional or latent capacity for complete expression and an inescapable human community" [*f*, 105]).

5 Joseph Conrad, *Heart of Darkness and The Secret Sharer* (New York: Signet, 1976), 21. Hereafter cited as *SS*.

and words meaning," a "wedge between intention (wanting-to-speak) and communication" (90), and a "disparity between verbal intention grammatically and formally apprehendable and ... verbality itself" (104). Yet Said draws back from the implications of the fault, fold, rift, or rupture that he names by reading Conrad's motif of *seeing* literally as representing an order beyond language. Citing Conrad's renowned preface to "The Nigger of the 'Narcissus'" — "before all, to make you *see*" — Said speaks of "Conrad's faith in the supremacy of the visible" (95), of his using language "for actual vision to occur, so that then language would no longer be necessary" (96).[6] Conrad's duplicity of language may itself extend to such strikingly misleading phrases. The visible as wordless presence contradicts visibility as a figure for reading, as when, in *Heart of Darkness*, Marlow convulsively links sight and its impossibility to naming and draws attention to the book that Conrad's readers hold: "that Kurtz whom at the time I did not see — you understand. He was just a word for me. I did not see the man in the name any more than you do. Do you see him? Do you see the story? Do you see anything?" (*SS*, 94–5). Yet *seeing* in the *SS* is explicitly linked to seeing and keeping something encrypted, "not visible to other eyes than mine" (*SS*, 50). If we read Leggatt as an unmodifiable figure of reading and the law, as the name suggests, we may well get suspicious as to what is — or is not — made visible before readers whose blindness mimics that of the first mate. In the *SS* what seems particularly in question is the "strangeness" of command, of mastery, of the law to itself (the captain's voice). The tale appears, at times, to be about a text's ability to totally block interpretation. If the tale also "reads" the production of Conrad as a sort of metatext, we recall that seeing and sight are linked not only to letters but to the sea (mer, mar) itself, from which the "headless" figure of Leggatt emerges. The sea appears in this text as a site of narcissistic engenderment ("The Mirror of the Sea") that nonetheless bars a specular system from truly emerging. The reflexive *se-* (in French) is heard in the sea, in see(ing), in secret, in the *Sephora*, and perhaps in the letter *C* as well. Such a return from the "infernal tale of the sea" to the material order of language is one place, now, where the fault of (and in) Conrad might be pursued.

---

6 Jameson calls this manifesto "the declaration of the independence of the image as such" (*PU*, 232), yet also does not raise the question of its essential duplicity, or whether the word "see" is, "above all," a screen.

Something about Conrad's sea seems to irk Jameson's will to historicize, since he represses it in a manner recalling Xerxes's commanding the sea be lashed for upsetting his navy's ships. He calls the sea the "privileged place of the strategy of containment in Conrad ... the absent work-place itself" (242), or "the non-place of the sea ... the space of the degraded language of romance and daydream, of narrative commodity and the sheer distraction of 'light literature'" (213), or "that unique place outside of place" (210). Jameson also terms Conrad's style "impressionistic" as a conventional means of asserting its descriptive, then Utopian, propensities. Yet from *Typhoon* he cites an example of "the Utopian vocation of Conrad's style" that betrays this mimetic premise itself: "The far-off blackness ahead of the ship was like another night seen through the starry night of the earth – the starless night of the immensities beyond the created universe, revealed in its appalling stillness through a low fissure in the glittering sphere of which the earth is the kernel" (230). The text seems to subvert any utopian rhetoric with a movement to a dystopia both inside ("in the glittering sphere") and outside of creation – a fault or fissure preceding nature or any mimetic figure in "another night." Jameson's suppression of such a figurative dilemma is apparent when he reads the pivotal figure of Stein in *Lord Jim*. Stein's butterfly collection ("as though on the bronze sheen of these frail wings, in the white tracings, the gorgeous markings, he could see other things") becomes the pretext for his ejection from the community of we who possess History: "the rhetoric of mortality is here but a disguise for the sharper pain of exclusion by history ... and of Conrad's own passionate choice of impressionism" (238). As with the sea, Jameson dismisses a certain material problem of figuration – here, Stein's butterflies – that represents a threat to a representational ("impressionist") hermeneutic. Jameson's hostility to the "sea" suggests a repression of a specular and prefigural site that demands a different historical reading than one focused on Conrad's "utopian" image.

In the *SS* the nameless captain narrates his concealing of a confessed, if potentially accidental, killer, his "double" (as we repeatedly hear), from his own crew – though to this crew he represents the Law, one that thereafter is divided from and within itself. The language opens a gap between meaning and performance, or action and figuration itself. It is a gap the text only seems to close with its asserted "perfect communion" of the captain with his ship when the narrative relinquishes Leggatt to the sea at the end. Since we may now read the "tale" not only as a story of ships but as a metatextual scene, two moments appear to be decisive. First, we note Leggatt simply passing through the text unseen. And second, while the analogy seems tentative, the assertion of achieved mastery over the ship at the end coincides, in Conrad's own canon, with something quite different. While one critic calls the tale a "microcosm of Conrad's fiction,"[7] we may read that against its position in the production following *Under Western Eyes* (1912), one that marks, as it seems, a radical decline of canonical "Conrad," almost as if the text precipitates a turn, faltering, or official decline in that writing itself.

In the concluding passages the image of the *mark* — linked again to *mar*, sea — and of ignorance stand out ("the saving mark for my eyes ... serving me for a mark to help out the ignorance of my strangeness" [*SS*, 60]). This *ignorance* suggests an inability to know the coincidence of the performative and semantic import of the text, for "help out" could grammatically imply not rescue from but a furthering of "the ignorance of my strangeness." The text also inscribes the (knowing) reader in the position of the blind, mechanical, and cliché-ridden first mate and crew. Why does Leggatt's erasure at least appear to help right the ship, heal the captain's strangeness, or help out his "ignorance," and what has this to do with Conradian writing, about which the tale seems also to be concerned? As a work of suspicion — and as the name Leggatt attests — it is a text not of the sea, or of command, or of male bonding, and so on, but of reading (*legere*) and its prevention. There is no way to close out this protested "doubling," since the tale says it is deceiving those most dependent on its word and law, just as there is no way to assert any real "doubling" is occurring. The text reiterates the figure of doubling so much so as to subtly undermine it, rendering it suspect with its too obvious literariness, since it could easily be read as using the topos of the "double" itself as a screen. For the interpretation of Conrad the point will be the role of a dissimulation or "lie" — similar to that which is thematized, say, by Marlow in his curious encounter with Kurtz's "Intended" — that both represents and is represented by a generative fault that seems always to precede (writing) itself, and effectually urges one mode of rhetorical acceptance over another. It proves vertiginous since the voice already betrays its own command as the law, and this

7 Introduction, *PC*, 29.

duplicity (like that Said notes) becomes the text's overt subject. It is impossible to say what "secret" is being concealed or shared by the text's openly drawing attention to that concealment (Leggatt), as the illusion that the reader is privy to it only further blinds that sight. The text revels in a disparity of readings that cannot be closed, yet end by asserting a foreclosure ("perfect communion of a seaman with his first command" [SS, 61]) whose hollowness recalls the text's most conventionally received interpretations.

Any discussion of a fault in Conrad suggests more a rupture in a reflective system of language (Said's "rift" between intention and verbality) than a moral or even epochal fault, though the latter is typically used to generate the narrative — be it as Jim's leap, Razumov's inaction or, differently, Leggatt's killing aboard the *Sephora*. The "strangeness" of the nameless "I" narrating the *SS* appears as an analogue for this rupture. Like the "event" in *Lord Jim* that was never quite an event, Leggatt is, uniquely in Conrad, passed through the hollow of the narrative (and the ship), divested in what is openly called "secrecy." What is being spoken of openly and yet kept secret about Leggatt in Conrad's script, if we read the *SS* as a metatextual performance? If we recall that Longinus depicts the "sublime" repeatedly as just such a *near* disaster (a ship perilously missing the shoal), the text or ship seems to stage its own "sublime" moment, using Leggatt's departure as an occasion. The ship describes a parabola by the dangerous shoal that is a parable of writing that almost makes a contact everywhere denied to words. This estrangement to his own ship recalls what de Man names the "radical estrangement between meaning and performance of any text" or the "*estrangement* between subject and utterance."[8] Yet this itself becomes a grammatical agent of Conrad's text ("My strangeness, which had made me sleepless" [SS, 22]).

The crime of Leggatt (strangled seaman, tongue out) *precedes* the narrative itself, while the *Sephora* appears at first, then, to name a figural site (the *phorein* of metaphor). The *SS* conveys or transfers Leggatt, stripped of name, outside of the scene entirely, off the chart ("the face of the earth"), as if the text existed to remove this figure from readability entirely ("Everything was as before in the ship" [30]). "I" and Leggatt are both "*Con*way boys," a figure stressing a

8 Paul de Man, *Allegories of Reading: Figural Language in Rousseau, Nietzsche, Rilke, and Proust* (New Haven: Yale University Press, 1979), 298, 289 (emphasis added).

cognitive agency (like the Congo, or of course Conrad). Preceding the narration it generates, Leggatt's crime occurs in the "forecastle" and the text is arrayed in series of *fore-* terms ("forehead," "forebitts," "forefinger," "fore-end," "forerigging," "foresail," "forebraces," "foreyard") that suggest an insistently prefigural site. Like Jameson's "place outside of place," the sea of Conrad precedes mimesis. Yet if the name of the ship of the crime, *Sephora*, suggests metaphor, it also bears in its name or carries (*phorein*) the reflexive *se-* or sea itself, and thus the name seems to invert metaphor entirely, feet for head, as what did the bearing (the sea) is now itself borne. Moreover, the *OED* defines the related cabalistic *sephira* as the "emanations by means of which the Infinite enters into relation with the finite." The "headless" Leggatt again suggests an order of crossed associations, including *legs*, which *carry* (transport) sense, as well as the law, legacy, and the legibility of *legere*, or reading. Leggatt emerges, then, as a material figure of reading out of the sea (specular *se-*, sight), yet one whose perception is linked to another structure called a "mysterious system" that is not at all specular. The writing of Conrad here resides over a fabrication of memorized words, as Jameson notes, as when the language teacher in *Under Western Eyes* writes that "man appears a mere talking animal not much more wonderful than a parrot." The "double" that emerges from the sea and reflects an obscure mechanics of reading in "Conrad" appears to evade being read. The figure that emerges as if headless from the sea names a *legs* (phonemes, letters, measure, inscription) upon which Conrad's tale, or style, might stand or fall.

"The Secret Sharer" may itself only double as a tale of doubles. Since it names and draws attention to doubling so much and so obviously, it also renders that suspect. When we hear from the narrator that "I felt more dual than ever" or "I took a peep at my double, and discovered that he had not moved" (*SS*, 36), we are not sure if it does not parodically appropriate the literary theme as yet another screen. The tale presents itself without any hidden reserve, since it knows, kens, or cons ("Conway boys") its own equally staged recess ("It was very much like being mad, only it was worse because one was aware of it" [37]). While the text turns on the question of control and visibility ("Can it be, I asked myself, that he is not visible to other eyes than mine?" [50]), it must warn itself (and us) against taking literally the very thing the narrator presents: "'We are not living in a boy's adventure tale,' I protested" (51).

If reading as *legere* is preserved from sight, from the crew and from the text's readers (who may see it as a boy's adventure tale), what does the emergence of Leggatt from "the mirror of the sea" imply? As mentioned, the *Sephora* seems, instead of being borne by the sea, to inversely bear the "se(a)" from which Leggatt emerges, while in an opening text the *Sephora* itself supplants the disappearing mail tug, transporting letters. While the captain's voice "represents the law" (32), the cabalistic sephira names as the portal to the "finite" a linguistic materiality bound to the sea itself. There is an odd reference to a Sephora in *Lord Jim*, indeed, to "the *Sephora* disaster," where a sailor returns to the sinking vessel to save a lady's maid ("gone completely crazy — wouldn't leave the ship"). What is seen from without as the two go down becomes comic in the absence of hearing their words ("like a naughty youngster, fighting with his mother"), until the sailor "just stood by looking at her, watchful-like" as it went down.[9] The vortex of this allegory that depends on a muting of language seems, at first, replaced by this *Sephora*'s survival precisely of a disaster, here due to Leggatt's strangulation of the unfortunate shipmate, to the point of producing a black face ("He was black in the face. It was too much for them" [28]). If I have been arguing that the *SS* involves a crime and a linguistic parable that inhabits Conrad's writing and determines a recurrent concept of "fault," it opens with a description directed to what is just beneath the sea's surface:

On my right hand there were lines of fishing stakes resembling a mysterious system of half-submerged bamboo fences, incomprehensible in its division of the domain of tropical fishes, and crazy of aspect as if abandoned forever by some nomad tribe of fishermen now gone to the other end of the ocean; for there was no sign of human habitation as far as the eye could see. (19)

The opening sentence rewrites the sea's descriptive surface as a figural domain that both precedes "human habitation" and is its uncertain product. It represents ("On my right (write) hand there were lines") a seemingly semiotic structure of "incomprehensible" division, which is at once prehistoric and historicizable. Like the term "preposterous" hurled later at the mate's suggestion that Leggatt is on board, the "my right hand" of the opening line may be taken literally as the hand that writes. The "mysterious system" that could

---

9 Joseph Conrad, *Lord Jim, A Norton Critical Edition* (New York: W. W. Norton, 1968), 91.

have been put under the surface ("half-submerged") by no human hand, the prehuman divider of "tropical fishes," or tropes, precedes this vista like a grammar:

To the left a group of *barren islets* suggesting ruins of stone walls, towers, and blockhouses, had its foundations set in a blue sea that itself looked solid, so still and stable did it lie below my *feet*; even the track of light from the westering sun shone smoothly, without that animated glitter which tells of an *imperceptible* ripple. And when I turned my head to take a parting glance at the tug which had just left us anchored *outside the bar*, I saw the straight line of the flat shore *joined* to the stable sea, *edge to edge*, with a perfect and unmarked closeness, in one leveled floor half brown, half blue under the enormous dome of the sky. Corresponding in the *insignificance* to the islets of the sea, two small clumps of trees, one on each side of the only *fault in the impeccable joint, marked at the mouth of the river Meinam* we had just left on the first preparatory journey of our homeward journey; and, far back on the *in*land level, a larger and loftier mass, the grove surrounding the great *Paknam* pagoda, was the only thing on which the eye could rest from the vain task of exploring the monotonous sweep of the horizon. Here and there gleams as of a few scattered pieces of silver marked the windings of the great river; and on the nearest of them, just within the bar, the tug steaming right into the land became lost to my sight, hull and funnel and masts, as though the impassive had swallowed her up without an effort, without a tremor. *My eye* followed the light cloud of her smoke now here, now there, above the plain, according to the devious curves of the stream, but always fainter and farther away, till I lost it at last behind the *miter*-shaped hill of the great pagoda. And then I was left alone with my ship, anchored at the head of the Gulf of Siam. (19–20; my emphasis)

If Conrad's language is anything but truly impressionistic here, this mime of a text's genesis appears informed by the first sentence's reversion to language's structure ("mysterious system"). The scene turns on a "bar" all but joining ("edge to edge") the lines, where normal personifications are reversed: the "barren islets" suggest "ruins of stone walls, towers" while the perhaps human "fences" become prehuman. Not only will the unfolding scene proliferate with dismembered bodily parts ("hand," "feet," eyes or islets, "mouth," "head"), but the "only fault" in the apparently "impeccable joint" occurs, it is said, "at the *mouth* of the river Meinam." The "edges" that, here joined, appear as a barely perceptible fault, and also represent those edges in and throughout the narrative that must, independently, be refolded, connected, and cut, in the process of reading.

Among them, one may read the "mouth of ... Meinam" as a figure of both meaning (*Meinung*, Mine-Am) and of the proper name (my nam(e)). While the "bar" dividing inside from out (the ship "outside the bar," "within the bar") itself erases the mail tug. This description seems disturbed only by "the great Paknam pagoda," where, like Jim's Patna or Patusan, an anagrammatic patronym seems at stake. This erasure of difference moves then into "a monotonous sweep of ... horizon" that threatens the ingesting, speaking, or muted mouth itself (Leggatt's disfigured victim is depicted blackfaced, tongue out). Even if one does not seek out the name Korzeniowski among the Malay underbrush, the assumption of names and letters lies among the passage's "ruins" (or runes), much as the looming "black mass of Koh-ring like the gate of everlasting night" (60) appears at the tale's end, resuming the pagoda's shape. If, for example, the name Kohring in the text can appear to recall the Englished Con-rad (*Rad* as the German wheel or circle), a circular encounter ("'She's round,' passed in a tone of intense relief between the two seamen" [61]) seems all but staged by the text as a figure of repetition itself.[10]

What logic is connected with the proper name, though, in Conrad? This Meinam, my name or *Meinung*, that yields the speaker "at the head of the Gulf of (S)iam" involves, at first, another removal from sight. What is portrayed as the loss of the visible trace of the mail tug itself does not seem arbitrary, since it disappears "behind the *miter*-shaped hill of the great pagoda." The loss of sight, of seeing or the sea, seems here doubled: what the eye follows is not the letter tug but "the light cloud of smoke" above it, which in turn now indicates it: like the inverting name *Se*(a)*phora*, the mail tug is transposed to an upper strata that is usually that of a signified itself ("the light cloud"), which, in

---

10 The name Conrad itself will return to our considerations. For now, we may note that the syllable or prefix *con* will have an itinerary of its own, and a distinct epistemological inflection. This is notable, too, in Melville, particularly yet not exclusively in *The Confidence Man*, where the multiple configuration of the term — joining (con), kenning, connivance, cognition, conning as tricking — plays out an arabesque determined, finally, by the non-word itself and the place of the letter *c* in Melville's own regime (where it links, as here, with the sea, and with the *third* (letter), and a cryptogram that depicts it as a vaginal pocket without inside). In Hitchcock's *To Catch a Thief*, Robie's pseudonym Conrad Burns is used to imply at once a figure of cognition (Con) and a Nietzschean circularity of time (Rad), each linked to a burning off of nature (trees) before the image as infinite replication without original. As I will note, this problematic returns not only in the figure of (ac)counting that links narrative to enumeration, but in Conrad's story "Il Conde."

return, itself indicates the carrying boat, the letters, and suggests the cloudlike transformations of paronomasia. The material carriers of meaning, in this text the ships of transport, are themselves the signifieds. One instance of this paronomasia occurs where the term *miter* supplants the "great pagoda" and a questionable *nom du pere* appears to be rewritten through a more diffuse *mater* or materialist dimension. The matrixal mother-tongue, like the submerged fences, in this case names, with miter, first a headdress, but secondarily the miter (or mitre) of a "joint" or "corner" made at right angles like an "L" shape ("edge to edge"). In another sense, however, the maternal metaphorics is itself a front and a false opposition to the authority of the pagoda – later openly named Koh-ring.[11]

The crime or fault of Leggatt aboard the *Sephora* that precedes the narrative also appears to precede representation. It is questionable what can depart the "mouth of the river Meinam," which has just metonymically consumed the letter tug that will be supplanted by the *Sephora*. In fact, the "ladder" that Leggatt emerges from will resume the figure of "letters" and "litter" it echoes ("littered, like any ship in port with a tangle of unrelated things," "the rope side ladder, put over, no doubt, for the master of the tug when he came to fetch our letters, had not been hauled in" [23]). If the headless Leggatt may signify the legs or materiality of Conradian writing, several figures are overturned as the patronyms front for matronyms shaped like L's (*elle*), and metaphorical boats become inversely the literal signifieds of their own trails of smoke. The maternal figure does not play into a gender opposition but rather undoes it, since it is linked to the sea and the materiality of language. The thematics of doubling becomes the estranged "gulf" of (S)Iam, while the panorama, with its enumeration of body parts, never departs from "my right hand." The reflexive possibilities of the writing become hectic – they might even provoke a sort of sui-cide, as in the official and fictive account of Leggatt's end ("Sui-cide! That's what I'll have to write" [42]). Thus, before the deceived Cyclopean watch of the chief mate ("round eyes ... trying to evolve a theory" [21]), we hear of a scorpion – spiderlike, poisonous – that "drowned itself in the inkwell of his writing desk." It appears that with Leggatt on board, all variety of paronomasias are unleashed, each further opening the gap between the placid surface of the tale and

---

11 The paternal is not so much set against a matrixal site as produced, and absorbed, by it in a movement that denies any binary or Oedipal plot.

a performative and allegorical dimension that the writing wants both to expel and claim.

If the "miter-*shape*" suggests a geometric edge, this *mater* or miter – an L or she (*elle*), *mer*(e), or *mar* – is also mentioned obliquely as a letter. The interior of the captain's cabin as scene of writing forms a recess like the letter *L*, a non-interior, where Leggatt is hidden:

It must be explained here that my cabin had the form of the capital letter L, the door being within the angle and opening into the short part of the letter. A couch was to the left, the bed place to the right; my writing desk and the chronometers' table faced the door. But anyone opening it, unless he stepped right inside, had no view of what I call the long (or vertical) part of the letter. It contained some lockers surmounted by a bookcase ... The mysterious arrival had discovered the advantage of this particular shape. Entering my room, lighted strongly by a big bulkhead lamp swung on gimbals above my writing desk, I did not see him anywhere. (30)

If the miter joints of an L can produce a recessive exterior ("above my writing desk"), the L cites the juncture of vertical and horizontal that graphs visibility as such.[12] For the capital letter L of the Law, Language, and Letter, of Leggatt and of the edge, is also that of "Literature" itself. It seems to depart from the system that precedes the specular sea (*mer*(e)/*mar*) and its surface, "half-submerged." The spatial play of the text takes on a letteral dimension, much as the S of the sea (or the SS) becomes in the paronomasia of the smoke trail that of seeing and of the letter C. For if letters and marks precede the placid surface of the mirroring sea, if no face is returned to this narcissistic site at the mouth of the river Meinam, the specular is itself marred and defaced ("headless"). This Leggatt knows and "I" (the narrator) wants to ignore. But this opens another possibility in reading "The Secret Sharer," where it is unclear what secret is or is not being shared. It may now appear that "I" wants to have Leggatt remain unseen, unread, for other reasons, and that this can become the subject of a subtext in its own right doubling as "a boy's adventure tale." The C of Conrad – as a letter doubled and reversed in the capital S's of the SS – suggests an enigmatic source, barely maternal, a pocket without interior, and an arc described by the ship's final thrilling turn as a broken ring or *Rad*.

---

12 Conrad subtly links the female – who, in *Heart of Darkness*, is said to be "out" of it (male discourse) – to exteriority in general, including that of language. The *elle* that lingers here is bound to the ship ("she") and the sea, even by exclusion. Much as the Congo recapitulates the *con* of Conrad, the *Nellie*, the ship of the narrative, represents a complex negation of this field.

When Leggatt projects flight it will be "off the *face* of the earth" (52), and, when reading the chart, he follows "his own figure wandering on the blank land of Cochin-China, and then passing off that *piece of paper* clean out of sight" (54). The "strange" narrator's concealment of Leggatt from all other eyes may suggest a contradictory suppression or erasure in Conrad's text.

The difficulty in tracking these ciphers is palpable, so let me resume what I was trying to indicate so far.

The *Sephora*, I suggested, implies not only a proper name for metaphor but the undoing of metaphor itself – a scene of defacement precedent to any narrative. Borne upon the sea, the metaphoric ship becomes by inversion the carrier of the se(a) in turn, and the natural ground gives way to another related to the "mysterious system" of the specular order from which Leggatt emerges. It would appear that this ship of metaphor is itself a misleading double, since in absorbing the disappearing mail tug it discloses a sharply literal, or letteral, capacity which, in turn, undermines the very transport that was the ship's purpose *vis-a-vis* the incarcerated Leggatt (as his escape implies). In narrating his story, Leggatt cuts himself off with an odd phrase directing his rage at the strangled victim he intercepted. Hardly a word itself, it nonetheless appears to traverse other writings of Conrad with a certain insistency: "You know well enough the sort of ill-conditioned snarling cur – " (*SS*, 27). Leaving aside the intriguing phrase "ill-conditioned" that may interest us later, the term "cur – " deserves comment. It appears, for example, in *Lord Jim* at a pivotal moment and is used as a term of self reference (Jim overhears the utterance, "Look at that wretched cur – " and thinks it refers to himself). The cutting off or curtailment of speech – as by a swollen tongue – yields a broken word or trailing syllable that, like the cloud of smoke, could be variably finished: cur – , Koh-ring, curse, cure: or more familiarly, as both a term for foreshortening and a name, Kur(t)z.[13] What, indeed, is the role of letters or the signature in the reading of Conrad today?

13 To pursue this syllable in its migrations would lead, for example, to Decoud in *Nostromo*. One must also give an allegorical reading to Razumov's punishment, that of broken eardrums, in *Under Western Eyes*, a text uniquely with a written narrative told by the word-alienated language teacher. The broken eardrums recapitulate the text's endless play on (not) being seen (or read) by confirming the mute world of the scriptive subject that doubles the political narrative.

In "Il Conde," a story written a few years before the SS, figures of counting, cognition, and conning merge in a way that draws an analogy between the point of a knife and figural contact, and where the conspiracy of anagrammatic destining appears as simultaneously erotic and lethal. In Naples, an aged Count is robbed at knife-point by a young man who had first been seen following him and afterwards seems indistinguishable, inescapable, and reproduced as the sinister "type" of various other young men who then seem numberless. Head or *capo* of a Camorra, a mafia-like organization, the young man sees "the Count" later in a cafe and notes that he did not yield a ring during the robbery and signals that he is "a marked man." The encounter and its web of conspiratorial dread leads to the aged Count's implied breakdown and his impending withdrawal to the north, a clime meaning for him certain death. Here (as in Faulkner) the South can double as the lower or material order of signification itself (sounds, names, letters), while the "point" or "spot" associated with touching and the knife implies at once an epistemological and a homoerotic reading ("a deucedly queer story" [PC, 621]). The violation of the Count's aesthetic space appears conspiratorial, much as the text seems increasingly determined by the letter C, or by ca-, co-, or co(u)n(t) and various cognates. While the narrator treats the Count's story with a degree of flippancy ("'What sort of knife was it?' I asked stupidly"), the Count's guilty hesitation to shout puts his account itself in question ("he might have said anything – bring some dishonoring charge against me – what do I know?"). Recurrent figures of the tale turn on a replication of signature similar to the seeming replication of the "type" of the young and sinister *capo*. A deadly circuit opens up for the Count tantamount to infinite recurrence. All the young men, for instance, start to look like the sinister *Cavaliere*: "It was he, no doubt at all. But that was a type. The Count looked away hastily. The young officer over there reading a paper was like that, too. Same type. Two young men farther away playing checkers also resembled" (628). Not only is this "type" apparently reproducible without original, but the prospect of innumerability undoes the Count's aristocratic sense of order. The connection of number (counting), narration (accounting), and cognition (conning) turns on this "spot." His evasion of an ultimate encounter only seals his fate, since to "go home amounted to suicide for the poor Count."

The Count refuses to part with his ring at the point of being "disemboweled," literally turned inside out. In Conrad it is often a non-encounter that becomes, like Jim's leap, temporarily the figure of an event. If the ring is not given up, that is also to say the Rad of (the) Con ("the signet ring of my father" [623]) – the circle of repetitions that is either closed, in advance, to the encounter (like a preserved virtue) or that, like the circling of "Koh-ring," attempts to repeat, restage, correct, or master a faulted scenario. The ring also represents retention (he does not give it up) or non-passage and yet mimes the replication of "types" that makes the lethal cognitive touch ("pressure removed from the sensitive spot") that of simulacra without original, a Nietzschean recurrence. "Signor Conde" cannot forget the implications of the encounter, where the "sensitive spot" is also the point of sense itself, of the sign(er). Conrad's title involves a slippage. He suggested that he inadvertently misspelled "Il Conde," combining an Italian article with a Spanish word in a ruse that mimes a conflict of languages. This should instead, of course, read *Il Conte*, though Conrad's insertion of the *d* appears a twofold diversion: either the tale is *de* or of "Con," or the word, name, or appearance of Conte would be too obvious for naming "the Count" as a figure of narrative (*le conte*), of accounting, and would present an irresistible feminizing pun he might wish to avoid. Though the event of the non-encounter is disfiguring ("His lifelong, kindly nicety of outlook had been defaced" [624]), the "C" suffers sheer, insidious replication – much as the Count's *orologia* was taken from him. A sort of Nietzschean entrapment of repetition and time is presented as the collapse of narrative, yet the Count's response is depicted by the narrator in a scorned mode. The signature "C(on)" or its syllabic variants make the Count "a marked man" in a double sense. Camorra, cavaliere, Count, capo, and "Sleeping *Car Company*" all crowd the closing passages like so many "types."[14] The knowledge that still appears dishonoring is mocked by the narrator who repeats the extent of his "*commiseration*," twice reiterating camorra, or the carrying, "Sleeping," *car* itself – rather like Bartleby's "prefer" takes over the Law Offices. The echoes inescapably return to a signature ("Signor Conde") and the citation of the saying

14 It is possible to read the *C* as indicating the number three, lethal to the fictive number one (or I), constitutive of the social group (three persons), which alone make possible the emergence of speech. It also cuts off speech by making the "I" a mere representation of himself, another third person. As such, the letter C – or, combined with vowels, ca-, co-, or cu-, the 3 : 1 combination, becomes a cryptogram for apostrophe, personification, or prosopopeia itself – the figure giving "voice" and hence preceding it.

Vedi Napoli e poi mori links seeing to this experience ("He had seen it! He had seen it with startling thoroughness" [629]). In such a fable of transgressive cognition (conning) connected to the avoidance of the "point," what emerges doubles as a knowledge of inscription (type) and evasion. What is interesting, too, is the vague contempt the narrator displays toward the Count's virtual abdication, or his hopeless flight from this (non)event.

As a "marked man" the Count serves as a relay to that "*remark-able*" man, as Kurtz is called, whose Congo the "mouth of the river Meinam" might ultimately itself return to. In positing Kurtz as the foremost of speakers ("I hadn't heard any of these splendid monologues on, what was it? on love, justice, conduct of life – or what not" [117]), Conrad nonetheless never has Marlow produce any of that "talk" directly. Instead, he mostly alludes to the overwhelming effect of an "eloquence" itself put into doubt by the tale's end in what is one of the most enigmatic and unaddressed aspects of the text. Narrative, like Marlow with his rivets, is here a delay, a waiting, *en route* to an "Interior Station." This inner point or station is problematized by various words formed with the syllable *in* (invoice, initiated, interior, Intended) yet is finally blocked, and voided by the unrelieved exteriority of the text's movement. This exteriority as such seems to be reproduced in the torn off and suppressed "postscriptum," not of Kurtz's manuscript but virtually of the text itself – Marlow's encounter, separated from and subsequent to the main text, with the personification of intentional meaning, the Intended.

If Kurtz is linked to sheer talk ("little more than a voice"), he is associated as an eloquent speaker above all with words, and words of appropriation in particular, of *Meinung*: "you should have heard him say, 'My ivory.' Oh yes, I heard him. 'My Intended, my ivory, my station, my river, my – ' – everything belonged to him ... The thing to know was what he belonged to" (121). The "motley" or "harlequin" figure of the Russian ("as though he had absconded from a troupe of mimes") functions as a mimetic foil to Kurtz in an unusual if much annotated way, since he seems to represent figurative language as such ("covered with patches all over, with bright patches, blue, red, and yellow"),[15] and renders Kurtz something beyond

---

15 Joseph Conrad, *Heart of Darkness: A Norton Critical Edition* (New York: W. W. Norton, 1971), 53, hereafter cited as *HD*.

figuration.[16] Kurtz's renowned last words, "The horror! The horror!" present a particular enigma, being among the most cited (if not analyzed) phrases in "literature." Indeed, it would be interesting to dismantle this notorious double apostrophe using other syntactic codes than the existential pathos and dark insight generally assumed to be transparent. Kurtz's very name appears cut off, *verkurzt*, like the "cur — " Jim hears himself called. The narrative is itself constituted by the deferral of his famous "eloquence," never heard, never ideally witnessed even in Marlow's own stammering, ruptured talk that mirrors it. The ultimate signified that *Heart of Darkness* announces with its title is a constitutive promise to — and manipulation of — the reader, very like that to and of the Intended herself. Like any penultimate phrase, "heart of darkness" invariably spawns a series a spectral referents without referentiality: the trip to the Interior Station is impossible since it discloses the absence of "interiors." As a figure of intentionality itself (and we recall Said's "disparity between verbal intention grammatically and formally apprehended and ... verbality itself" [*WTC*, 104]), "the *In*tended" must be the oddest of allegorical figures, a virtual linguistic personification unrecognizable as such because unlooked for, and essentially displaced. Moreover, she is displaced in the *mise en scene* in which she finally appears, after Kurtz's death, to the position of message-receiver, "lied" to, and, like women in Marlow's conception, "out" of the textual play ("Oh, she is out of it — completely. They — the women I mean — are out of it — should be out of it"). She is the figure of a permanent exteriority that the entire narrative turns on.

If the "Suppression of Savage Customs" begins as "a beautiful piece of writing," it is later appraised as bad writing — on almost aesthetic grounds — and is then virtually erased by the "note at the foot of the last page," the torn off "postscriptum" (or ps.): "Exterminate all the brutes!" *Ex*-termination is a double negation, even as "brutes" itself recurs to sound, to markers, to "unspeakable rites." The insidious postscriptum that must be torn off, suppressed from the "Suppression," is like a repressed content that emerges simultaneously with the main text, only to erase or invert its pretext. It overtly throws hermeneutic logic to the winds — and, under-standably, the end of the text will show Marlow trying to reclose this

16 Kurtz's Russian, in this regard, may be compared to Fortunato in Poe's *Cask of Amontillado*.

Pandora's box. If we again ask what, in the tale, corresponds to this torn-off text, it is of course the scene with the Intended herself — virtually another postscriptum. Only in this remarkable reversal, the nameless personification of "intention," who appears to be deluded and self-referential, is depicted oddly. Rather than questioning a text about its or the author's intended meaning, she appears to question the hermeneut-as-liar, Marlow, about the words of the "*re*markable" Kurtz. The system is inverted, virtually, yet also kept from being read as such by its very obviousness ("the Intended"). We typically read these "last words" of Kurtz ("The horror!") again as an ultimate cognitive insight into some "heart of darkness" in prehistory, the primeval Congo, in Western civilization, or humanity. Yet in fact that insight is always indirect at best, and it is the impossible duplicity of the scene itself that becomes the proper subject, if not the "horror." What emerges is the question of the "name" of the Intended.

Kurtz, as he is dismantled, turns out to be not only without a "voice" but without vocation ("he gave me to understand that Kurtz had been essentially a great musician"). We learn, in fact, "that Kurtz really couldn't write a bit" (74), as he may have been "a painter who wrote for the papers, or else a journalist who could paint." In each case, the figure of an impassable translation emerges.[17] When it is recommended that "Kurtz's proper sphere ought to have been extreme politics 'on the popular side'," it does not matter which political party ("'Any party,' answered the other"), and what is left is a hollow relation to sheer rhetoric. With a reduction to the meagerest of traces or "broken phrases," there "only remained" two things, "his memory and his Intended" — the barest premises for speech or writing, memory, and intention. But if this could be said of any text, what the postscriptum stages may amount to is a different extermination beyond any dialectical reading.[18]

What is in question seems an inverted allegory of all hermeneutics, then, with Marlow as Hermes the messenger, a go-between of the dead and the "living." If we extend this to include the Orpheus myth, however, it gets quite bizarre. Rather than rescuing the dead beloved

17 One recalls Nietzsche's trope of the "painter without hands" in "On Truth and Lie in an Extra-Moral Sense," an image of the impassability of translation or analogy in language.

18 Even the word *exterminate* is decisive here, since if terminate includes both ending and word (terms), the "ex-" involves a double negation that would be akin to a dialectical sublation of sorts. "Brutes" then could be read as sound, or marking.

with his song, the spellbinding Orpheus (Kurtz) appears as the already dead one. Rather than representing the lost linguistic referent, Eurydice, the Intended, appears deceived and parlour-bound, as the *Intended* questions Hermes about the now dispossessed speaker's shade, in an ironic configuration that is justly abysmal. She is of course told, finally, that his "last words" coincide with her, that they were in fact her "name." Too many substitutions and reversals occur here to trace at once (including the reader's appearing as the Intended). Instead of asking of Kurtz's (or even Conrad's) words what they, or their speaker, intended, we have the Intended asking Marlow what were Kurtz's words, or at least his last ones. Nowhere does a Conradian fault appear more nakedly addressed and nowhere more unreadable, since the duplicity, if it is read, destroys the reader's assumption of a narrative contract and complicity with Marlow:

> "His last word — to live with," she insisted. "Don't you understand I loved him — I loved him — I loved him!"
>
> I pulled myself together and spoke slowly.
>
> "The last word he pronounced was — your name."
>
> I heard a light sigh and then my heart stood still, stopped dead short by an exulting and terrible cry, by the cry of inconceivable triumph and of unspeakable pain. "I knew it — I was sure!" ... She knew. She was sure. (79)

Marlow's double talk deceives us into thinking we are in the know, though in her deceived capacity at least the Intended can reflect Conrad's own generic reader, assured of his or her own self-referential interpretation of the text ("She knew. She was sure").[19] It is telling that the text ends with a skit about the containment and falsification of information or meaning — one subject of the narrative. It is a gesture that both contains Conrad's own "modernist" premises and allegorically abandons or betrays them, sealing them from sight. It is a text that, at the least, veers in two directions that cannot be reconciled. The scenario of this "lie," while an extraordinary textual allegory, also suggests where Conrad — like "Il Conde" — abdicates stylistically by

19 The standard address of this "lie" and its moral recuperation are paradigmatic of how it continues to promote a deceived reading parallel to the Intended's supposedly intended understanding (itself duplicitous). See Kenneth A. Bruffee, "The Lesser Nightmare," in *Heart of Darkness*, 239: "Thus the paradox of the lie which establishes a condition of truth is resolved. By denying superficial 'integrity,' and by putting himself at the service of a passion to maintain, however tenuously, man's humanity, Marlow at last manifests the unexpected, wholly unideally devious forms that man's 'innate strength' or 'capacity for faithfulness' may tale. Marlow's lie establishes a condition of truth."

choosing to reinforce the lies of mimetic narrative at the very point they have historically been broken with. It would be compromising to retain these premises at, or beyond, this point, which Conrad of course does do. He will continue to write almost as if nothing has changed, while the fault within his style becomes – as in the *SS* – a chasm. By helping Leggatt go unseen, Conrad's captain in a sense relinquishes any post-"modernist" direction that inhabits his writing, as Jameson points out, from the outset. In the scene with the Intended, however, the break, or estrangement, with intended meaning is so complete that it can be recoded, demonically staged with rotated referents. Yet in a way this is the same device used in the *SS* where the reader, by being as if privy to the drama of Leggatt's concealment, may in fact be prevented from reading the parable of his own sightlessness – like the deceived first mate who the reader is encouraged to find both simple-minded and deluded.

Aside from the apparent send up, with the Intended, of the self-referential reader ("She knew"), the text clearly overwhelms Marlow's *own* controlling irony and double talk, rendering him a blind and ignorant Hermes. For it is equally possible that she is right, or that (unwittingly) Marlow does not lie, is just the uncomprehending vehicle of a truth; or perhaps "The horror! The horror!" might actually be or coincide with the Intended's "name." Much as the syllable "con" can generate a text like "Il Conde," the possibilities of these celebrated words or non-words are daunting – including the doubled play on or-or, error, or the *hors-hors* that names her as the outside (of an outside). If the "he*art* of *dark*ness" suggests a moral and historical nightmare, it is also, plainly, of a linguistic and representational order and it is this that Marlow is breaking down in the text's course. The empty clang of the word "horror" both divests the ideological machinery of Kurtz and suggests the alternate horror of a determination of language by presemantic elements. We need not play out the possibilities of reading the utterance as a linguistic event, which unleashes a *combinatoire* passing through apostrophe, aural repetition, time (*orologia*), exteriority, and what precedes semantic depth altogether.[20] In any event, it names not only a repulsion before

20 A more exacting reading of "The horror! The horror!" as paronomastic riddle might begin with the successive echoes of *her, or-or, heart, hear,* and *hors* (outside) that interlace and are disfigured by the apostrophic mode and the definite article. Since the utterance lies beyond decoding and represents that beyondness, a

what "my Intended" signifies, but falsely covers the "rift" of intention itself with the economy of double talk. Given the dismantling of Kurtz from eloquent voice to beautiful writing to bad writing to inarticulate phrases and ultimately vocationless fraud, Conrad's clear interest is not only in the duplicity of discourse but of interpretation itself and the text's mimetic and historical authority. Conrad's inverted parable of signification addresses a fault within discourse so precisely, and potentially comically, that it has, as perhaps intended, proven unreadable. One can hardly be more explicit than in personifying the text's nameless "Intended," who waits for the word, outside (yet within) the main text. What does such a rhetorical fault, however, tell us when applied to the *SS*?

If a fault in Conrad repeatedly involves an attempt to represent a rift within (his) language in moral or historical terms, to say this is not merely to aestheticize Conrad's complex political thematics. If the fault within or between a word and its meaning — '*Twixt Land and Sea* — is part of the captain's estrangement to his ship in "The Secret Sharer," then the narrator is put in the position of the Intended, only now in relation to his own text. A scene parallel to the Intended's interview occurs when he affirms his understanding of Leggatt: "'The rest ... I only hope I have understood, too.' 'You have. From first to last' — and for the first time there seemed to be a faltering, something strained in

putative "unnameable," a literalist reading might begin with the repetition itself: why twice, why two exclamation points? The repetition that begins as emphasis may be read as citation (is the second "horror" a denial of the first?). To read Kurtz outside of the attempted pathos that Marlow alternately manipulates and empties is to remove ourselves from the (apparent) position of the Intended as blind, self-referential receiver of the (non) message of the (doctored) text. The utterance explodes any intertextual dynamics by naming a structural dilemma in language, yet it poses as penultimate signified and signifier — a promise that is undeliverable, as Marlow finds and then repeats to others. Despite the apocalyptic context of last words, one can always ask the question what Kurtz actually meant or intended, despite the fact that this can seem both self-evident and totally unnameable: by naming the unnameable, the text has absurdly seemed obvious, and it is that permanent deception that is a "horror." Yet Kurtz — or *Co*(n)*r*(a)*d* — could have meant, intended, or been thinking "about" almost anything, including going back to the Intended from his "unspeakable rites," or something in his last meal. The chain of signification returns to the phrase as a marker, and the *or-* repeated twice resounds in numerous names or terms (K*ur*tz, he*ar*t, d*ar*kness, Marlow), and may represent where a prefigural signifier compels a deferral (or-or) of semantic excess. There is a tension between the phrase and every translation compelled to resolve it.

his whisper" (SS, 55). This faltering, folding, and faulting cannot be contained, taking into its crevices every variation on a linguistic *and* epochal break that shakes the cognitive pretext of the captain, of Conrad's style, of his rhetoric of the "double," the uncertain illusion of doubling itself. The ship is literature itself, and will be left by Leggatt, voided. As a faltering in the promise of identification, it momentarily confirms the captain's own rhetoric, too, as being simultaneously the reverse of everything the reader first takes it for; it cites his "strangeness," for instance, as more glaringly deceptive, down to the details of the narrative he openly speaks of omitting, down to the final assertion of a "perfect communion" that places his voice in the role of the Intended and splinters the law he personifies. The work relinquishes, purges in Leggatt, a figure of reading emerged headless from a sea no longer natural but reflecting its "mysterious system" of prefigural language. In the narrative, we are never clear why the captain and crew of the *Sephora* universally side against Leggatt: is his version correct, though he will not be able to argue it, or must he be ejected for other reasons? It is possible to say that one secret left unshared by the SS is that it reads and rewrites, erases and leaves "as before" the legacy of Conradian writing, weaving in and out of a fault that can only be gapingly ignored, uncovered, and covered, until it appears as subject or passes elsewhere. As if the text were reading itself in reverse, Leggatt will not only be erased off the "chart," or the "face of the earth," but does so without any mark, as when he notes, "It would never do for me to come to life again." The final whisper of recognition by the crew ("She's round" [61]) also echoes the Cyclopean "round eyes" of the first mate that represents the surveillance of a reader and his deception (endlessly "accounting"). Getting "round" becomes an evasion of sight, like getting around something, and the black mass of Koh-ring becomes an empty or, like Polyphemus, scorched eye, in a scene that inverts the black on white of writing, perception, or visibility ("White on the black water"). Contrary to Conrad's supposed aesthetic credo about making the reader "see," the pretext of mastery seems measured by what is kept from surveillance or reading and one does not begin to "read" the SS until one places the captain under severest scrutiny *vis-a-vis* reader, crew, Leggatt, or, as he openly avows, himself. The narrator's assertions of full understanding and "perfect communion" are ruined as the tale repositions itself as a fore- or pretext for the very scene it stages: Leggatt, carried from the "fore-castle" passes to a site that is technically after it, or "preposterous," never acknowledged as on the captain's ship. If Signor Conde's lethal knowledge ultimately came from the unreadable syllable ca(r) – as in the secret *Camorra*, the "Sleeping Car Company," or the eviscerating "cur – " – and if such *car*rying (*phorein*) permeates the *SS* it is not only in the Sephora, or the "legs" of Leggatt, but the "phosphorus" of the last scene.[21] In the closing sequence, what warns the captain back is a markless "mark," white on black, likened to a blank sheet of paper, an erasure of writing itself: "What was needed was something easily seen, *a piece of paper*, which I could throw overboard and watch ... White on the black water. A phosphorescent flash passed under it. What was the thing? ... I recognized my own hat" (60). The inversion here becomes "the saving mark for my eyes," itself a white sheet, meant to protect Leggatt "from the dangers of the sun" – though it, here, becomes the bearer-of-light, a non-solar light, "phosphorescent." It suggests a phenomenality other than that of the sun or natural description, emerging from beneath that "mysterious system" that links perception and marking ("A phosphorescent flash passed *under* it"). It reverses the direction of reading ("the stars ahead seemed to be gliding from right to left").

Jameson's remarks on Conrad's "vocabulary for which we ourselves have no contemporary equivalent" remain acute, though what seems at stake is not a lost historical index. It is the "strangeness" of every text for which Conrad's relation to English merely serves, now, as a special, unmarked instance. This compels us to seek another index for historicizing a "rift" that cannot be contained, but that inhabits many of Conrad's narrative pretexts and the nostalgic "modernism" he stands, clearly, beyond. Rather than focus on "psychoanalytically charged terms and ideological, public slogans," words such as conjunctions and prefixes fall into this alienness of the narrating "I" on his own ("my") ship. If "the *ignorance* of my strangeness" is both an ignoring of that strangeness and an active unknowing, the "perfect communion of a seaman with his first command" must suggest less a reconciliation than an absolute break within and between codes.

---

21 In "Amy Foster" a casual line links phosphorus to *thought*: "if it's true, as some German fellow has said, that without phosphorus there is no thought" (*PC*, 159). Such a bearing of light proposes another dimension of phenomenality itself, as the hat was to guard against "the dangers of the sun" (*SS*, 60). The passage through "Sunda Straights" links the sun to sundering, a passage between a rift in the authority of the natural order.

Rather than an asserted mastery over the ship of writing – seemingly reflected in the purely crafted tale – the "perfect communion" recalls that asserted by Marlow for the Intended.

How affirmatively does the tale end, as the narrator imagines the figure of Leggatt ("a free man, a proud swimmer")? I have been arguing for a reconsideration of the material element of language and of where Conrad's "modernist" pretext remains "strange" to itself, demanding a more suspicious and reflexive reading than it traditionally receives. If we choose to read the "perfect communion" announced by the captain negatively, as I would argue, then Leggatt's celebrated escape indicates not a triumph but an erasure and abdication internal to Conrad's text, one along the lines of Signor Conde when confronted with the seemingly lethal knowledge of simulation and inscription. (Indeed, in Leggatt's imprecation, "*ill-con*ditioned snarling cur – ," we hear echoed "Il Conde" itself, as well as the pre-letteral bar-series which informs consciousness with another authority.) We may appropriate Said's insight here that "Conrad's writing tries overtly to negate itself as writing" (107), though Said means by this primarily Conrad's use of the "voice."[22] It is possible to read the *SS* through the image of the legal or official "suicide" attributed to Leggatt, in which the text obliquely writes (of) a negation of Conrad's own fiction. Rather than a "microcosm" of Conrad's fiction, "The Secret Sharer" becomes a figurative metatext that folds into itself and erases that "ill-conditioned" production.

Conrad in his letters associates blackness with "mining" words ("quarrying my English out of the black night, working like a coal miner in his pit" [*HD*, 158]) yet if the entire tale occurs at the writing desk, on his "right hand," in fact, the parabola sketched is a parable of parabolic writing. When the narrator navigates the double shoal of the shore and of Conrad's style to unload his "double," the asserted mastery seems to be the successful generation of the text from a traceless encounter. Conrad writes and keeps the "piece of paper"

---

22 Said's complete remark reads: "Conrad is generally unhappy with the idea of writing, so much so that when he is not complaining about it he is always turning it into a substitute speech, ... Conrad's writing tries overtly to negate itself as writing. Of negation Freud has said, though, that it is a way of affirming what is repressed .... For Conrad, writing and its negation constituted a way of permitting himself a number of things otherwise impossible" (*WTC*, 107). This last becomes almost a psychological banality, except that the "repression" of writing involves a double negation that cannot be contained.

white against the black. One may simplify this, by suggesting that in Leggatt, Conrad hosts the specter of a post-modernist style that would entail a stylistic shift, a relinquishing of nineteenth-century mimeticism (or "impressionism") that served as a rhetorical pretext. The legs that uphold include the legacy or anteriority of received language (or trope). The legal lie of the suicide becomes the lie of the official, legal interpretation that Leggatt is erased by, from which he is safe so long as he is concealed in the L-shaped cabin, and which the narrator assumes his position in as the law. But if Conrad is writing a text that appears to read or rewrite "Conrad," it is also because it refuses to do so at all. It wants to get rid of, by loving or doubling, its fault.

If Conrad is writing a text that appears to "read" Conrad, among the secret sharers that the title designates is the only representative "reader" in the text. The first mate, with his "round eyes and frightful whiskers" (*SS*, 21), speaks in the most clichéd discourse ("Bless my soul, sir!" — his "usual ejaculation"), and is perpetually evolving "theories" by taking "all things into earnest consideration." We might recall what the model for this *theorizing* was:

He was of a painstaking turn of mind. As he used to say, he "liked to account to himself" for practically everything that came in his way, down to a miserable scorpion he had found in his cabin a week before. The why and the wherefore of that scorpion — how it got on board and came to select his room rather than the pantry (which was a dark place and more what a scorpion would be partial to), and how on earth it managed to drown itself in the inkwell of his writing desk — had exercised him infinitely. (21)

This passage reproduces, in part, the reader's dilemma in "accounting" for the *SS*. Like a text that lulls one through "public slogans" without real correspondence, the *SS* encrypts its secret fissure within a false specular model of literature. Its style must appear "edge to edge," an "impeccable joint." It is the mate who notes a suicide (of writing) in the scorpion's enigmatic drowning in "the inkwell of his writing desk," which above all provokes an effort to read or "account." The blackness of the ink, like that of the sea on which the phosphorescent hat appears like a "piece of paper," or the face of Leggatt's victim, does not return a reflection. Bearer of a poison that may stage a pharmakon-like cure (or "cur — ," *scor*), spiderlike, the scorpion seems at once a figure of "bad" writing ("a boy's adventure tale") that obfuscates by exercising one infinitely, and of a "high" writing that takes its own "descriptive" and interpretive rhetoric as its subject.

That the anagrammatic scorpion — or sc(o)r(i)p(t)-on — "drowns" *itself* in the inkwell, returning black to black without the detour over white, bears a parallel to Leggatt's legal "suicide," also a drowning. We are now in a position to ask if what is here recapitulated is a break within Conrad's style, a leave-taking, or merely another repetition, not unlike the system the Count is caught in. If the first, then the scorpion's demise indicates that Leggatt can be read as actually drowning after his plunge into the sea — now in a double sense, at once both fictive and textual. The text's asserted mastery over I's "strangeness" to his ship literalizes the fiction of Leggatt's "sui-cide," the perfect communion of a false, "legal" hermeneutic preventing his being pursued. In letting Leggatt pass through his text and beyond, in preserving him (reading) from being seen or read, Conrad's "perfect communion" stages not mastery but a total break in two levels of interpretation, mimesis and figuration, performance and meaning. That he thereafter falls largely back into narrative mimesis, the "infernal tale of ships," the "boy's adventure tale," appears both a regression and a cover. It is in Conrad's resistance to the periodizing concept of modernism that the historicity of Conrad's style, in every sense, lies.

8

Miss Emily, *c'est moi*: the defacement of modernism in Faulkner (inscription and social form)

It sometimes seems that one of the missions of traditional Faulkner criticism is to return his text – like the runaway slave Tomey's Turl in the story "Was" – from subversive representational forays back to the plantation order of representational meaning. This happens especially when Faulkner is celebrated (or fetishized) as a regionalist. In doing so, we tend to ignore where even "the South," at least as a trope, may have more than one referent. If we think of the South, for example, as opposite some figurative North, we see where "it" can simultaneously be identified with a lower or material order of figuration – the sound and fury that generate metonymic chains for Benjy out of random signifiers (the call, "Caddy!"). Until recently this bias of Americanists had kept Faulkner's text relatively isolated from theory, as the Morrises note in introducing their *Reading Faulkner*: "No American writer's work opens itself for critical displacement more readily than Faulkner's, yet for many years the critical tradition largely repressed that openness for the purpose of a certain edification" (7).[1] One focus that remains in need of further theoretical attention is the problem of black representation in Faulkner. Because the issue of black experience and slavery is one with considerable political and historical pathos, it is less often asked where black figuration serves roles outside of historical reference, or where it may

1 Wesley and Barbara Morris, *Reading Faulkner* (Madison: University of Wisconsin Press, 1989), 7. Today, a theoretical revision of Faulkner is underway in many works, though these remain on the whole mimetic. Among those most interested in the figurative problems of language would be John T. Matthews, *The Play of Faulkner's Language* (Ithaca: Cornell University Press, 1982), James A. Snead, *Figures of Division* (New York: Methuen, 1986), Richard Moreland, *Faulkner and Modernism: Rereading and Rewriting* (Madison: University of Wisconsin Press, 1990), and Minrose C. Gwinn, *The Feminine and Faulkner: Reading (Beyond) Sexual Difference* (Knoxville: University of Tennessee Press, 1990).

exceed and even actively revise the representational order within the writing – an order that sustains or defaces institutions of meaning, and hierarchies of cultural investment. While Eric Sundquist argued that race is the most pivotal theme in Faulkner, the trend has been to approach that exclusively in mimetic or historical ways.[2] As a vehicle for rethinking the politics of mimesis itself, Faulkner's treatment of black figuration has yet to be traced.[3]

The role such figures play may be substantially more problematic if considered within the entire textual order. Thus we could also read black figuration as resistant to representational truth – as if blackness itself has something to do with materiality, anteriority, or allegory. The old order of "the South" would then correspond to a certain regime of meaning, and the black ex-slave class to a long effaced materiality of language within that regime. A certain paradox comes out of this hypothesis that is itself interesting, since the more one attempts to recuperate black characterization as achieved subjectivity, the more one tries to return this site to the oppressive aesthetic or mimetic order that denied that all along. At issue, instead, would be how to evaluate Faulkner's defacement of that order through an identification his text establishes with blacks.

The issue can be seen particularly in the treatment of *Go Down, Moses*. When Sundquist asserts, for instance, that in returning to the subject of black lives in *Go Down, Moses*, Faulkner returns from his experimental modernist style to a seemingly more direct, nineteenth-century, *pre*-modernist one – to direct personal truths, and the heart – we recognize the critic's myth of a return from an inaccessible

---

2 Craig Werner, in "Minstrel Nightmares: Black Dreams of Faulkner's Dreams of Blacks," notes: "The first stage of the Afro-American response to his work consisted largely of correcting Faulkner's misconceptions. This stage resulted in what I think is a fairly clear consensus that, while Faulkner was a good observer, he consistently interpreted Afro-American behavior in static rather than kinetic terms, substituting 'endurance' for 'ascent' and 'immersion'" (in *Faulkner and Race*, ed. Doreen Fowler [Jackson: University of Mississippi Press, 1986], 37).

3 The moment Jim Bond emerges as an unaccountable remainder at the end of *Absalom, Absalom!* (New York: Vintage, 1972) is suggestive here. The relevant closing passage (Shreve's) is a well-known example of the power invested in the *runaway* black figure: "'Which is all right, it's fine; it clears the whole ledger, you can tear all the pages out and burn them, except for one thing .... You've got one nigger left. One nigger Sutpen left. Of course you can't catch him and you don't even always see him. But you've got him there still. You still hear him at night sometimes. Don't you?' 'Yes,' Quentin said" (378).

"modernism" to a direct mimetic truth.[4] If the narrative of black ascendancy in Faulkner (however tentative) suggests the rise of something material, prefigural, or anti-mimetic to a more prominent role in the writing itself – the rise of the legs, or slave-cipher, to the position of the head – the result would be a shift the text demands in the entire order of reading or signifying, with the result that *Go Down, Moses* might be considered more post- that pre-modernist, or perhaps even amodernist in some more problematic sense. Here "modernism" appears as a term of edification itself, suggesting complicity with a rhetoric of authenticity and mimeticism in contrast to the figurative nihilism of its supposed other – post-modernism. For black ascendancy to be realized as a double project – a social history and an infra-linguistic shift – the interiorizing model of humanist reading would have to be closed, and the very trope of the subject displaced by a materialist model of language that appears anti-mimetic. This might jeopardize the regionalist commodity value of Faulkner's literature in general, opening it to a different reading than that it seems largely caught in. From the point of view of Faulkner's text, the doomed possibility of a disruption of social hierarchy seems wedded to a revolutionary rehierarchization of reading/writing. It is not arbitrary, for instance, that in the text in *Go Down, Moses* that most epitomizes this (failed) transition allegorically, "Pantaloon in Black," the assumed name Rider echoes both writer and reader at once. If, as the Lacanian Zizek argues in speaking of Hitchcock, the "postmodern" effect can appear to lie in the negative epiphany of the Thing disrupting codified symbolic meaning, that would seem associated with the site of *black* figuration in Faulkner's text. In turn, something at work in Faulkner's use and depiction of blacks with which his textual project identifies, leads not to representation but into a discourse of inscription, hypograms, and subtexts that gives the term *black figuration* a second sense almost connected to a collapse of figuration itself. If the very politics of mimetic representation itself stands to be altered by the narrative of black ascendancy, then precisely when appearing to return

4 In *Faulkner: The House Divided* (Baltimore: Johns Hopkins University Press, 1983), Eric Sundquist notes of *Go Down, Moses* that "as in *Absalom, Absalom!*, Faulkner is moving further away from his own early 'modernism' and placing himself, deliberately or not, more clearly in the tradition of classic nineteenth-century American fiction" (133). He adds: "*Go Down, Moses* may be Faulkner's most honest and personally revealing novel, even though it is clearly not his best" (153).

to a *pre*modernist style *Go Down, Moses* may be doing the opposite and, as the title implies, exceeding the Mosaic laws of modernism or casting down that logos. There are times in Faulkner, to repeat, where the figure of the old order seems to apply less strictly to the old South than to a mimetic regime in which his own writing originates. It is also clear from what I have suggested that as a means of opening up Faulkner's text, we have drawn a corollary between represented black characters and what can be called *black figures* in the text.[5] In the following discussion, I want to examine this issue indirectly, not by turning to *Go Down, Moses*, but by asking where the politics of signature, intertext, and gender converge and can be read as actively defacing the *mimetic* aesthetic of modernism that can be identified with patriarchy itself. I will use here only a short and very familiar tale to explore this problem.

In addressing the subject of pedagogy, Gregory Jay depicts "A Rose for Emily" as an example of the complexity of a certain sort of subversive text. Miss Emily, poisoner and necrophile, has represented to some a female revenge on the patriarchal order, yet she can simultaneously depict a reconfirmation of that order which she ends by identifying with, re-enacting, and eviscerating in the preservation of Homer Barron the (already dead) father. To most close readers of the text this will immediately make sense but render the story more confusing, since the two movements seem to cancel one another in an endless traffic:

Emily Grierson, then, presents a hermeneutic puzzle. As a feminist subject her story speaks of a revolutionary subversion of patriarchy: as herself a figure of racial and class power, Emily also enacts the love affair of patriarchy with its own past, despite all the signs of decline and degradation. She is a split subject, crossed by rival discourses. What the text forces us to think, then, is the complex and ironic alliance between modes of possession and subjection, desire and ownership, identity and position. (*America the Scrivener*, 334)

5 It is a commonplace to note, as does Fredrick Douglass, that the black slave who is regarded as property takes on the dimension of a speaking thing – which, from the perspective of (the master's) discourse, lends the black character or speaking face the aura of a double prosopopeia. Within the realm of sheer figuration, blackness further doubles as a set of associations in the culture leading into materiality, anteriority, "evil," otherness, absence, death, and so on. For an important meditation intersecting with this problem, see Toni Morrison, *Playing After Dark* (Cambridge, Mass.: Harvard University Press, 1992).

What is passed over in this reading is the most central problem, and that which I want to return to here. It is the fact that an "act" appears perpetrated in the text — murder, necrophilia, violation of the reader and community, and it needs to be assessed. I will ask not where the tale can, as is so clear, generate numerous allegorical readings with more or less persuasive claims to validity, but where the work itself forecloses in Faulkner's writing a "modernist" aesthetic model — antifiguralist, representational, mimetic — that is itself identified with a deadening political or discursive social patriarchy. It is where the tale itself seems to shift from the supposed position of the narrator and his communal "we" to that of the psychosis of Miss Emily in which that community is asked to read itself that will interest me at first; a movement beyond identification and subjectivization, in effect closing out the rituals that constitute it as consumable regionalist "literature." What is at stake in my approach is where the destructive patriarchy situated in Emily's father and Colonel Sartoris, as it were, extends not only to the manner in which the community (or ourselves) produce the narrative of Miss Emily and our allegorical readings of it, but where the story seems to identify the modernist or mimetic habits of interpretation with that patriarchy itself. At the center of this reading I will place the enigma that is seldom addressed in this text, that is, the import of the *title*.

The story is of use in questioning the central traditions of interpreting Faulkner. More than other "high" modernists, Faulkner has at times seemed protected by the thematic investments of his American readers, reluctant to accede anything like the linguistic and theoretical import of a writer like Joyce to his text — as if such an address would disrupt the very value of the historical narrative at stake in the questions of race, Oedipal narratives, and his regionalism. So absorbing are these elements that it has seemed a formalist intrusion to draw attention to even mild intertextual problems. This sort of formalist game, if game it is, has always seemed instead the province of a type of metafiction, as when Nabokov in *Pale Fire* mocks the determination of sense through complex verbal pattern-ing as a game of word *golf* (strike it and watch a complex word reconfigure meaning as it skips across the text's surface). Even where writing in Faulkner is openly thematized, as it seems to be in part four of "The Bear," the subject is by-passed as a secon-dary import to Isaac McCaslin's moral struggles with the repudiation of his slave-owning patrimony. Compared to the elegiac themes of ritual hunting, education, race relations, and the disappearing wilderness, a sustained metatextual address seems trite, at least at first.[6]

By even addressing a problem like intertextuality in Faulkner, one usually understands the endless process of revision within his own work – the recurrent and rewritten scenes and characters and their networking overlaps.[7] Broader unexplored examples that come to mind might be the reference to *Madame Bovary* in Horace Benbow's pocket with its obscure references to reading in the opening of *Sanctuary*, or the covert rewriting of Plato's *Phaedrus* at the end of *The Sound and the Fury* in Benjy's closing carriage ride. In each case the alluded to text is the basis for a violent and parodic parable about Faulkner's own authoring. And something of the sort appears in "A Rose for Emily," though in terms so totalizing that, rather than placing Faulkner in any tradition of simple revision, it raises an entirely different sort of question for reading.[8] Indeed, we would not be amiss in looking at Miss Emily Grierson herself, first, as a figure who can only be misread by every attempt of the community. If "A Rose for Emily" does not seem an obviously relevant text here, it nonetheless involves the somewhat dislocating move for us of identifying Miss Emily as one surrogate signature for the author (as one can read the initials M. E.), though this in itself certainly presents several problems. While the trope of necrophilia can imply the fetishization of a textual

6 The Morrises' Bakhtinian depiction of *minstrelsy* remains essentially mimetic in its mock-Bakhtinian premise: "The focus is not on the aesthetic illusion of direct quotation, a kind of ventriloquist's trick, but on the sense of otherness or difference his black characters represent. The reader must ask of Faulkner, What is the difference of your difference? The answer is entangled in the speaking relationships between black characters and the authorial voice and between black characters and other characters" (*Reading Faulkner*, 229–30).

7 While Michael Grimwood notes in "Faulkner and the Vocational Liabilities of Black Characterization" where "The Bear" seems flooded with figures of writing ("That part 4 of 'The Bear' is about writing Faulkner confirmed by filling it with books. It is as replete with manuscripts and published texts as the rest of *Go Down, Moses* is empty of them – a contrast that reinforces an implicit discontinuity between literary and nonliterary experience" [*Faulkner and Race*, 266]), Grimwood turns this reflection into Faulkner's relinquishing a too-difficult style for the promise of communication – a sort of abdication on a par with the Faulknerians' will to mimesis.

8 Thus the Morrises can note that to "adequately measure Faulkner's struggle to represent racial difference we must read at least three novels intertextually" (230), for them, *Absalom, Absalom!*, *Go Down, Moses* and *Intruder in the Dust*.

past as much as a personal one – certainly a standard interpretation of the story, as an allegory of the South's fixation on its past – Miss Emily's own unreadability before the community's repeated attempts to interpret her acts mark (mis)reading as itself a subject of the story.[9] Repeatedly, as in the incident of the odor from beneath the house, or the purchase of the arsenic, the incorrect reading of gossip-like information helps turn Emily into an aesthetic object for the community, called a "monument." Whether or not the monumentalized reading of Faulkner itself is also attacked by identifying the reader with the narrator's "we," Emily appears positioned not only beyond its powers of reading, but from the first refusal of the new sheriff's "letter" asking for her taxes, outside the contractual *law* and economy of that community.[10]

There is evidence at the beginning of the story for a metatextual reading. Indeed, if allegory is defined as the commentary of signs on anterior signs, then Miss Emily's act of killing and preserving the absolute past – rather like a Hegelian *sublation* gone awry – simulates an allegory of the cancellation of allegory itself. In works like *Absalom* or *Sanctuary* the gothic "house" appears as if as a character and has associations with language itself or even literary tradition: *Sanctuary's* gutted "old Frenchman's place," for instance, is discretely associated with Flaubert's *Madame Bovary*. Miss Emily's house is also initially associated with metaphors of writing: "white, decorated with *cupolas* and spires and *scrolled* balconies in the heavily lightsome *style* of the seventies ... – an eyesore among eyesores" (489; my emphasis). Here "style" and "scrolled" are terms that can be called scriptive, while "cupola" may be rewritten as the copula, the predicate of being echoed in the black "manservant" named *Tobe*. Even the "eyesore among eyesores" suggests the redoubling of a fault or rupture that, like the sidewalks Homer Barron will be brought down from the North to repair, must be somehow righted. For Homer to come down to repair the site where feet move, indicates a reparation that is more far-reaching on the part of the text. One of the facets of Miss Emily's role as a *pharmakon* for the community – one who is separated and

---

9 The text of "A Rose for Emily" is that of *The Portable Faulkner*, ed. Malcolm Cowley (New York: Viking, 1967).

10 Jay notes: "The narrative point of view in 'A Rose for Emily' puts 'us' in a strange position. It is 'our town,' and our position toward Emily is initially that of the narrator and the community. They are the subject who is supposed to know, but this posthumous narrative turns on their lack of knowledge" (332).

sacrificed by the community to play a symbolic role that mirrors its own crimes, a role echoed in her trip to the druggist to buy poison ("But the law requires you to tell what you are going to use it for" [496]) – is the manner in which she holds negative power in the community, particularly over the men. In fact, by being called "a fallen monument" in the first line, her role as disempowered woman of the upper class ("the high and mighty Griersons") places her in a role that is prescripted and instituted by Colonel Sartoris' relieving her of her "taxes" at her father's death, a gesture, nonetheless, that places Emily *outside* of the economy, a *gift* that is a further castration. This law's first gesture is to reveal itself, anyway, as a *fiction* in Colonel Sartoris' pretense that Emily's dead father loaned the city money which the city will repay by remitting her taxes.

I have noted that throughout the story the community fails to read the signs Miss Emily leaves. In an article on "Pantaloon in Black," John Limon argues that the mourning black laborer Rider is totally beyond readerly comprehension, and that this is one point of the text; he is definitively outside any "interpretive community" such as the one Stanley Fish theorizes must be present.[11] Miss Emily complicates that break with the interpretive community, since rather than being a black effaced by the system (hence unreadable to it, as, it is assumed, is the character Rider of "Pantaloon in Black") she is the resented product of the class the community existed, in the past, to sustain ("the high and mighty Griersons"). Though used by the community for *aesthetic* value (that of infinite gossip), the relation they have to her is one of the power of interpretation, as when she would be contained by the language of pity ("At last they could pity Miss Emily" [493]). The law is associated, first, with a double patriarchal or communal discourse, with Emily's father or Colonel Sartoris, and the male communal "we" the narrator refers to. This connection is essential because it addresses the moment the townspeople burst into her locked bedroom in what is a symbolic rape of her space ("The violence of breaking down the door seemed to fill this room with pervading dust" [500]), only to be themselves *violated*, in theatrical fashion, by the sight and text of Homer's corpse left behind. The holding of the unreadable Emily at the center of community attention throughout had been an act of aesthetici-

11 See John Limon, "The Integration of Faulkner's *Go Down, Moses*," in *Critical Inquiry* 12 (Winter, 1986).

zation as well as of voyeuristic rape. Her symbolically complex deed — of revenge, incorporation, or fixation — represents an aggression against the reader, in turn, for whom the aesthetic act is not innocent either.

Yet we must draw nearer, since what is violated here is distance. The "law" in the text, we said, is itself introduced as a contingent fiction, one that changes: "that day in 1894 when Colonel Sartoris, the mayor — he who fathered the edict that no Negro woman should appear on the streets without an apron — remitted her taxes, the dispensation dating from the death of her father on into perpetuity" (489). Yet when the law is altered again by the next generation, it and they are dismissed by Emily, for whom the decree had become fact ("Perhaps he considers himself the sheriff" [491]). It is associated not only with the father but with an act of desexing and suppressing black women. Women and blacks, in this text, are potentially transfixed and dispossessed by the power of a patriarchist discourse ("only a woman could have believed it") that Emily is at once victim of and reverses. Not only does Miss Emily simply turn away the men and the law from the beginning, greet with blank silence the druggist's request ("'But the law requires you to tell what you are going to use it for'" [496]), or refuse integration into the postal system ("When the town got free postal delivery, Miss Emily alone refused to let them fasten the metal numbers above her door" [498–9]), but the word Negro is used until the law, Judge Stevens, uses "nigger," which afterwards takes over the text. The smell thought to come from *below* the house is implicitly allied to a menstrual odor ("'Dammit, sir,' Judge Stevens said, 'will you accuse a lady to her face of smelling bad?'" [493]), marking the flower of southern womanhood as a repressed order of death.

One of the puzzles of the work is the title, which has no *reference* to or in it. Faulkner ducked a question about it once, pretending that it was self explanatory, but the fact is there is no rose in the story, nor any clear sense of who — aside from the text, unless that is the "rose"? — is *gifting* one to Emily. Why "A Rose for Emily"? But what is a "rose," or rather, what does or can it signify, which seems rather the point: the title raises the question, in turn, of what signifying itself may entail? On its face a rose is an emblem, one that generates, however, numerous possible meanings. For example, it is used in courtship or victory or admiration or mourning, or it is a token of the past, like a flower preserved between pages as a book mark, like

Homer's body. Yet the word may also be a kind of interpretive guide precisely because it is *not* in the text.[12] The only mention in the story of anything like roses occurs in the early verb form of *rising* ("They rose when she entered – a small, fat woman in black" [490–1]), or in the color *rose* in the final scene ("upon the valence curtains of faded rose color, upon the rose-shaded lights" [500]). The play on the forms of *rose* returns us, nonetheless, to its value as a word or signifying agent as such. For while a "rose" can signify many things it does mark that act of generating reference when it has no obvious cipher. It is itself an emblem of interpretation, as one could almost hear the word emblem in the name Emily itself, or as if anticipating the *antho*logies the story would be forever entombed in. If Emily herself is raised to the status of a figure that signifies, primarily, by incorporating other figures, the violent nature of her aestheticism – she gives painting lessons – becomes the more ominous for our relation to Faulkner's own writing.[13]

Miss Emily's act of poisoning becomes the problem to interpret – or does it? In fact, signs in the story never quite point to their conventional meanings, just as the smell is misread as that of dead rodents. One may well hear in the name Miss Emily some variant of *mis/sema*(ly), like a signature for a rupture within the signs that the text names as a subject. It is this rupture that seems cloaked in the narrator's voice, and it makes the various ways to read the necrophilia depend on our act of choosing between signifieds. If we start with the fact that the killing of Homer *repeats* the death of Emily's life-robbing father and her first attempt to retain the father's corpse, it is not sufficient to say Homer's murder is designed to keep him, a potential husband, from also leaving her simply. The father, who may or may not have raped her as well, who may or may not have desexed her by

---

12 That is, Faulkner implants verbal riddles in his titles that far exceed the attention they are usually given and remain unique entrees into difficult verbal patterning and their figurative consequences. *Light in August*, "Go Down, Moses," and "Pantaloon in Black" are immediate cases in point.

13 It is not accidental that, at the end of *As I Lay Dying*, the text most overtly experimenting with "voices," what emerges with the new "Ms. Bundren" is the *graphophone*, that is, a machine of reproduction that acknowledges these voices (or dead "I's") as mnemonic fictions that – like the rereading of the novel – are artistically projected inventions of memory, scriptive repetitions, and figural traces. For a very different reading of the graphophone as an implement of modernization invading the rural world, see John T. Matthews, "*As I Lay Dying* in the Machine Age," in *Boundary 2* 19:1 (1992).

not raping her and thus did anyway, is first clung to after death in the denial of that death – but it is not clear whether that is done as if to perpetuate the life, or because he died before she could avenge herself first and was cheated, and must repeat the act to appear to master it in a standstill: "We remembered all the young men her father had driven away, and we knew that with nothing left, she would have to cling to that which had robbed her, as people will" [494]). Is the "past" and the destructive patriarchy foreclosed in this act, repeated and controlled, or fixed and simply perpetuated? Is her act emblematic of our hermeneutic appropriation of a poetic text ("Homer"), or are we actively violated in our own act of voyeurism, left with a dusty corpse as Emily eludes our reading? The psychosis depicted stands, in a sense, beyond dialectics. The reader can only account for the murder of Homer in successively irreconcilable ways by inscribing it in a reversible, if serial, narrative: either Homer's murder repeats the father's death, to master in repetition what was impossible to control the first time, thus preserving the "past" in a fetish-form; or the repetition is a gesture of freedom from a position of entrapment, and thus erases the "past" at the expense of the present (being thus sacrificed by the sacrifice), and so on.

It is here that we seem to reach the limit of a discursive and representational reading. Unless, that is, we understand the patriarchal language to be that of the community, of "we," and hence of the eluded reader as well, in which case a certain anamorphic turn to the act of interpretation occurs. To return to my early considerations, we might recall that the author appears inscribed in the initials in Miss Emily's name (M. E.). What is at stake is the (impossible) repetition of an always (pre)originary violation, an attempt at revenge or righting that spirals further into loss – an implied identification (with the father). The text, it should be noted, places Miss Emily in a *gray* zone of sexual difference, heard in the name Grierson, increasingly rendering her mannish even as it puts Homer's sexuality in question ("he liked men, and it was known that he drank with the younger men in the Elks' club" [496]). Homer's grecian proclivities to the side, if Emily is depicted as already sexually transgressed, as the townspeople assume during her buggy rides ("Poor Emily"), she is simultaneously a figure of virginity perpetuated, as at a wedding night held indefinitely at the point of consummation by death. Yet the name Homer Barron is openly problematic. For instance, if we take Homer to imply the name of a father, it can only be that of the "father" of poetry as such, and we see a bizarre yet unavoidable parable of Faulkner's own incorporation of precursor textuality or his sense of defaced authority. Inversely to how Popeye keeps Temple locked in a brothel room (a sort of Memphis-Albertine), Miss Emily keeps Homer – only as corpse-text. When the pair go on their joint carriage rides, we are encouraged by the repetition of the term "sun" to give the skit a vaguely allegorical reading:

And as soon as the old people said, "Poor Emily," the whispering began. "Do you suppose it's really so?" they said to one another. "Of course it is. What else could …" This behind their hands; rustling of craned silk and satin behind jalousies closed upon the sun of Sunday afternoon as the then, swift clop-clop-clop of the matched team passed: "Poor Emily." (495)

The carriage ride, like Benjy's ride with Luster that ends *The Sound and the Fury*, manages subtly to suggest a mythic figure of transport. Yet where Benjy's ride inverts and rewrites the Platonic myth of the poetic flight in *Phaedrus*, Miss Emily's carriage ride seems to be a figure of an Icarean course belonging to a writing project (of M. E.) and its potentially solar trajectory ("the *sun* of *Sun*day"). Yet if the *carriage* is a vehicle of metaphoric transport, the "clop-clop-clop" also represents the absolute reduction of language and perception to a repetitive series of sheerly differential and material signifiers, marks or bars preceding and containing even Homer, or placing the two as if synchronously in the carriage *together*. Indeed, such a reading is not at all far-fetched given the general theme of secret inscription and encryption that the story presents; moreover, it does not contradict the social subversiveness of the writing, particularly since what is being undone is the dual "paternal" order of past authority and patriarchal discourse. Indeed, we may hear in the name "Barron" itself another such cipher, since aside from its suggestion of nobility (or, as sometimes historicized, "robber barons") it includes the word "bar" as well as a Greek signature of *being* itself, Bar-*on*. The name Barron now suggests, like the word "rose" that can generate all but will not surrender any specific referent of meaning, what is also (a) *bar to being* as such – like a poetic precursor one cannot quite get beyond or digest, yet also like the materiality of language depicted by the clopping of the carriage.[14] In this case, we see such a reading confirmed cryptonymically in the references to cupolas/copulas as in

14 A tradition for this sort of anagram certainly exists in literature, as noted in the treatment of Melville's "Bartleby."

the name *Tobe*, who "walked right through the house and out the back and was not seen again" (499).[15] Tobe services Emily's narrative and then appears as the figure of a remainder or excess, like Jim Bond at the close of *Absalom, Absalom!* – a role in which Faulkner equates blacks with what is unrepresentable and suppressed or enslaved in the semantic order.

It is at this point that the "psychosis" we attribute to Miss Emily becomes problematic, since it departs from the fairly endless reading of the emblems and symbolic markers the tale cannot stop generating in its readers. Indeed, it indicates where a certain Faulkner, like Emily, practices a defacing violence against the communal reader who tries to break in the door, or penetrate his recessive text. For in reading for the exposed "meaning" we discover the empty indentation, sacrificing the entire paternal or literary order from which his words generate references (like the word "rose"). The psychotic allegory of Faulkner's narrative unsurely confers on Emily, or his own text, the murderous defiance of being a sacrifice to – and of – an inherited model of reading in which his work is ritually produced and consumed. This dimension of the story allows us to read in Miss Emily, somewhat surprisingly, the allegory of Faulkner's own murderous relation to the symbolic or linguistic order in which he produces his modernist works.

For Faulkner to write the "autobiography" of his authorship through Miss Emily's *psychosis* underlines the aggression with which the community of readers is itself treated. It reminds us that behind the authorial image which the thematic criticism has projected stands an alternate "voice," as approachable as Miss Emily's, whose project may be to deface the reserve of thematic readings by which the community canonizes his text. It equates the community's treatment of the "woman" Emily with that of the author Faulkner.

Yet there is another footnote to this reading. So far we have attempted to move from where the text generates recurrent allegories (the south's fixation on the dead), to where it explores the subversion of social and discursive patriarchy. And since Gregory Jay noted where these two readings cancel one another, or can, we proceeded to

---

15 Jay decodes this mimetically as a reference to the situation of black subjectivity, rather than a more enigmatic marker of writing in the text itself: "The servant's name is Tobe, a punning appellation that echoes Hamlet in signifying the black man's split being and the deferred futurity of his achievement of any authorized subjectivity. Such subjection is literally the business of Homer Barron, a construction company foreman ..." (334).

what could be called an "autobiographical" reading of Faulkner's subversion of the literary modes of production he works within (the refusal of past textual authority, the defacement of hermeneutic institutions). In so far as we have moved from a "modernist" reading that resists figuration to something else, for which the name "postmodernist" will not quite substitute, the question remains how and where Faulkner marks his overthrow of the modernist or antifigural hermeneutic in his writing, where it is already identified not only with the dead Homer (the sacrifice of the traditional poetic project?) but the patriarchal model itself, now understood as desexed itself and almost universal. In "A Rose for Emily," the legal fiction of paternity is deflowered. From this perspective, the first reading we marked – those which generate more meaning from the text than it can account for, that which places it in every college anthology – is complicitous with patriarchist conventions. To the extent we satisfy ourselves with (re)producing a mimetic reading of the tale, we are ourselves lying in the indented discovered space of Emily's bed. While one place to trace this shift in writing in Faulkner generally is through the narratives of black figures in *Go Down, Moses*, another seems to be in a detail of the story we only mentioned in passing and must return to. It is the startling detail about the erosion of sexual difference in both ostensible "lovers." If Emily's gray hair ("a vigorous iron-gray, like the hair of an active man") suggests a site in between binaries like white and black, male and female, it can only in part be explained by identification with a "father" she assumes the position of; it in turn exposes the patriarchist site as feminized, homoerotic, or a fictional regime of representation – as arbitrary as Colonel Sartoris' two decrees. Of these two – that freeing Miss Emily from her taxes, and that demanding black women wear aprons in the street – it is the sartorial excess of the latter, in its desexing and removing the black woman from the patriarch's desirous gaze (that is, publicly or for the reflected gaze of the white woman's concerns), that is telling. The patriarchist gesture is here desexing to women, not only because of the threat of aroused male desire, but to *conceal a desexing of the male order that precedes it*. We must return to the discovery of her indentation in the *bed*, next to Homer's body.

That Emily can be termed a gender outlaw does more than place her in the normal domain of woman as carved out in the text's premises. In the "tableau" earlier presented we see the father "clutching a horsewhip" as if guarding her from any other males ("a slender figure in white in the background ... the two of them framed by the back-flung front door" [493]). Male power here threateningly guards against a male intrusion that objectifies the woman, yet it does this through an instrument that marks its own dismemberment, the whip we also see Homer wield. This scene presents Emily as both suspended and oriented, through the father she stands behind, toward a male order, or body, one she identifies with in its empowered and, secretly, feminized or dismembered form. As presented to us in Emily's father or Colonel Sartoris, old male power is violent to the degree it covers its own castration — evidenced in the war — by the arbitrary fiction of its decrees or law. The paternal order here is a fiction enforced with a whip. What is guarded, and subverted, can also be read through the index of what Eve Sedgwick has termed "turn of the century male homo/heterosexual definitional panic" — understood here, however, against a dismantling of gender itself.[16] In her account, this is also the site of the ideology of modernism. Of this "definitional panic," she argues that abstract "modernism" and its suppression of figuration involve the suppression — and virtual encrypting — of "a very par-ticular body, the desired male body":

Postmodernism, in this view, the strenuous rematch between the reigning champ, modernist abstraction, and the deposed challenger, figuration, would thus *necessarily* have kitsch and sentimentality as its main spaces of contestation. But insofar as there is a case to be made that the modernist impulse toward abstraction in the first place owes an incalculable part of its energy precisely to turn-of-the-century male homo/heterosexual definitional panic — and such a case is certainly there for the making, in at any rate literary history from Wilde to Hopkins to James to Proust to Conrad to Eliot to Pound to Joyce to Hemingway to Faulkner to Stevens — to the extent the "figuration" that had to be abjected from modernist self-reflexive abstraction was not the figuration of just any body, the figuration of figurality itself, but, rather, that represented in a very particular body, the desired male body. So as kitsch or sentimentality came to mean representation itself, what represented "representation" came at the same time signally to be a very particular, masculine object and subject of erotic desire. (166–7)

Since I began by noting how in contemporary readings Faulkner seems to be caught in what Sedgwick calls "antifiguralist modernism," and I have ended suggesting that Miss Emily's act involves relinquishing just that reading, we may ask, again, *not* where such a

16 Eve Kosofsky Sedgwick, *Epistemology of the Closet* (Berkeley: University of California Press, 1990), 167.

transition by Faulkner from a modernist to a postmodernist reading is marked – but whether, finally, what is really at stake is a core *a*modernism whose materiality marks and refuses the "modernist" enclosure to begin with. For instance, can we say that "antifiguralist modernism" is represented by the tableau image of Emily's sex-robbing, panicked, or castrating/castrated father? If he stands for the "modernist" or representational reading with its criminal restrictions and fictive laws (literally "a spraddled silhouette in the foreground"), Homer's murder seems meant to ritually both re-enact and inter that. We can now ascribe to the use of the name Homer itself a sort of totalizing or destroying parody of the modernist technique of citing past works (as practiced by Eliot, Pound, or Joyce).[17] By murdering and transfixing patriarchy in its own name, much as Faulkner emblematically names the "father" of all western poetry as the beloved-victim-substitute, the text implies a space in which the entire metaphorics of fathers, Oedipal models, and precursor authority is suspended, as if itself preceded. Faulkner positions his work within a post-humanist project predicated on emptying out the models of interiority which the encroaching community, in vampiric fashion, seeks affirmation *of* in his corpse-text.

To return to the role of the male body, we may hypothesize two things as taking place. First, Emily is presented as negating her own female body when she cuts her hair following her father's death, as in the opening she is presented as obese ("She looked bloated, like a body long submerged in motionless water" [491]). If, following Sedgwick, we say that one place "antifiguralist" modernism is spawned is by its suppression of (and fixation on) the eroticized *male* body, Miss Emily's poisoning seems oriented to that fact – or almost, since it preserves that body in the person of Homer. As a corpse, in bed, and in a position of erotic embrace, Homer's body at once exemplifies and eviscerates any literalization of this logic. Once again, as we release or unbind the story from its modernist (historicist, mimetic, revisionist, allegorical) reading, a number of antagonistic and deadly signifieds appear generated. (Indeed, we might read Emily's visit to the pharmacy and use of arsenic through Avital Ronell's *Crack*

---

17 It may be illuminating to compare Miss Emily's double and more startling sacrifice to that of Isaac McCaslin in *Go Down, Moses*, whose "repudiation" of his patrimony – part of a cursed system of property including slavery – involves the loss not only of the inherited past but, as it turns out, of progeny, or the future itself.

Wars, where the role of "literature" as drug (and poison) is intricately theorized – and where the white "crack" is both rupture and a vaginal trope that balances Emily as avenging hero against Emma Bovary as literary martyr.)[18] In this case, what appears enacted is simultaneously the essence of a modernist gesture (the fetishization and suppression of the desired-male-body, the figure of figuration itself) *and* the foreclosure of that modernist-as-text body as a corpse, an absence. Not only does "A Rose for Emily" allow the patriarchist model to *execute itself* through Emily's act (Faulkner's writing), it does so through the "criminal" sexualization of a feminine love refracted through a homoerotic principle. It is not simply a *male body* that is metaphysically desired here, as if in parody of Sedgwick's thesis, for that is clearly abjected as well – the screen or pretext for a materiality sought beneath the seductions of descriptive language.

We again see why the isolation of the word *rose* – as word, emblem, phallus, vagina – is a problem to the text, a vacuum through which the mimetic surface is transfigured. Its refusal of reference in the story presages the death of the antifiguralist reading of Faulkner himself, even strangles it by suffocation or poisons it with the *gift* of itself, since if it is not ignored as an interpretive problem and simply repressed, it can *only* compel successive figural readings that undermine figuration and approach psychosis. To this extent, the story might be called an anthology of Faulkner's career in its Icarus-like trajectory from representational "modernism" – the aesthetic symbolized by Emily's father – toward a subversive (a)postmodernism, a trajectory that all along may have been at stake. The "rose" thus extended to Emily as a figure of the figuration, extended by Faulkner to (another) Faulkner, is a movement the text equates with the auto-subversion of a ruinous semantic and social order that it also exemplifies. Self-sacrifice is accomplished in the demonstration of the impossibility of sacrifice, or purging the system that allows that staging to begin with: and Emily is the hero of this. The "old" South here becomes an emblem for an entire metaphysical and aesthetic order, in which blacks, like the materiality of language, were/are repressed. As it turns out, this same story of "escape" from representational limits is told over and again in the quilted tales of the stylistically regressive or seemingly "premodernist" *Go Down, Moses*, specifically in those tales of black figures. Such repeated attempts to escape a closed order or system –

18 Avital Ronell, *Crack Wars* (Lincoln: University of Nebraska Press, 1992).

as in Isaac's "repudiation" of an inherited model of property and slavery, or Rider's story, or "Butch" Beauchamp's return – may be read as the stutter of the authorial Moses who, as lawgiver, is also the dismantler of that mosaic system "going *down*," himself not able, however, to cross over to a subsequent stylistic land.

What does it mean, then, when we read in the text, this open signature that says M. E. or "me" in *Miss Emily*, which says not "I am Madame Bovary" but, rather, and with all the successive ironies this implies, "I am Miss Emily"? Indeed, the announced closure of the project begun in *Madame Bovary* and the modernist style can be read, in this sense, in the opening scene in *Sanctuary*, where Horace Benbow is carrying that novel in his pocket, something Popeye draws attention to ("'A what?' 'Professor,' Popeye said. 'He's got a book with him.' 'What's he doing here?' 'I dont know. I never thought to ask. Maybe to read the book'").[19] Popeye, not black but called that "black man," will be later compared to the black stuff that is said to come from the imaginary corpse-mouth of Emma, a "stuff" that suggests the citational amalgam that flows from the endless anteriority of a collapsed textual past that Faulkner would rewrite, assassinate, sublate, or close with Homer ("He smells black, Benbow thought; he smells like that black stuff that ran out of Bovary's mouth and down upon her bridal veil when they raised her head" [7]). Indeed, says Faulkner, with a certain inaccessible hauteur and castrate outlaw pride, to all those readers who monumentalize him in the fetishistic domain of reading: "I am Miss Emily." The prospect opens a different (re)reading, one that is perhaps beyond the mock opposition of postmodernism with a strategically nostalgic iconology of modernism itself, as it is, potentially, from the regionalist commodity literature to which Faulkner's canonicity is inversely indebted. These interpretive stances may remain the surest way to evade what is transfiguratively and historically at stake in his linguistic representation of blacks.

One last point. It may be that we should read *Go Down, Moses* not as a return to a pre-modernist style but as metatextual writing in which the conditions of signification themselves stand to be altered – in reading Faulkner's black figures, that is, as struggling to exceed the plantation system of mimesis whose Mosaic logos would be cast *down*. It is this system Faulkner, like Miss Emily, is both arrested in and stands to overthrow. We might better address the problematic of

19 William Faulkner, *Sanctuary* (New York: Vintage, 1958), 8–9.

black representation by accelerating a reading of the invisible terms of Faulkner's own writing. Moreover, if Isaac McCaslin can be said to repudiate the inherited system of property in Faulkner's name, the latter seems to similarly indict the mimetic aesthetics of his own production as one that could be redeemed by a new Moses, as it were, a counter-text within his own figural writing. It is interesting that after this novel, Faulkner seems to do the opposite, that is, to fall into a more pronounced mimeticism *and* more ineptly literal attempts at fable.

In this way, Miss Emily — M. E. — is already a post-humanist figure, a cipher more in the tradition of a cybernetic other than a hysterical female, her/himself violently post-gendered, about whom all the structures that supposedly uphold the Faulknerian canon and the ideology of Americanists — mimesis, Oedipus, interiority, meaning, regionalism, historicism — are disarticulated, herself representing what Deleuze in speaking of Kafka might call a deterritorializing "minor literature." From this perspective, M. E. presents the signature of a future or future writing that bears no inscription, like "Tobe": that materialist allegoresis whose primary transformations seem sketched out in *Go Down, Moses* — a work about the throwing down of the Law that presents the stutter of a crossing-over that (itself also Lethe-like) occurs after the official style's (own) death, a mosaic in which the patterned emergence of the black figure or remainder alone escapes the mimetic tedium of patriarchist reading.

9

Hitchcock and the death of (Mr.) Memory (technology of the visible)

This essay is about the way that memory in Hitchcock is marked and effaced to account for the absence of origin in his narratives. I am not speaking of how the recovery of "memory" is a goal, sometimes overtly, as in the plots surrounding amnesia in *Spellbound* or *Marnie*, but rather how memory itself is used as a machinal figure that conceals a catastrophe of sorts. Memory appears as the machinal enforcer of mimesis out of which the ideological closure of identification and subjectivization occur (the domain of the symbolic police), yet as a machine of repeated re-marking, it is also that which breaks up or destroys mimesis when figures, syllables, sounds, letters, and visual puns, or objects emerge through repetition.[1] The problem of memory becomes one means of addressing Hitchcock's handling of language and the various *signifying agents* that are marked across his production. These generate a sort of hyperbolic *writing* covering the surface of the film text: markings or puns (at once aural, visual, nominal, and intertextual) which may be manifest in citations, numbers, body positions, or objects. They traverse the production and establish scenes of reading between works. Such Hitchcockian *writing* seems largely untracked today in any criticism because it ceaselessly *inter*rupts the pretense, which the spectator *desires* — identification, the appearance of subjectivity, the wholeness of the body. Since *The Thirty-Nine Steps* presents the earliest and most thorough theorization of memory, and in ways is a metatext about Hitchcock's own poetics, I will use it as the basis to explore this question. What I will argue is that the machinal place of memory as personified by Mr. Memory in *The Thirty-Nine Steps* is so relentless that it compels the surface of

---

1 Frequently, this catastrophe is linked to *representation* itself. It is marked at the outset of the film by an association with photography (*Secret Agent, Lifeboat*), or some murder, fall, or car wreck which, as in photos of the car accident in *Rear Window*, suggests an arrestation of movement (cinema) itself.

Hitchcock's text to be traversed by a folding back (re- and dis-remembering) that ruptures the contemporary rhetoric of the "gaze." In doing so, I will argue for an approach to Hitchcock in which a model of reading seems installed prior to any discourse of the "gaze," in which *seeing* is itself an effect of reading signs, graphics, or marks. If "memory" always denotes in Hitchcock a problem of signification, it also reveals a machine-like function that eviscerates the interiority of any subject, and can threaten to dissolve the representational pretext of (the) film itself.

If the compulsion in Hitchcock to repeatedly mark the (absent) "secret" of origin always *re*folds against this radically emptied site or machine of memory, there are several consequences. First, viewing Hitchcock's film as an anamorphic surface of marks, graphics and, again, aural and intertextual "puns," draws our attention to how he treats the materiality of language itself – which is not to say mere "dialogue." Second, not only is "narrative" in its traditional sense blocked by a machine of memory that precedes and generates it but by a certain dis-remembering of the body, but a segmenting and monstrous rearrangement also occurs. We might say that the lower or *material* order of the body or of the sign itself – letters, sounds, marking, signatures – usurps the position of the head (the centered subject). In a film with "steps" in its title that goes on to tell us that these are merely tropes (a code-term for a band of foreign agents), we might question the import of the *legs* which traverse *The Thirty-Nine Steps* and rise up, literally, at the end. This occurs with the dance of the chorus girls at the Palladium, whose legs are positioned above the slumping head of the dying Mr. Memory as he recites the secret formula for the silent warplane.[2] Finally, if there is such a textual dimension that Hitchcock marks in his text, one we have only just begun to read on its own terms – that is, one whose "agents" are understood to have a defacing and aggressive, rather than entertaining role – one implication is that the *mimetic* status of the film image on which our habits of identification and representation depend could be dissolved.

2 Feet or legs, marked and utilized emblematically *throughout* all of Hitchcock, very clearly recall Derrida's use of the term legs itself as I have been using it thoughout the book. "Steps" or legs in Hitchcock leads us to *legere*, or reading as a *material* problem.

1. Zizek's economics of "beyond"

Because I will return to the role of language in Hitchcock it is useful to position my remarks in relation to a recent commentator who has opened a more radical and "postmodern" scene of interpretation, Slavoj Zizek.[3] Zizek is particularly useful since he explicitly turns against the identificatory, inter-subjective, and narrative responses to Hitchcock that have been most influential in the criticism. What I will suggest, however, is that in going "beyond" such models to explore where the play of the symbolic and the real disrupts this identification, Zizek does not go far enough, and precisely by misreading the material problem of "language" itself. I should add that the stakes are not insignificant, since the main interpretive traditions of Hitchcock interpretation are variously invested in the subjectivist and author-oriented models that might seem at risk. Broadly speaking, Hitchcock criticism is invested in various forms of intentionalist interpretation, authorial surrogacy, identification (with characters), or subjectivization. These for Zizek remain within the domain of the symbolic, creating narrative meaning such as psychological or thematic interpretation does.[4] In some respects, Zizek's writings on

3 The works of Slavoj Zizek that will be cited here include *Enjoy Your Symptom! – Jacques Lacan In and Out of Hollywood* (New York: Routledge, 1992); ed., *Everything You Always Wanted to Know About Lacan ... But Were Afraid to Ask Hitchcock* (New York: Verso, 1992), hereafter cited as *EYAW*; *For They Know Not What They Do* (New York: Verso, 1991), herafter *FTKN*; *Looking Awry: An Introduction to Jacques Lacan Through Popular Culture*, hereafter *LA*; and *The Sublime Object of Ideology*, hereafter *SO*.

4 From Eric Rohmer and Claude Chabrol's *Hitchcock: The First Forty-Four Films* (New York: Frederick Ungar, 1979) through the excellent thematic readings of Robin Wood's *Hitchcock's Films* (New York: A. S. Barnes, 1977) to William Rothman's *The Murderous Gaze* (Cambridge: Harvard University Press, 1982), hereafter cited as *MG*, and even Tania Modleski's *The Women Who Knew Too Much* (New York: Methuen, 1988), variations of the controlling god-figure allow for a simplified rhetoric to accrue that implicitly sustains a subjective model of meaning. Treatments of the technological elements in Hitchcock – such as Elizabeth Weis' approach to sound in *The Silent Scream* (London: Associated University Presses, 1982) – remain at best semiotic. In Rothman's case, the reliance on a pre-critical model of authorship is treated decisively in Fredric Jameson, "Allegorizing Hitchcock," in *Signatures of the Visible* (New York: Routledge, 1990). Given the fact that the "gaze" itself, largely via Laura Mulvey's influential "Visual Pleasure and Narrative Cinema," had taken on a similarly subjectivist turn (however politicized or gendered), we might ask how much the central paradigms of Hitchcock reading depend on a mimetic blind-spot that is specific to the lack of

Hitchcock have implied a decisive, if not always obvious, turn in the criticism. This involves not only a near total investment of authority in Hitchcock's text (a gesture which, familiarly modernist, is also entirely persuasive), but the staging via *late* Lacan of a movement "beyond" the humanist terms of canonical criticism.

A great deal in Zizek's text involves the shift from the familiar middle Lacan, identified with the "Seminar on the 'Purloined Letter'," who is preoccupied with inter-subjectivity, the symbolic, and metonymic chains of signifiers, to the late Lacan, who moves "beyond the wall of language" to the irruptions of the real – that unrepresentable "kernel" of exteriority whose post-modern and negative epiphanies Zizek tracks as "the Thing": "what lies beyond is not the symbolic order but a real kernel, a traumatic core. To designate it, Lacan uses a Freudian term: *das Ding*, the Thing as an incarnation of the impossible *jouissance* (the term Thing is to be taken here with all the connotations it possesses in the domain of horror science fiction: the 'alien' from the film of the same name is a pre-symbolic, maternal Thing *par excellence*)" (*SO*, 132). The move is one from earlier viewing the symbolic (the order of cultural language, the "dead" law) as being "beyond" the pleasure principle – where the resolution of analysis involves integration into the symbolic order through acquiring a narrative – to viewing the symbolic as itself still part of the pleasure principle, a machine of gentrification, and its *beyond* as the unnarrativizable domain of the real. Implicit in his depiction of the late Lacan, however, is Zizek's attempt by analogy to contain "poststructuralism" as a whole (and deconstruction specifically) in the idea of the symbolic, or the middle Lacan's reliance on the signifier's play, and to move beyond it. What Zizek opposes to the play of metonymic chains "caught in the signifier's network" (*SO*, 132) is the uninterpretable or unnarrateable effect that conveys the "answer of the real" (*LA*, 34). For Zizek this irruption of the real defines one kind of postmodern moment and Hitchcock is its theoretical exemplar.

This shift "beyond" the symbolic, or post-structuralism, or the signifier, to the encounters with the absent Thing is mapped, finally, as that from the *symptom* (the infinitely interpretable effect of the symbolic) to the *sinthome*. Whereas the symptom denotes the infinitely

attention to language or the model of reading in film theory? A useful critique of the rhetoric of the "gaze" itself is presented in Joan Copjec, "The Orthopsychic Subject: Film Theory and the Reception of Lacan," *October* 49 (Spring, 1989).

interpretable effect of the symbolic, the Lacanian neologism indicates the uninterpretable moment that anchors the subject ontologically.[5] The *sinthome* bears the weight of this late Lacanian shift, since it fuses the "sublime object" with a signifying agent that seems to operate outside any signifying function, with a kind of implicit transparency or inert thingness itself.

Zizek's move is accordingly pixyish, since by ascribing all play of the signifier to the Lacanian symbolic he consigns interpretation as hermeneutics (an activity of the symbolic) to a zone that can be gone "beyond." As the realm of the real corresponds to a psychosis that resists narrativization, the privileged text of this for Zizek is, naturally enough, *Psycho*, which is the basis for the brilliant programmatic essay closing Zizek's edited anthology *Everything You Always Wanted to Know About Lacan ... But Were Afraid to Ask Hitchcock* (1991), " 'In His Bold Gaze My Ruin Is Writ Large'."

Zizek's reading of *Psycho* virtually reproduces in Hitchcock the same moves he elaborates in the late Lacan, creating a system that reads, potentially, "Lacan/Hitchcock." For Zizek the hoary epiphany of the Thing signals the "answer of the real" breaking through the "gentrifications" of the symbolic and representation, to reveal in perpetually "uncanny" fashion that the gaze of the Thing was all along the depthless space of the subject itself, "not a relapse into subjectivity, but an entry into the dimension of the subject beyond subjectivity" (*EYAW*, 255). This is the site in which the subject is always already occupied by a dispossessing exteriority or *extimite*, the model for which subject can be the cyborg or living dead. This critical operation makes *Psycho*, or the "psychotic core of Hitchcock's universe" (*EYAW*, 241), one site where the narrativizing, subjectiv-izing discourses of film theory may be demystified — "the theological dimension of Hitchcock's *oeuvre*" (211) represented, differently, by Chabrol or Rothman. These approaches and others represent potent critical territory in which the discourses of interiority, authorial surrogacy, inter-subjective narrative, and above all identification return. For as long as those models control "interpretation," Zizek

---

5 According to Zizek, the "symptom as *sinthome* is a certain signifying formation penetrated with enjoyment ... a particular, 'pathological', signifying formation, a binding of enjoyment, an inert stain resisting communication and interpretation, a stain which cannot be included in the circuit of discourse, of social bond network, but is at the same time the positive condition of it" (*SO*, 75).

implies, a false or pre-Lacanian subject remains in place. To establish a site beyond all of this (post-structuralism as well as hermeneutics) Zizek locates *Psycho* in the collapse of any inter-subjective (symbolic) model, a *"destitution subjective"* (Lacan) that constitutes "the very abyss of the subject not yet caught in the web of language" (245), which in turn forces us to "identify with the abyss beyond identification" (226).

Compelling as Zizek's gambit is, his insistent move "beyond" is compromised by the means in which it is, repeatedly, staged. There arises an inevitable rhetorical trap which he confronts but does not entirely negotiate: that of recuperating inversely in this "beyond" the very terms that have been dismantled and emptied out. Despite Zizek's aligning of the symbolic with language as such, "beyond the wall of language" (245) there tends to be, in some form or another, still more material language. When Zizek maps the move from the symbolic to the real it covertly brings back the function of metaphor, symbol, and identification, as opposed to metonymy or the disseminating play of signifiers. The place "beyond" language, in short, tends to look like a metaphoric use of language that stages itself as the phallophany: "it is not possible to present the transphenomenal Thing-in-Itself within the domain of phenomena, so what we can do is present this very impossibility and thus 'render palpable' the transcendent dimension of the Thing-in-Itself" (*FTKN*, 144). The Thing presents itself as gaze in a radically negative immediacy, a place that reasserts the transparency of a language less gone "beyond" than provisionally backgrounded.[6] Accordingly, while Zizek closes the model of identification and subjectivization, he does so by moving to the perverse endpoint and inversion (emptying) of those same discursive terms — not quite "beyond" it.

We might look for a limit to Zizek's turn in what he calls the Hegelian "negation of negation." It functions economically, since "the whole point is just that we come to experience how this negative,

---

6 Zizek openly opts for metaphor over metonymy in Lacan's name — the very function that the *sinthome*, however objectalized, represents in pretending the end all signifying chains. This is, of course, the antithetical move to de Man, for whom metaphor, like symbol, involves a mystifying and totalizing function. Zizek's main modification (and it is significant) is to posit that "metaphor" as itself over an empty site: "The 'original metaphor' is not a sustitution of 'something for something-else' but a substitution of something for nothing: ... which is why *metonymy is a species of metaphor*" (*FTKN*, 50).

disruptive power, menacing our identity is simultaneously a positive condition of it" (*SO*, 176). The economics of the "negation of negation" are central to Zizek's rhetorical arsenal. They are present, for instance, when the Lacanian subject is presented not as the end of the Enlightenment, but as its (unwitting) definition all along; or when Derrida's deconstruction of identity is said to be nothing but the definition of identity all along.[7] This partial recuperation, in which the first term is denied its oppositional status and returns in an emptied form as what was, we hear, all along the case anyway, is visible in Zizek's own incessant return to fairly traditional interpretations of Hitchcock – relying on Oedipal scenarios, didactic inter-subjective formula, or discussions of the family.

One of the ways Zizek partitions the *two* stages of Lacan involves asserting the difference between a metonymic "signifier" in middle Lacan, and a "sign" that elicits the "answer of the real" ("the 'sign' is given by the thing itself" [*LA*, 32–4]). Beyond the "wall of language" seems, again, only another term for language which effaces itself in manifesting the effect (beyond signs) of the impossible Thing. Yet if we call it *sign* instead of *signifier* and assume its potential to present the obscene kernel of "the real," we have less erased *or* preceded language than done something else. We have allowed it to secretly return to an emptied function that we might align with metaphor or symbol, and other suspect ideologies of transparency.[8] Of course, Zizek locates those moments that bring signifying chains to an end in the figure of the *sinthome*, or enjoyment, or even the "gaze" – yet in each a problem lingers.

On the one hand, Zizek inverts film theory's long problematic subjectivization of the Lacanian "gaze" by locating its radical Otherness at the point the subject can never occupy. The "gaze" is never coincident with sight ("the gaze I encounter 'is, not a seen gaze, but a gaze imagined by me in the field of the Other'" [214]), and yet

---

7 "The impossibility (of identity) unearthed by Derrida through the hard work of deconstructive reading supposed to subvert identity constitutes the very definition of identity" (*FTKN*, 37).

8 The odd written title text opening the second *Man Who Knew Too Much* suggests, in Hitchcock's intricate marking, an annulment of the logic of "symbols" in the very pun that identifies a "crash of Cymbals" as the enigmatic agent of the film. The "single crash of Cymbals" that dislocates an American family indicates the *priority* of the disruptively emptied ("crash") signifier – sound, the punning relay – barring any pretense of symbol?

its claim to immediacy and epiphanic power is enormous, indeed, without parallel in the terms Zizek mobilizes. Thus "the ultimate lesson of *Psycho*" (257) is that the "final dissolve of Norman's gaze into the mother's skull" is a "Beyond" that "is itself hollow, devoid of any positive content" since "this Beyond coincides with gaze itself" (257). As such, "*Psycho* indexes the status of a subject which precedes inter-subjectivity – a depthless void of pure Gaze which is nothing but a topological reverse of the Thing" (257–8). The gaze as that of the inanimate Thing reflects the subject's empty personification over an inanimate or dead site:

"In so far as this subject dwells 'beyond the wall of language', its correlative is not a signifier representing it, marking its place within the symbolic order, but an inert object, a bone which sticks in the subject's throat and hinders his/her integration into the symbolic order ... From our perspective, however, this 'transsubjective' dimension is precisely the dimension of a subject beyond 'subjectivity' ... the 'impersonal' abyss we confront when we find ourselves face-to-face with Norman's gaze into the camera is the very abyss of the subject not yet caught in language – the unapproachable Thing which resists subjectivization, this point of failure of every identification, is ultimately *the subject itself.*" (245)

Following the technique of a "negation of negation," the Cartesian moment of Hitchcock must return to its position in the most *heimlich* of sites, that of the old subject of the Enlightenment – now represented best by the vampire or undead ("Norman's gaze is utterly 'soulless', like the gaze of monsters and the living dead" [257]). Accordingly, Zizek returns at this point to a kind of weird identity with Rothman's *The Murderous Gaze* (who locates the "gaze" in the "machine (camera) itself" [256]) – that is with a Rothman who uses the precritical discourse of authorial control and surrogacy.[9]

Since I am arguing, instead, that the "Cartesian" space Hitchcock treats is always in advance displaced by a more radical *exteriority* located in the interstices of endless semiosis – that, in short, the psychotic "beyond" of language is in a sense language itself – it is important to see how Zizek addresses Hitchcock's other signifying practices. I return here to his discussion of the *sinthome*. It is a term

9 Earlier, Zizek's adaptation of Rothman's theological-auteurist model causes him to move toward a reductive notion of rhetoric: "one is even tempted to say that Hitchcock's films ultimately contain only two subject positions, that of the director and that of the viewer – all diegetic persons assume, by turns, one of the two positions" (*EYAW*, 218).

that, after putting the weight of his reading on (and naming one of his book-things after), he tries, and curiously *fails*, to import into Hitchcock. Typically, Zizek depends on a special use of binaries that seem to present a false narrative. Time and again, these are set up — modernism/postmodernism, post-structuralism/late Lacan, desire/the drive, signifier/sign, symbolic/real, symptom/*sinthome*, and so on — in such a way that the first term becomes a figure of identity out of which the second emerges as the more radical moment, but which, then, can be seen to have preceded the first, itself the latter's "gentrification" or forgetting. The rhetorical technique cannot be separated from its conservationist value, nor conceal the fact that the operation itself is so pervasive as to be suspect of a strangely recuperative role.

In the case of the symptom/*sinthome* operation, the latter is applied to Hitchcock in a central contribution to his edited anthology, "Hitchcock's *Sinthomes*." Surprisingly, what results might seem to some a kind of quick retreat, a face-saving getaway before a potential disgorgement or loss of control. For after beginning to outline Hitchcock's recurrent leitmotifs, repeated figures that blast open a film surface and arrest or dislocate the official "narrative," Zizek not only adduces the most mild and bizarrely evasive examples (for instance, the glass of milk in *Suspicion* and *Spellbound*) but then breaks off the entire discussion *after only three pages*. What could easily constitute a major book is begun and fled from — as if a domain of signification opened by the *sinthome* (a fascinating conceit which, notwithstanding, can regress to what may be called an emptied symbol-thing) threatens to overwhelm the controlling purpose of the construct. Rather than generate "meanings" by virtue of their repetition across films, Zizek finds that Hitchcock's *sinthomes* "designate the *limit of interpretation*: they are what resists interpretation, the inscription into the texture of a specific visual enjoyment" (*EYAW*, 126).[10] What is denied to these

10 Zizek: "How, then, are we to interpret such extended motifs? If we search in them for a common core of meaning ... we enter the domain of Jungian archetypes which is utterly incompatible with Hitchcock's universe; if, on the other hand, we reduce them to an empty signifier's hull filled out in each of the films by a specific content, we *don't say enough*: the force which makes them persist from one film to another eludes us. The right balance is attained when we conceive them as *sinthomes* in the Lacanian sense: as a signifier's constellation (formula) which fixes a certain core of enjoyment, like mannerisms in painting. ... So, paradoxically, these repeated motifs, which serve as a support of the Hitchcockian interpretive

figures is the very signifying dimension they advertize, themselves (like the chapter) foreclosed as inert figures, fixed as "a specific visual enjoyment" alone. One must add at once, that the list of *sinthomes* could well be almost endless, and certainly would involve almost discrete figures like hands, birds, feet, dogs, certain letters (M, P, F, R) and numbers, and so on. What Zizek here does is curtail a pseudo-symbolic function only to neutralize its signifying, threatening import. What Zizek suppresses is that here the signifier itself has become the Thing by virtue of reflecting back on its emptied status as material signifier – agent, leg, step – which destructively intrudes in the symbolic realm itself. At this point, Zizek himself has unwittingly become an agent of the symbolic (which he clearly requires rhetorically), endeavoring to "gentrify" what threatens it.

Here the Lacanian machine gets, unexpectedly, clogged. In Zizek's model, one is arrested by and before what could only undermine a rhetoric of the gaze. What Zizek cannot entertain, for it would conflict with the rhetoric of the "beyond" on which everything hinges is that the reification of the symptom-qua-*sinthome* involves a reflexive moment in which, isolated from context by virtue of its repetition, the "fact" of memory becomes a sign which prioritizes its own radical materiality. The irreducibility of this materiality provides the very loop in representation through which Hitchcock's radical allegories derive authority: the "Thing" is never, in short, staged beyond representation; it is, instead, sought in the loop of representation, repetition, and anteriority. This removes Hitchcock, finally, from the classic model of representation Zizek remains, ultimately, within. It is not the *sinthomes'* resistance to interpretation that is the problem, but the excess they can produce – the threat of emptying interpretation by generating innumerable relays and chains of associations (what Hitchcock seems to call knowing *too much*). This Zizek would contain: "The postmodernist pleasure in interpreting Hitchcock is procured precisely by such self-imposed trials: one invents the 'craziest' possible shift from the film's 'official' content ..., whereupon one is expected to stand the test by proposing perspicacious arguments on its behalf" (127). This radical materiality is not a subject before language, which is impossible, but a subject beyond subjectivity that is already the radical effect of a language that Hitchcock endeavors,

delirium, designate the limit of interpretation: they are what resists interpretation, the inscription into the texture of a specific visual enjoyment" (*EYAW*, 126).

hopelessly, to control by breaking down into its rock hard components (language become Thing). He then sets these dismembered feet loose in the text.[11]

I will try now to open up the terms of this other Hitchcock. The revolution of Hitchcock reading is not, then, Zizek's move beyond traditional subjectivization – a model he successfully critiques, but only by moving to and inhabiting its endgame inversion. Rather, it is beginning to read Hitchcock's detail and text as the site of a radical *hyper-writing*. I use the phrase "hyper-writing" to indicate the manner in which Hitchcock turns film into a surface amalgamating a multitude of material and technological markers beyond the mimetic images; the way in which the least detail, phrase, sound-effect, or emblematic repetition can organize an entire reading of the text. *Hyper* names the reflexive excess that Hitchcock repeatedly marks (as in the recurrent phrase "too much"), and which describes the potential flood of sense or erasure that alternately occurs in this networking (and intermittent collapse or emptying) of signifying chains. Zizek's interpretive dilemma arises not from using Hitchcock primarily as an "example" of Lacanian theory, as when the *sinthome* is invoked to contain a Hitchcockian rupture of signification by placing it "beyond" reading, but from Hitchcock's own theorization of language (which may be "beyond" Lacan). If Hitchcock never leaves a material conception of "language," he nonetheless breaks it down into dismembering elements which operate silently (including sound) as relational, transvaluative, and destroying agents. When the attempt for language to mean fails – as exemplified by Hannay's inability to communicate – language aspires to sheer materiality, but this fails as well; language cannot *not* mean even though meaning cannot be controlled (indeed, it leads invariably to identification, subjectivization, and narrative). Hence where agency fails, *secret* agency returns and cannot be done away with.[12]

---

11 This subject beyond subjectivity recalls where, in *The Lodger*, the transmogrifications of anonymous *faces* in the wireless scene follows the panorama of the giant printing press, the subject as the repository of dead newsprint ("The Evening Standard").

12 My thanks to Betsy Dillon for this characterization and to both her and Sarah Pelmas for their generous critique of this paper.

2. Secret agency and the chorines' legs

The Thirty-Nine Steps opens with neon lettering spelling out Music Hall and a headless figure buying a ticket and entering. The price is unremarked, but the economic and ritual nature of the transaction precede the show (or film). The figure (Hannay) takes a seat in a darkened theatre in which all heads are anonymously turned from us, while the master of ceremony takes stage to introduce the act of Mr. Memory. It is a raucous lower-class crowd, emerging, as does Hitchcock's cinema (one corollary to the Music Hall), to usurp the space not only of theatre but "high" culture as such. There is no barrier between stage and audience. It is a scene in which consciousness seems staged at its emergence by forgetting the ritual and repetitive nature of the scene itself. This fact is so astonishingly allegorized in the personification of Mr. Memory that it seems, on the contrary, entirely unremarked by critics. The setting mimes consciousness' own seeming engenderment through the vaudeville act of questioning the "re-markable" Mr. Memory, who memorizes a thousand "facts" a day. It is also a scene returned to in the denouement at the London Palladium – where the reference to Pallas suggests, ironically, wisdom and revelation. It will later turn out that the spies are using Memory to transport the complex warplane formula (later recited by the dying Mr. Memory) out of England. After an anonymous shot is fired in the Music Hall, the veiled many-named "Annabella Smith" under a sexual pretense chooses Hannay to bring her home. When she is murdered at night, Hannay is "interpellated" in her place into a narrative machine in a pursuit that leads *up* to Scotland and back *down* to London. The circularity of the narrative, in which Hannay is both the object of pursuit (by police and spies) and pursuer, assumes the form of a negative *Bildungsroman*. When Hannay returns to the scene at the Palladium, which replicates the Music Hall (in one sense having "gone" nowhere), he calls out to Mr. Memory the question of what "the thirty-nine steps" are. Since Memory cannot not answer a question, he publicly discloses the spy ring – at which point he is shot by the Professor (the spy leader) from a box-seat. Throughout, direct speech seems barred for Hannay, making him the cipher for a position that has no prepared voice in the cultural order.

The whole film is structured around a series of questions, and the loop of answering is peculiar: in Memory's case, as a vaudeville act, there are only memorized "facts" (that is, no interpretation), and

Memory will always ask if his answer is right (the questioner is supposed to know the answer to his own question). Memory will be associated not only with the odd figure of origin (which is itself, clearly, a repetition) but with a disaster – as when a shot goes off, spoiling the aesthetic economy of the show, and emptying the Music Hall. Indeed, the spillage into the street erases any inside and outside opposition, much as the interaction with the audience had, between the stage and the crowd.

Everything depends, it seems, on which questions are asked – and Hitchcock points out that the interpreter too is in this bind: by asking of the film itself only certain questions (will the couple come together? what does the death of Memory signify? is order restored at the end and England saved?) – generic, prescribed questions or questions of genre itself – we are guaranteed the same answers, that is, we are guaranteed not to see or hear. What are the other questions we can ask, then, to break away from this machinal or cultural loop or bind? Or differently, how does a recurrent rupture in the attempt to *produce* narrative in this space proceed? How does Hitchcock address this, if not through his own *secret agents* – agents that elude the surveillance of the law, the gaze, the big Other, the viewer? We might even say that if there are "events" in history, they occur at sites in which the machine of reproduction, copying, and repeated questions (Memory) is altered, disrupted, or submitted to revolution – and aesthetically, this means intervening in an aesthetic or representational order, such as the pretext of *mimesis* itself that film, above all other mediums, seems to enforce. Perhaps, a new question might be: how does Hitchcock organize his text as a war-machine designed to sabotage the mimetic regime ("England") within which it operates – like Verloc in *Sabotage* issuing bombs in film cannisters from his movie theatre, the Bijoux?

Understandably, questions put to Memory tend to be about origins (as when the old man, cut off three times in the Music Hall, cannot quite get the question to be heard, "What *causes* pips in poultry?" – disease in *already* flightless birds). Yet while Memory must answer whatever question is put to him, *must* exteriorize what is already inscribed (what Zizek calls "the ethics of the signifier"), we as listeners may have to pretend, like Hannay on hearing the formula recited, to recognize what we don't know when Memory asks: "Am I right, sir?" Thus when Hannay asks at the Palladium what "the thirty-nine steps" are, and is told a band of foreign agents, we may assume the McGuffin is "out." But there is a McGuffin of the McGuffin that inverts the relationship of pretext to narrative, particularly when we recall that *The Thirty-Nine Steps* is also the film that Hannay is in. (Hence the question may be like asking, What is "life"?)[13] Accordingly, we ignore that in fact we still have no idea what "secret agents" are, or who they are.[14] Thus there is a second McGuffin (even as the first involves no real revelation), but it is even stranger, since it simulates an absolute revelation — that of the secret formula for the silent warplane, which Hannay tells the dying Memory he got right even though Hannay can have no way of knowing, especially since Memory discloses only *a string of numbers and letters, wholly ungrammatical and untranslatable.* Are these numbers and letters, agents or "steps" of the silent yet war-like sublime too? Signifying agents which carry explosive messages out of the country, and which by naming *agency* connect acting as performance to a subversive or disfiguring act itself?

Hannay pretends to "know," as we do ourselves — as when assuming that the point of the film is to produce the couple, or that Hannay learns something from his circular career. Yet as the backs of the policemen (guardians of symbolic ignorance) close around Memory, only Hannay's hand is left — he too, as at the opening, is headless, reabsorbed by the symbolic (with the spectator) rather than in a position of knowing. The film ends pretending revelation but actually performing *fore*closure (rather than closure). This replaces us at the opening — only now in a clearly circular way, like a Moebius band twisted again, at which point the headless Hannay enters the film

13 Or, to be technically more precise in describing this signifying loop: what is the "structure" that narrativizes "me"? Or again: in what apparatus am I inscribed and dispossessed by in even posing this question?

14 The curiosity about the McGuffin is that we may *still not understand its logic.* Its riddle is hardly put to rest by being assigned a role in the Lacanian cosmos as the *objet petit a*, a hole or lack generating narrative desire. In Hitchcock it is (also) something other than the very thing that he *seems* to call it. The anecdote goes: When asked about a package on the train rack, a man answers, "It's a McGuffin." When asked again, he explains, that is a device for hunting lions on the Highlands. When told there are no lions in Scotland, he answers that it is, then, not a McGuffin. Repeat: the "McGuffin," too, is not a McGuffin. First, the story tells us that we still don't know what a McGuffin is (we are not on the side of knowing), and second, that it covers a *signifying loop* that is close to implosion. What Zizek does not note is that even the McGuffin is *not* itself — not a mere "hole," but a desperate signifying loop that is destructively, vertiginously close to collapse within the narrative generated (sometimes hysterically, always as excess) to manage, contain, sacrifice, or absorb this space.

again, like one stuck in a timeloop, or an *eternal recurrence*.[15] Only in this case the dismembered letters and numbers return as well, and right away, one after the other, in a phosphorescent row: *M-U-S* ... Thus memory involves an operation of referring back, of folding, against which "narrative" cannot quite progress – even remembering the musical motif, for Hannay, compels him to go back, to fold back, to (Mr.) Memory.[16] And not only headless, if we understand that the name Hannay also suggests a *negation* of hands.[17] We need only consider the handcuff scenes which have a subtext beyond the erotic. Like dismembered feet, *hands* signify throughout Hitchcock, only here with a difference: for if the cuffs resemble a projector – as do, in other Hitchcock films, bicycles or spectacles – then the cuffed hands imply an inability to write *directly*, yet also, inversely, a kind of hyper-writing that will pour across the surface of the film in puns, and through "secret agents," like Hannay's political double-talk before the public Assembly Hall in Scotland (like Albert Hall, an A. H. signature).

When Zizek attempts to account for Mr. Memory, he is presented as "a personification of pure automatism and, at the same time, the absolute ethic of the signifier" – that is, he is the symbolic, surpassed by the united couple in "the Oedipal voyage in pursuit of the father" (*LA*, 100–1). Yet, as we saw, it is the "big Other" that absorbs Hannay with the policemen's headless backs in a kind of return to

---

15 We may think of Hannay opening the film immediately after this conclusion, caught in a time loop that precisely parallels the endless rerunning of the film spool itself. That Hitchcock intends this to be marked as a Nietzschean recurrence could be argued from other film evidence, including a reading of *Rope*.

16 Just how much the *fold* of memory structures the "fiction" of narrative is apparent in the very road turns of the opening car chase in the Riviera hills in *To Catch a Thief*. Followed by a strange aerial shot surveying the treeless landscape, the police car turns back after the pursued (but empty) car encounters sheep, a citation of a scene in *The Thirty-Nine Steps* evoking Memory. Moreover, in a text that equates tourists with viewers, it is explicitly echoed when the insurance agent calls Robie's villa "travel folder heaven." The phrase, broken down through a series of puns, implies the circularity involved in "seeing" what we are already looking to see from the example of a photograph or model: seeing, in this sense, is caught in the loop of being predicted by (a) memory already. It is a loop which dissolves nature (the absent trees). Travel (cinema) folds – or folds back to memory, and in the process becomes "heaven": a place of cheap gratification involved in the recognition, and also a place always already dead or an afterlife. "Fold" is also used to imply collapse, or obliteration, as when Robie (Cary Grant) describes his origin as a thief in a *travelling* circus that folded.

17 Hitchcock's use is not limited to hands themselves, but names (Handel Fane, Iris Henderson).

unknowing in an irreconcilable rhetorical split in the image at the end. (Mr.) Memory, accordingly, appears to take place over (and as) a much darker sort of machine, one that at once generates and destroys in advance concepts like the symbolic: he is pure anteriority, and nothing but the machine, to begin with, of recirculation without interpretation. Yet by virtue of repetition it is the same "facts" that become the facticity of hollow signs. The difference is, that for Zizek the encapsulation of Memory as the symbolic automaton allows for getting beyond him (or it) to a space "rendering possible the amorous couple's final reunion, their 'normal' sexual relation" (101). Yet in fact, all the end gives us is two dismembered hands, one white, one black (gloved), with a dangling cuff or zero in between – a clutch entirely tentative and cut off. What, then, is this machine about, one which gives the world, "life," as already dead, as inscribed "facts"?

A hint is present in the emergence of neon letters endeavoring to spell "Music Hall." As the *opening* of the text they subtly suggest sight or consciousness to be dependent upon something like letters, or reading. And with the visually decapitated Hannay not yet a "subject," the back of his head being turned to us in the dark theatre, the opening syllable (*M-U-S –*) is also marked when the master of ceremonies introduces Memory, that "*remarkable man,"* as one who will donate his brain to the "British *Mus*eum."[18] The repeated syllable crystallizes as the word Muse, and through the agency of the syllable the dimensions of Hitchcock's totalizing conceit emerge. We understand from this that Mr. Memory should be read or interfaced with the epic muse Mnemosyne. But the modernist allusion is still more unexpected and penetrating, reaching through and gutting the high epic tradition itself. The scene in the Music Hall is, impossibly enough, meant to be read through the opening invocation of Hesiod's *Theogony*, of the muse of memory, Mnemosyne, the giver both of consciousness and poetic text. We grasp, too, that Hitchcock's text is not only mass cultural entertainment, but that it is also consciously usurping the social power of both theatre or even the popular novel – and the

18 The reference to the "British Museum" intentionally cites *Blackmail's* concluding scene, where the blackmailer – named Trac(e)y (alternate spelling included) – plunges through the skylight of the museum dome. That is, in the process, he falls through frozen history, back to the giant Egyptian stone face, the origin of writing.

entirety of the western "sublime" epic tradition back to Hesiod.[19] This makes the presence of the other dark muse, the pseudonymous "Annabella Smith," suggestive, since the name implies a going-up, an anagogic path in the Platonic sense used in the *Symposium* – in which the sound itself twice rises and falls (Anna-bella). Yet it is an anagogic path in which the *aesthetic* itself is at issue and intervenes (*bella*). As a circular epic of (un)knowledge leading to the catastrophe of Memory in the Palladium (taking Hannay "up – or down – the garden path," says the Professor), there is a question of what the aesthetic means here, echoed in the "sublime" we may associate with the *flight* of a silent warplane.

The "aesthetic" can be momentarily understood as the material, or even the linguistic, following the sense suggested by the neon letters opening the text in which sight or perception (the Greek *aisthanumai*) appears linked to reading or even the bar-series that William Rothman calls Hitchcock's "signature" and which appears in every film – that sheer alternation of differences out of which consciousness emerges, or emerges as already ruptured, barred, and dead. To invoke the Hesiodic sublime also suggests a certain reversal of it. This is implied by the raucous lowlife in the theatre and the attempt to ground Memory in mere "facts" – the most banal, least sublime figures imaginable. The Hitchcockian anti-sublime actively subverts, we might say, not only the mimetic ideology of the western tradition but also a certain romantic notion of the sublime itself linked to *interiority*. For Hitchcock, it would seem, this technological sublime involves the active evacuation of any interiorizing model of consciousness, while linking the sublime to the banal, and the scriptive, to *feet* or *legs*.

The question of the aesthetic or the sublime is not irrelevant, since both will be defined, through Memory, in the most abysmally banal

19 In his treatment of Hitchcock's *Murder!* in *The Murderous Gaze*, Rothman makes much of Hitchcock's competition with – and vertiginous incorporation of – theatre itself. His claims are too modest, since one can trace where Hitchcockian hyper-writing is conscious of dispersing and absorbing the "high" and "low" of popular genres. Certainly, Hitchcock rethought the danger introduced by talkies, where the reading of the silent or mute film would be displaced by the illusion of the subjects communicating personality or ideas. For him, as he tells Truffaut, dialogue is first "sound" – that is, a resource of signifiers to be networked, as signal and pun, with other dismembered sound for diverse purposes. Hitchcock consciously incorporates not only opera and the novel, then, but the "sublime" epic tradition itself. Indeed, *The Thirty-Nine Steps* must be called a circular or even negative epic.

and irremediably *material* terms – if, that is, we understand material (in which *mater* echoes) to pertain to marks, letters, and sounds. One should be aware, of course, that as with the "*re*markable" Mr. Memory, the syllable *mar(k)* irradiates through numerous proper names in Hitchcock (Marnie, Mark, Marvin, Margaret, Margo, Martin, and so on), framing this alien and metalingual token at the heart of nominal and visible identity. Moreover, the banality is that of feet, of mere "facts" without elaboration, which (Mr.) Memory, unlike some divine muse's voice, simply inscribes and repeats; in the process, however, he transforms them from referents to potential, if empty, signifiers: it is not clear if this is the fallen, technological anti-god of mechanical reproduction, stuffed into the cyborg Memory, or if this was, all along, the very stuff of Hesiod's Mnemosyne as well, however disguised. Memory's "feats," as they are called, intentionally echoes "feet" (a spectator raises this point of confusion as a joke). The pun ties the idea of action, or agency, to the implication of, well, feet, mere "facts," prefigural events – disremembered feet or legs brought up to the level of the head itself. How, indeed, asks Hitchcock's cinema, is one to write or fabricate a technological sublime out of mere unembellished "facts"? If from the first, Memory is a destroying origin that exists as machinal copy (that is, produces what it has killed in advance as the condition for production), successive repetition imbues the "facts" with the possibility of being isolated emblematically (as, say, *sinthomes* even). On the other hand, and this is crucial, Memory clearly resembles a camera, reproducing facts through pure mimesis: the film itself begins – yet is also displaced from – the image of letters. The reason it is Mr. Memory who would smuggle the "formula" for the silent warplane *out* of England, is that memory seems to do two things: first, it (or "he") appears as the machinal enforcer of mimesis, or representation, out of which the ideological closure of identification and subjectivization occur (the domain of the symbolic police), yet as a machine of repeated "re-marking," it is also that which breaks up or destroys mimesis as figures, syllables, sounds, letters, and visual puns or objects (*sinthomes*) that emerge through being repeated.

If I take you through a casual run of such signifiers, here, it is only to begin a demonstration of the dance of Hitchcock's agents at the heart of this seemingly low-mimetic fare, the movement of these feet, as well as their foreignness to the "mimetic" pretext of the film. It is the feet/feat of these "secret agents," then, which would produce an *anti*-sublime starting from entirely banal, material, or inscribed "facts," dismembered and dismembering signifiers that represent sheer *exteriority* as such. This is why, as we saw, even the M of Music Hall is flagged, becomes a *sinthome*, and one specifically with three triangles (as in the tripled instance of 39), up and down, yet also why this hieroglyph (M) is repeated twice with its inversion (W) in the questions put to Mr. Memory. In the first, "How old is Mae West?" Memory declines to answer ("never tell a lady's age"), while the chosen character, Mae West, also signals that "gender" is already a purely performative construct (as with a female impersonator who becomes, thus, "manly") – an important lesson, utterly wasted on a Hannay who can only enact it. Yet this is echoed in the latter's own question to Mr. Memory about the distance between Montreal and Winnipeg, in which the inversion of W and M reminds us that they are the same, and also without distance (like the Music Hall and Palladium). In addition, the syllable *Mon* of Mon(t)-real decouples as a trope of subjective appropriation of meaning/*Meinung*, which is echoed later in the Palladium billing for "Crazy Month" (shown with letters askew), a title hurled by Pamela at Hannay in a manner invoking menstruation – the emptying out of life before generation – with the connotations of hysteria applied to *him*. In this sense, the Professor's missing finger is not, as Zizek rather banally notes, "an ironic allusion to castration" (101), but a disclosure of the pointless pretense of castration itself, apparent in the pipe/"gun" figure Hannay carries in his pocket (an object that, again criss-crossing visual and aural, echoes the "*pips* in poultry," a phrase that further isolates the *p* for use elsewhere, as in "Portland *P*lace," the site of the murder).[20] It turns out that the plot(ting) of the Professor (that is, Hitchcock) is to generate a "sublime" that is also a war-machine silently able to destroy, or

---

20 If one wished, for instance, to pursue the course of the letter "P" in Hitchcock, one would eventually end up in *Torn Curtain*, where the code for the underground in East Germany uses the Greek *Pi*, at one point traced *underfoot* in the sand. As such, the Pi is also the Pythagorean formula (3.14), which invokes Hitchcock's signature 1–3 triangulation (often transliterated into words beginning CA or CO). It could elsewhere be shown why the "one" and "three" combination is also a code for the emergence of "voice" or utterance itself, and the curtailment of the subject by the very prosopopeia or apostrophe that brings him into existence. In *Torn Curtain*, moreover, a casual reference to a "Pete's Pizza Parlour" confirms this focus on "Press," presenting an allegorical aside that determines on the voice (parlour) as superimposed over the stone dead subject (Pete), at a site that links the *Pi* with the alphabet in general (Pi-z-ZA).

sabotage, the mimetic ideology we may associate now with England itself.[21]

We can return to the final scene, that of the death of Memory – for we see, now, why the "destitution of the subject" does not reside *beyond* "the wall of language" but is that field itself. And why the letters and numbers serve a dismembering function reflected in the dancing chorines legs placed above the dying head of Memory – a sort of postmodern *pieta* composition. We might here speak of a Nietzschean moment to *The Thirty-Nine Steps*, where the material agency of representation is not recuperated for a familiar model of the (Enlightenment) subject, but posited in a non-transcendent, destructively ironized yet transvaluative mode. I have come to believe, in fact, that positing a Nietzschean agenda becomes more and more necessary to return to Hitchcock the force of a critically transformative project that is everywhere staged, even as failure, in the various plots of his "thrillers."[22] In this film, that manifests itself with a citation of how an eternal recurrence or loop is inscribed in advance as the catastrophe of the mnemonic machine; and secondly, how a materiality – raising the legs of sense above the putative Cartesian head, inverting "Platonism" and its remnants, the corporeal signifier itself usurping the phantasmal space of the signified – is evinced in mere or banal "facts" meant to precede metaphor as such, a banality that rewrites the sublime and empties every interior model of meaning. What might be called an "external" mechanical force emptying out narrative in advance, and making the latter generate itself over its impossibility, is one result of this site. At the close of the film, we can read the chorines, legs cut off

21 As at the Music Hall, the "aesthetic" itself is totalized as the material, the real, the revolutionary, politics, "life" – since it emerges as the root of the world or knowing.

22 One may well undertake an overt study of the unmarked presence of Nietzsche in Hitchcock – the only open allusion to whom is in *Rope*. One might look for it, however, in the aesthetic materialism announced in *The Birth of Tragedy* as well as the project of transvaluation in *Genealogy of Morals*. What I mean by invoking the "dance" of material semiotic effects in the figure of the chorines is the image of a text that, unlike Zizek's, does not try to escape to a beyond of "language" as such (again), but in which the aesthetic text is mobilized as a destructive and transformational agent, rather than an exemplar – as in the Lacanian reading – that returns to a familiar ("Enlightenment") notion of (emptied) subject. To call Hitchcock a materialist or Nietzschean in this sense is to affirm where his text becomes a kind of "minor literature" (in Deleuze's sense) that deterritorializes the reigning aesthetico-political hegemony and writes this into its narrative allegory repeatedly.

and raised to the top of the frame, as an explicitly Nietzschean dance – an affirmation of the "play" of signifiers outside of a nostalgia for origin (or a *beyond*). If one of Hitchcock's aims is to exceed the mimetic pretext of film – a project carried forth only most explicitly in the supposedly "expressionistic" films (like *Secret Agent* itself) – the dance of the steps, *pas*, or legs suggests several things.

Zizek borrows from Jameson a fairly standard triadic history to map Hitchcock – one divided into a realist (or Oedipal), a modernist, and a postmodernist period, chronologically conceived. Yet the close of *The Thirty-Nine Steps* seems to refuse this division, much as the earliest texts tend to be among the most radical in their representational experiments. Hitchcock's text is inhabited in advance by a machinal order that, in some ways, narrative attempts to forget, occurring itself in or as a sort of parenthesis. This makes it more important to read what is at stake in the closing scene of the chorines. It is interesting that when the clowns come on stage and say, "And now – we will *sing*," they proceed only to tap-dance, as if at this point, the legs have become the thing, the Thing, not as an epiphanic other, but as a mobilized script that pervades the text. The reaction to the chorines' upkicking legs has been one of condemnation and defense, as if they represented a prurient eroticism.[23] What, indeed, is it so necessary to suppress about the dancing legs? What in them announces an active

---

23 This appears in Rothman as a curiously male repression, moralistically invoked under the guise, strangely, of *feminism* in a redemptive mode. Charles Silet, in "Through a Woman's Eyes: Sexuality and Memory in *The 39 Steps*," seems repelled by the chorines' *legs*: "The delicacy of the film's concluding sequence is hard to capture in words. On the one hand, Mr. Memory's backstage, confession-like recitation of the Air Ministry secrets redeems Hannay and confirms the liberating power which the exercise of memory can have, and almost off-handedly resolves the 'spy' plot. As if to confess and confirm their own memories – Hannay's of all the women he has encountered, Pamela's of Hannay – each quietly seeks the other out, their hands entwining as the image fades. Hannay and Pamela thus come together voluntarily, without the restrictions which manacle the other couples in the film, a fact symbolized by the now dangling and useless handcuff which hangs between them as they stand together, backs to the camera.

"On the other hand, as William Rothman points out, the recollections invoked in the final shots, specifically those connotations clustered around the initial Music Hall sequence, carry decidedly negative implications, evidenced chiefly by the line of high-stepping, barely clad chorines visible in the background while Mr. Memory confesses to Hannay. Their presence is intended to calm panic and to reassert the Music Hall norm, sexuality as gag or display, as something not serious, which replaces or displaces the life or death drama just enacted (it literally takes the place previously occupied by Mr. Memory and Professor Jordan)."

defacement of the Cartesian subject, including the inter-subjective, humanist, mimetic, identificatory, and authorial approaches to the screen?

There would seem, now, to be three ways to read the chorines' high-stepping legs and the death of (Mr.) Memory. First, the "death" of Mr. Memory is a *modernist* gesture, announcing an epochal break with *classic* scriptive culture, in this case doing so by citing Hesiod and his muse. Hitchcock then is noting that the place of writing is being usurped with the machinery of his cinematic text. Second, the "death" of Mr. Memory can be read as a *post-modernist* gesture, involving Hitchcock's reversal of the Platonic model of the sign by placing the feet in the place of head, the signifier over the signified, a move annulling the mimetic and humanist subject of commercial cinema ("pictures of people talking," as he calls them), turning to an affirmative Nietzschean dance of *material* signifiers, steps, and agents that actively rupture memory, stamp out and actively forget references, a dance generated by the machine of mechanical reproduction. Such a poetics would supersede the now headless Cartesian subject and redefine "man" according to the sheer exteriority of this new order of signification. Yet a third reading of the death of Mr. Memory might be called *post-"postmodern,"* since it, precisely, cannot locate itself even in a ruptured historical trajectory. It says, in effect, that "memory" has always been, back to Hesiod, this machine that, in a sense, represents a radical exterior, something material and alien that dispossesses the forgetful present. In this reading, the silent warplane that would rain destruction on a certain order of representation (mimesis, identification) had already been functioning, forgetfully, from the "beginning" of the film, a beginning it cannot but loop back to, in the process erasing even this knowledge. Indeed, the "sublime" warplane also *is* the text, which can be seen as starting again at once after the end, forgetfully preceding itself, erased and citing itself in Moebius fashion, the formula unscrambled as M-U-S ... and so on. This last reading, which contains the other two, has the value of opening up a future reading of Hitchcock's secret agents, in which the reflexivity of the text is not conceived of as a property of reflection, but as an active and violating project of transformation from which no categories — life, politics, or gender — are secure.

(*Hitchcock Reader*, eds. Deutelbaum, Marshall and Leland Pogue [Ames: Iowa State University Press, 1986], 120–1).

If Hitchcock supplants a model of *seeing* with one closer to the radical discontinuities of *reading* itself,[24] it is interesting that he repeatedly marks his films with a device that supports no explicit mimetic or referential "meaning" – the repeated prefigural instances of (aural) knocking or alternating bars. I allude to what William Rothman, in a unique insight developed nowhere else, identifies as a bar-series which he calls Hitchcock's "signature."[25] Rothman struggles to interpret this non-figure, which recurs in each film, psychologically or as a *symbol* suggesting containment (the character feels trapped, and so on): "I call this pattern of parallel vertical lines Hitchcock's / / / / sign. It recurs at significant junctures in every one of his films. At one level, the / / / / serves as Hitchcock's signature: it is a mark on the frame, akin to a ritual cameo appearance. At another level, it signifies the confinement of the camera's subject within the frame and within the world of the film ... It is also associated with sexual fear and the specific threat of loss of control or breakdown" (*MG*, 33). In fact, *it* actually suggests an invasive marking-effect that is preletteral and even presemiotic, a relentlessly infinite yet minimal semiosis based on alternating *difference* into which series the word, letter, face, sign, or image – that is, all perception and temporarility – struggle not to be resolved. As such, the "signature" can imply narrative, cutting, allegory, semiotic "death," sheer difference, and so on, but is also what supersedes any representation. The series suggests less a psychological enclosure (Rothman) than a machinal repetition that cuts off in advance any allegory of "castration," and which makes the myth of castration itself recuperative. The bar series is a skeletal parallel to the upkicking, dancing legs, only permanently installed

---

24 We can see why Hitchcock, in his first cameo in a "talkie," that is, in *Blackmail*, appears not only reading a book but reading on a train (that is, a metonymic figure of cinema as movement). Moreover, he is *interrupted* repeatedly, by a bullying boy. It is the interruption of an interruption. "Reading" thus represents a hyperbolic acceleration of reflexive signs, anagrams, puns, and citations that, at any moment, can blank out, and collapse their relational networks, as when the screen whites out or a character falls in a swirl. The image is reproduced on the cover of *The Hitchcock Reader*. Tracking the import of reading and "books," as with letters, across Hitchcock is certainly a project of its own.

25 So dependent is Hitchcock on the *bar* figure that it migrates, as in *Vertigo*, from being a series to being a single bar (clutched in the opening by the detective's hand alone) to being inserted into a name (Judy *Bar*ton), much as, elsewhere, it establishes itself in punning references (*To Catch a Thief*'s line about "an alcoholic at a bar on election day," or the bar in *Frenzy* come to mind).

across Hitchcock's production. In a sense, it is this "installation" which opens the prospect of a *post-"postmodern"* reading.

I propose, briefly, to examine one further way this agency is represented.

3. Hitchcock's black sun

It is interesting that Zizek, in trying to apply the notion of the *sinthome* to Hitchcock, turns haltingly to the first *Man Who Knew Too Much*, "perhaps the film which most directly calls for such a reading" (*EYAW*, 127).[26] We recall this figure, which represents "the limit of interpretation," and mediates "tension between the 'official' content of the totality of the work and the surplus that comes forth in its details" (126). I say haltingly, since in fact he does anything but give the work such a reading. On the contrary, he breaks off with a few parenthetical asides, after ascribing the underlying text "behind the 'official' spy plot" to "a story about family" and the intrusion of a "charming foreigner" — that is, the most banally mimetic of pretexts. What, indeed, in this text draws Zizek's eye and then blinds it so utterly, virtually fleeing his own trajectory after three pages?

26 It is interesting and typical that the address (or evasion) of the *sinthomes* concludes with a glancing pass at a key and little addressed scene, that from the first *Man Who Knew Too Much*: "When, at a party in a Saint Moritz hotel, the mother dances off with the seductive stranger, the remaining part of the family (father and daughter) pin to the back of the stranger's dress-coat a thread from the woollen pullover on the table, so that the dancing couple gradually unravel the pullover, symbol of the family bond — the shot which, during the dance, kills the stranger is clearly a punishment for his intrusion into the closed family circle. (It is highly significant that this shot exerts a kind of deferred action identical to that usually encountered in cartoons: Louis Bernard first just casts a surprised look at his chest — that is to say, he falls down only after he beomes aware of the bullet in his chest, as if the detour through consciousness is necessary for the shot to become effective ...) In the preceding scene, a shooting match, the mother misses the clay pigeon, demonstrating thereby her agitation due to the impact of the seductive stranger ..." (*EYAW*, 245). This passage is, in ways, typical of one sort of Zizekian encounter. The first explanatory sentence is almost painfully traditional, an account fetishizing the family and locating punishing causal connections with moral import — Hitchcock as (transparent) manipulator, specular other of the assuaged moral reader. Then, in parenthesis, a detail, a "surprised look" that opens onto an other significance — but it is parenthetical, the *sinthome* ending in being remarked. Thus his account ends on a shallow and recuperative note: "One is thus tempted to say that the film is 'actually' the story of the two shots: of a mother who, a second time, rectifies her aberration and regains her capacity to shoot straight."

Moreover: *why* is every reference of his to a scene either erratic or distractedly looking for a cause – as occurs when Zizek notes that in the early marksman's shoot in the St. Moritz, the "mother misses the clay pigeon" because of agitation caused by the stranger (Louis Bernard)? Zizek's error is instructive (she is in fact distracted by the sound of a jingle held by her child, the same one that betrays Peter Lorre hiding behind a door at the end), since he turns to an inter-subjective pretense to evade a dispossessing sound. Rather than confront the disfiguration of the *sinthome* itself, Zizek returns to the very inter-subjective model he would empty out under the aegis of the Lacanian machine.

The first *Man Who Knew Too Much* (1934) presents the problem of an allegorical reading in its full scope – one which nothing in Zizek's remarks focuses on.[27] Although the narrative involves a political assassination attempt and the kidnapping of a child to silence the parents who unwittingly gain knowledge of it from the dying agent Louis Bernard, it cannot be dealt with as a familial order setting itself right. Indeed, the references this plot supplies to the only title that Hitchcock will return to and remake hardly explain where *excess* and *cognition* are put into play. Even if we focus, instead, on the attempted use of a single sound or cymbal crash to cover the assassin's shot in the Albert Hall sequence, figures of excess overrun the text from the opening ski accident of Louis Bernard to the final gun battle's innumerable shots at the false Temple of Sun Worshippers, the spies' hideout. What seems generally unnoted is the way that a metaphoric concern with the sun centers the problematic of knowing in classic tropological terms (Plato's sun as Idea or paternal origin). Indeed, one may even locate a "sun" figure as target in the early clay pigeon shoot – only it is black. The difference is that, in this film, "knowing *too much*" seems covertly associated with falling, losing consciousness, or blacking out, as if the excess in question were uncontainable and erasing.

It is not arbitrary that several early films – this one, *Secret Agent*, and *The Lady Vanishes* – include scenes in the alps where conflicting languages are spoken at once (Italian, German, French, English, Swiss-deutsch, and made up tongues), dissolving into a Babel of noise,

---

27 As Zizek notes quite appropriately: "the strongest 'ideologico-criticial' potential of Hitchcock's films is contained precisely in their allegorical nature" (*EYAW*, 219).

making "English" itself another such alien tongue.[28] The Babel-motif, for Hitchcock, returns not only to where the "voice" is already a supplement (to silent film), but where, as he tells Truffaut, "dialogue" is itself primarily sound – the stuff of punning connections extraneous to a speaker, and also the catastrophic matter of signifying before representation. If the problem with the *sinthome* in Hitchcock is that while appearing as a symbol it becomes an object, a thing, Zizek stops short of noting that this decontextualization does not end in itself but reifies a signifying function. Perhaps the problem of a hyperbolic excess of cognition – of what we can "know" if memory only repeats what is inscribed in it – is best addressed in the first *Man Who Knew Too Much*, where what is excessive or "too much" is marked not by a fullness of knowledge but, on the contrary, by characters passing out vertiginously (Jill), being knocked out (Lawrence), hypnotized (Clyde), or dying with a blank and uncomprehending look – as when Louis Bernard, first shot on the dancefloor, must look down at his lapel to know he is dying (semiotic "death" is a matter of consciousness) and then proceed to act it out. Knowing too much or passing out in this way mimes the sheer acceleration of relational meaning across the film's surface, registered when the screen too blanks. Hence the "McGuffin" this time is slightly different: the assassination of an ambassador, named Ropa, by the circle of spies that Peter Lorre (Abbott) heads. Yet in the name Ropa we hear the term *rope* which recurs across Hitchcock's texts and lends its name to one film. In it we hear *hang*, the suspension of the "I" between undecidable sites (as in the "half-cast(e)" Handell Fane's suicide), yet also narrative weaving – as when Lawrence ties Jill's knitted "jumper" to a dancer's button, which is then *un*ravelled by the entangled *legs* on the dance floor: narrative as if undone before it begins, superseded, as the *pre*mise of the plotting itself. The purpose of the assassination is, in fact, to

28 The problem of memory is not far to seek in Hitchcock, particularly when he seems to address the broader problematic of *agency*. I use the term, not only because it opens up the issue of "secret agents" (why they are necessary, who controls them), but because it traverses the break between cognition and action, the aesthetic moment and historical intervention. "Acting" shifts from its meaning as performance to its meanings as *action* (historical intervention), and agency as such. Accordingly, agency names not only what might be broadly called the problem of the "subject" (which returns Hitchcock to *Hamlet* repeatedly), but what *effects* a transition from text to history – as does Brandon's implementation of Ruppert's empty theorizing about the aesthetic of murder in *Rope*.

overleap or undo narrative time by using the mechanics of narrative – as Robie says in *To Catch a Thief*, "The biggest problem is time." The shot is rehearsed, in the Temple of the Sun Worshippers, to a recording of the "Storm Cloud Cantata" so as to be covered by a single cymbal clash. It is rehearsed, that is, to coincide with and cancel a machine of repetition – a phonograph, not incidentally, that we see in Norman Bates' bedroom, arrested, sporting Beethoven's *Eroica*.

This seems reflected by Hitchcock in the early *mark*smanship match between Jill and the assassin-kidnapper Ramon (the "shot" always also being that of a camera). Here we witness the most bare rendition of a central problem in Hitchcock – let us call it, for now, that of the *black sun*: a figure that precedes figuration, a Hitchcockian black-hole that mimes deadly origin and sheer simulation at once, the agency of agency that both guarantees "death" before all (screen or animated) life, and is the sheerest trope of materiality, disaster, and empowerment that traverses, and makes possible, the film surface.[29] That is, in the black clay pigeon seen repeatedly crossing the sky and shot at just after Jill tells Betty she will be with her "presently," a marked disturbance traverses Hitchcock's text that is the target of the narrative it generates and all but renders impossible by preceding – the figure of simulation, the hole in the symbolic order, the obscene "Thing" that also *is* not, which is here both representation itself and yet bars any return to presence as other than *its* effect (the sun, knowledge, and so on). For when Jill and Ramon compete, a black disc as clay pigeon repeatedly passes across the blank sky – rather like the inky black dog darting across the white snow that causes Louis-Bernard's first *fall* on the slopes.[30] As the black-sun-as-skeet crosses

29 I intend no specific reference to Kristeva's use of the "black sun," or any single theoretical utilization. The term, it seems, has a determinate course of its own, in which the figure of (universal) eclipse – what separates the sun's presence as light and life from us – first becomes a trope of absence and representation itself, and then proliferates as a figure of the copy at the source of (or before) origin or the sun itself. At this point the "black sun" absorbs not only the solar absence (as ur-representation) but a destroying flaw within any solar configuration (as is apparent at the false Temple of Sun Worshippers in *The Man Who Knew Too Much*). At that point the "sun" itself absorbs the blackness, we might say, in an implosion equal to a vertiginous fall (as Hitchcock certainly uses it) through a collapsed, thing-like loop of representation itself. Accordingly, the figure itself re-emerges in Hitchcock as, again, feet, black dogs or cats, excrement, or the blank materiality of sound or writing.

30 Louis Bernard's "fall" in skiing downhill ends by tumbling in a white cloud, where the limbs of the protagonists and villains (Lorre) must be disentangled. Snow may

the sky, we see what we cannot see, the anamorphic space of an invasive external figure that, nonetheless, like the innumerable black birds of *The Birds*, makes reading or visibility possible. Thus we can even hear in the name of the assassin Ramon, a presumptuous anagram of *No-Mar*(k), a negation of a negation irrecuperable and, hence, different from Zizek's. This reading seems confirmed when the scene then shifts to the spies' hideout, the false Temple of the Sun Worshippers — a trope for a movie house in which the spies take the worshipping dupes' money while plotting the overthrow of an entire representational and symbolic order.[31]

The question is what do the spies want to overthrow with Ropa? The answer, I would suggest, is the political and aesthetic hegemony of representation itself. The anamorphic logic of the skeet shoot seems to be this: if the black hole is hit, it does not put out the sun or return us to the real sun from its simulacrum, but only engenders another copy. The black disc is a hole in the tissue of the heavens, a negative eye and anti-body that destroys yet also engenders narrative as its pursuit, as the account of this invasion and attempt to abject the abject; as such, it is at once a black hole of pure anteriority and its erasure. It is the archetype of all "legs." This accounts, in turn, for the parodic subtext of the "thriller," a hyper or Hyperion-like solar leap (echoed in Jill's "jumper," in the first day of "spring," in the "too much" itself) at excessive knowledge (inverted in the opening fall on the snowy slopes) that would also mark the overthrow of a political and aesthetic regime — that which we may call *mimesis* itself. In a sense that would need more elaboration, what is called in Lacanian terms the

here be read as Mallarméan whiteness — sterile and yet ideal evacuation of sense — over which the black dog running presents the incision of a mark. (Ramon will later be called by Lawrence, jestingly, a "dirty dog.") Bernard's fall also invokes the problem of (staged) chance, which can again be possible to read in the Mallarméan sense of *le hasard*. Throughout his production, Hitchcock allows "narrative" to be generated by the incision of a chance event that is also, precisely, staged or calculated.

31 This recalls, of course, Verloc's acts of subversion in *Sabotage*, starting with the ineffectual putting out of the lights that only elicit laughter at the opening, or with the plunderers of *Jamaica Inn* who, to fund Charles Laughton's (or Hitchcock's) aesthetic projects, lure ships as if to safety with a lamp, much as people seek escape from reality into a movie-house, only to wreck, rob, and (as if representationally) murder them. The name Ramon, in this context, harbors other traces as well: here the Egyptian "Ra" (sun-god) shifts into the R(e) or "repetition" attached to the appropriative "Mon-" of mine, or meaning, which we hear in *The Thirty-Nine Steps* "*Mon*treal" or "Crazy *Mon*th."

"symbolic order" would seem to be a myth, in part, that functions institutionally through mimetic ideology as such – a fact that links the word symbol and mimesis.

Zizek opens his essay by turning to the *Wrong Man*, on the assumption that a failed Hitchcock text would tell us more of the system (failed, in this case, because it attempts to by-pass the space of allegory). I must choose a different "failure" to indicate a more sweeping aspect of Hitchcock that, displacing any logic of the "gaze," also takes us to the place where visibility is itself technologically staged. The black *excess* which traverses the *Man Who Knew Too Much* in the guise of a solar poetics, which Hitchcock seems never done with, is both a representation of representation and is also what simulates the sheer exteriority or materiality of language as such (sound, letters). "It" returns, for instance, as the covert and unread subject of the later film, *Secret Agent* – a "failed" thriller about the search for and attempt to kill an unknown "secret agent," in which the *act* itself cannot quite be done by the drafted writer put in the role (Ashenden). It is not accidental that in seeking a gloss on Hitchcock's secret signifying agents we should turn to the film named *Secret Agent* itself. Ostensibly, the narrative turns on drafting a novelist (John Gielgud) as a "secret agent" to hunt down and kill a German agent in Switzerland. He is given as a cover a fictional wife (Madeleine Carroll) with whom a romance of course develops and the aid of a fairly unsecret agent (Peter Lorre), the hyperbolic many-named "general," who speaks with no known accent and is virtually half-caste (dark skinned). Lorre, as a trope of sheer figuration, is capable of incessant action while Gielgud hangs back, unable to decide or commit murder, and the text moves through failed attempts to generate narrative. The actual agent, Marvin, turns out to be the American "college boy" all along (Robert Young), while a pursuit on a train to Constantinople brings an aerial bombing and derailment. The deaths of the "general" and Marvin occur without Gielgud's doing them. The text, however, seems to metaphorically enact a wild exploration of what *agency* may mean on a material and semiotic level, and where the aesthetic passes into the murderous domain of actuality. In the process, the film presents a raw encyclopaedia of Hitchcock's figural explorations of language, translation, sound, telepathy, and the machine.

Indeed, just as the impossibility of agency or "acting" (in both senses) is embodied in John Gielgud – the inability, in effect, of two rhetorical levels to coincide – so the narrative cannot quite *begin* but, seeking to uncover the foreign agent (its actual plot) stops in dead ends, veering into mock-improvisation that actually occurs on the screen (as between Robert Young and Madeleine Carroll in the carriage). This is why the guiding figure behind *Secret Agent* is the spymaster called "old man R" – the letter R that is, which we see also on Rebecca's burning pillow in *Rebecca*, or Rusk's tie-pin in *Frenzy* – where R may be read by us at once as the signature of repetition, anteriority ("old man"), or the Lacanian "Real." And it is also why the *black disc* reappears as uncancellable, always in and yet spawning a metonymic series turned back into itself that includes a black dog, feet, deafening sound, the Babel of languages, Peter Lorre, a button, excrement, a phonograph, chocolate, a giant machine, and transcoded letters (the spies' "post-office," as it is called).[32] Zizek would separate the "Real" from the trajectory of the letter; Hitchcock, as *Spellbound* avows, only "represents" the traumatic kernel of the Real by and through the collapsing segmentation and radical anteriority of letters beyond words, and figures of prefiguration.

What is the secret agent or agency now – and why does Hitchcock's text turn back to it, like an origin, though it is experienced as a cutting that produces excess, empty sites within the symbolic, loss of "consciousness," and incessant simulacra? It seems to be the object of pursuit which ruptures narrative in advance with its excess; a lodger that, when uncovered on return to the Palladium as Mr. Memory, babbles numbers in a sort of double talk, presents a false answer that is allegorically too true. Let us recall the scene from *Secret Agent* in the hotel when the "agent" of excess – this time a character, Peter Lorre's dark-skinned "general" (as opposed to "particular," echoing, and curtailing *gen*eration), who alone can act or kill but never does accurately – is driven to a hyperbolic tantrum. Peter Lorre's ambisexual, alien-tongued, many-named Mexican General, neither white nor black, is a figure of deadly figuration; neither Mexican nor a general, he constantly reverses word order. At one point he wanders into the hotel bathroom to throw a tantrum at "*old* man R." Rolling the *toilet paper*, he complains that it is "too much," while in the background we glimpse a *phonograph* on a toilet seat. Here the inert chains of associations accumulate, like a bomb, themselves ready to accelerate or lie unread or dormant. What is the connection between

32 It is also, much later, the black cat of theft and representation that stalks the roofs of Nice in the opening of *To Catch a Thief*.

the barely seen phonograph – machine of the (re)production of sound
– and the General, between sound and shit, machinal reproduction and
the black sun as record disk? Here the phonograph marks where the
"voice" is originally a replay of an inscription, where phonocentrism
is doubly dispatched on the screen. What may be interesting is not
where the giant bell in the subsequent Langenthal church scene (the
name cites both Fritz Lang and, simply, *language* itself) reduces all to
deafening sound in the shot of a single deafened ear. The bell of the
tower like Poe's poem of that name eviscerates all speech practically,
much as it inherits the single organ note, ringing in the valley, which
is associated with the discovered *corpse*. What is interesting is how this
leads, also, to the later roar of the gigantic machines in the grotesque
Chocolate Factory, a cover for the spies' "post office," where
messages are coded and relayed: the roar of the machinery, the
conveyor belts, and the absurb crowd of faceless white-coated
workers fleeing. Nothing prepares one for the gargantuan impudence
of this scene, which presents the site of production of the McGuffin
itself, or the unrepresentable exterior which stalls the narrative
repeatedly, yet which it is dedicated to accounting for in its double
economy until the accelerating and metonymic train to Constantinople
is derailed by a warplane's bomb.[33] "It" traverses the text through the
agency of terms collapsing representation itself, such as the black sun,
shit, dogs, feet, sound, and now *chocolate*. Hitchcock's narrative here
seems designed to contain the uncontainable, which itself is produced
by looping back to a deadly pre-structure: thus, typically, the secret
agent sought and to be terminated is behind them, too close, too
heimlich all along, English and not German, the American "college
boy" *Marv*in. This is why the image of "mother" which irradiates in
Hitchcock is not Oedipal at all, but is mother as machine that destroys
what it generates, like film, by cutting, or cutting off from any natural
order. The foremost example of this is not the disembodied voice of

33 Constantinople makes use of a frequent Hitchcockian pun – the use of the syllable
"con-" to suggest cognition, consciousness, or a reference point for "knowing
too much." Variants include names like Constance, Constantine, or, in the second
Man Who Knew Too Much, Jo Conway. Naturally, the other implications of *con*,
such as conning or deceiving, are implied. Alternately, "ken" is used in the same
capacity (from kenning or the German Kennen), as with Dr. Mc Kenna or Eve
Kendall. "Constantinople," which of course is never reached, in this sense
represents the allegory and rhetoric of cognition that underlies the entire "spy"
plotting and the problem, to begin with, of secret agency.

"mother" in *Psycho* but the uniquely good mother in *To Catch a Thief*, who is briefly seen putting a cigarette out into a sunny-side up egg: the image of production as itself a process of self-cancellation in which the egg of generation, like the eye or sun itself, is put out. Yet the Chocolate Factory does other things than present a deafening parody of Lang's *Metropolis* while *preceding* any site of production for the text's unrepresentable X and excess, its "secret agent," the anamorphic backloop of representation. The black hole of the chocolate transforms the *obscene* trope of excrement into the chocolate bon-bon of mass cultural entertainment, the film canister that, in *Sabotage*, contains the saboteur's bomb. The other turn, more interesting for our purposes, is that the Chocolate Factory is itself disclosed as a front for the spies' post-office. It is less a site of production than a central *relay* station where letters – that is, both missives and letteral characters – are transcoded and sent out across past and future Hitchcock texts.

There is an intolerable visual-verbal pun in the first *Man Who Knew Too Much* that presents some unwelcome commentary on this sequence – itself unintelligible, but for the fact that, like the factory itself, it is marked as the site from which "intelligibility" itself is blindly generated as evasion. On the second floor of the false Temple of Sun Worshippers, there is a female helper or housekeeper for the spies, frumpy and clearly something of a Hitchcock surrogate who wants to leave – discomforted, perhaps, with keeping the kidnapped child. Abbott (Peter Lorre) indicates instead that he wants his henchman to remove her skirts so that she cannot leave. She returns, to malicious laughter, showing instead her black stockinged *legs*. At this point, Hitchcock has the henchman who brought her back reach behind her rump – as she bends over in the foreground – to get a chocolate from a lower shelf. While this character virtually consumes as chocolate her or Hitchcock's shit, the bon-bon of the thriller entertainment, Lorre – the plotter who cites Shakespeare – is engaged in another word-play, involving a verbal reference to the *sea* that echoes seeing itself. In the impenetrable punning cluster, out of which numerous black rays can shoot, Hitchcock locates a certain blinding production of sight itself, of reading and its erasure. While its temporal location is uncertain, it can be said with some assurance to occur before, after, or "beyond" the recuperative invocation of the gaze.

To return briefly to Zizek, we can conclude that the late Lacanian apparatus with which he attempts to close down a certain subjectivist and identificatory model of interpretation is powerful indeed, yet seems itself to move to the endpoint of the same system, at best inverting and eviscerating it. It is not a Hitchcock "beyond the wall of language," but one, perhaps, merely beyond Lacan that we should seek. Such a return to the question of material language in Hitchcock suggests yet another trajectory for reading this text, one that further closes out our own interiorizing, mimetic ideologies and remains a vehicle of transvaluation. Rather than submit his text to the specular game of shuttling between modernist and postmodern agendas, Hitchcock actively seeks that moment where performance becomes a defacing action or event, where film-writing intervenes in history, where (as with *Sabotage*'s Verloc) cinema becomes a totalizing front for politico-aesthetic sabotage. Instead, he mobilizes his project on behalf of a cultural transition to a post-humanist space. To date, the specular doubling between modernism and postmodernism, it seems, has been a distraction or delaying tactic before this genuinely historical shift.

❖❖❖❖❖❖❖❖❖❖❖❖❖❖❖❖❖❖❖❖❖❖❖❖❖❖❖❖❖❖❖❖

Post-humanist reading

❖❖❖❖❖❖❖❖❖❖❖❖❖❖❖❖❖❖❖❖❖❖❖❖❖❖❖❖❖❖❖❖

In the 1991 film *Terminator 2*, sequel to the cyberpunk classic, *Terminator*, there is a curious intertextual problem within an otherwise lazy time-loop narrative. A series of reversals of the first film seem at first noted and effaced: the Linda Hamilton character is now in an asylum, and society is silencing her mad knowledge of the future disaster (nuclear holocaust, cyborgs taking over), which renders her a psychotic-heroine; Arnold Schwarzenneger has returned in the same form as before but is reprogrammed from the future, he is now a *good* terminator (he was, in the first version, supposed to destroy her as the mother of the future resistance leader); and "T2" – the newer model who shows up looking entirely normal, only he is able to assume myriad anamorphic shapes as liquid metal, a virtual melt-down through all representation (becoming people, a floor, and so on) – is cast as the to-be-evaded assassin this time. Yet assassin of what? And why is that which burns through all representations including the commodity form of the human, *evil*? All sympathy is drawn to the newly dysfunctional mock-nuclear family, with mother Linda Hamilton as hippy guerilla, Arnold the neuter *pater*, and the kid an obnoxious L. A. urchin with sufficient hi-tech skills to rip-off ATM machines. Despite the hi-tech promise, a reactionary or retro drift is evident as almost all the violence – aside from T2's transmogrifications – is bewilderingly *low-tech*, including shotguns, truck chases, and so on. Yet this is only the first gaping rift between what is going on and what is projected as going on. What becomes apparent (much as with Arnold's German named alter-ego in *Total Recall*, Hauser, who turns out to be a thorough fascist and, indeed, the real Arnold virtually) is that what the film is fighting against in T2 is the invasion, from a fantasized "future," of an *anti*-representational and post-humanist logic. What is perhaps not obvious, but bleeds through in odd ways, is that the status quo of the human which mother-Hamilton means to protect – yet by whom she is at first imprisoned and persecuted in the sanitarium at the film's opening – is itself a thoroughly commodified, Hollywood, machine-like, low-tech representational or *mimetic* version of the human. It would not take much to reverse our sympathies.

Thus it does not seem to matter that Arnold as the now good Terminator 1 model (T1) happily knee-caps a squad of police or destroys two people who only want to help the kid, since what is being defended is the *representationalism* of Hollywood against an anamorphic logic, humanism's low-tech mimesis against the implementation of the supplement. In turn, the destroying and robotic future implies a time in which "humanism" is revised through an anti-mimetic or figural logic. So here, then, is the secret inversion: "T2" manifests himself not only as an invading "real," but as a figure – opposed to Arnold, whose non-humanity is now avuncular, paternal, and fuzzy-warm by comparison – whose primary trope is anamorphosis and who burns relentlessly through the empty commodity images of mimetic reality. Indeed he performs this demolition of representation by exceeding it, exploding it, and replicating anything he touches. The film, subtitled "Judgment Day," strives to put an apocalyptic slant on what is a recurrent aesthetic evasion on which the future may indeed be said to rest. Humanity as a now empty trope opposes, here, the post-humanism that grows out of its own logic, and it opposes that with star power. Here the pseudo-humanism of Hollywood representationalism (parodically symbolized in the real machine-man, the Kennedy-Republican Arnold) beats off the invasion of French post-structuralism and non-representational logic, cast as a threat to the human, as materiality as such. Yet what also emerges from this reading is the inversion that inhabits the totality, the painting of the new holy family – android, "mad" Linda, fatherless brat – as an endangered norm, the savior cluster misread by the paternal order which Arnold (T1) now stands as paradoxical simulacrum of. (The father figure, though, is actually T1's or Arnold's master, the kid himself who in the future becomes the adult rebel who sends his own "father" first to copulate with his mother in the past: the computer-hacker/spectator as auto-parthenogenitor.) Hence Linda's opening scenes in the asylum as rebellious truth-holder and mad seer imprint her first with the *terror* of the American panopticon whose blind inertia will lead, according to her knowledge of the future, to its own displacement by a more dreaded metallic Other. What this shows and hence allows us to forget, particularly when a token black scientist is brought in to represent a politically correct techno-culture (he is, quickly, killed off), is that Linda is fighting for the *terror's preservation*, for the familiar panopticon that is responsible for California techno-capitalism. The battle of "judgment day" appears, as always, between mimeticism and its supposed Other, between a late *faux* "humanism" represented by T1 (oddly, of course, since he is also a machine) and an anti-mimetic Other, T2, presented as radically *exterior* yet which, as with T1, can be assimilated as all-too-human. Of course, in this scene the machine-as-human, Arnold, must go through the misleading gesture of (human) self-sacrifice at the end, virtually erasing not a terrifying future but the opportunity of the "human" present to read itself. The (inhuman) "human" wins out over the real — suppression is restituted.

To some extent, this may seem a parable of reading itself, or of where the management and suppression of an irrupting "real" we associate with literature — and of a certain materiality that transforms the definition of the human — is performed by institutions of interpretation, in which commodified forms of humanism prevail through a mimetic ideology that suppresses figural logic. Figuration itself, which can derive from a scenario of repression and persecution, has a transformational role to play if what it designates as the "official" cannot be segregated from the regime of representational meaning itself.

What this parable suggests, today, may be the role that reading "materially" has in thinking through transformations in the cultural definitions of personhood — that is, less identity in the subjective sense than the definition of human experience or being. It also suggests that the manner in which we encounter canonized works often involves a systematic reversal of value-polarities and significations, a machine-like pre-inscription by which works already have entered the socialized or symbolic sphere of interpretation. To suggest this as an institutional given is to note that it may be part of the social function of such works to organize communities of readers dedicated implicitly to the the foreclosure of specific irruptions that occur within them, that, if developed, would put such communal icons — and the values based on them — at risk. Accordingly, canonical works are often preserved and transmitted not because they uphold the humanistic values of a cultural program for which they become the icons, but because they have the power to radically disfigure the very values they are, once inscribed, used to uphold. Such a relationship, of course, is not surprising, since it is as familiar as the Boccaccio tale of the sinner who, dead, ends up being worshipped as a saint — the very story that we hear Bakhtin, who knew something about literature and could predict his own faux iconization, wanted to hear again at his deathbed. The model may be a general one since it reproduces the same move over and again, through which the radically other is placed, invisibly, at the heart of what passes as the same. To begin to trace how such institutions function, ones in which our own discourse and values are inscribed is, perhaps, a continuing project of criticism in a post-humanist milieu — a milieu, in which a more complex and exteriorized definition of the human's constitution through language is being prepared.

In a sense, such a view presupposes that we always already encounter a primal ideological (re)inscription in any instituted "canonicity" itself, a set of controls experienced through this sometimes predictable inversion of the subversive powers of a work. Perhaps in this regard, a premier model of cultural re-inscription is presented in Aeschylus' *Eumenides*. Specifically, in the closing epilogue, when the terrifying Furies are re-assigned a recuperative role in the community and then renamed as the positive Euminides in the world about to be inaugurated after ending Orestes' flight. What emerges is Athena's attempt to write the inception of the symbolic order into or as the founding of "Athens," to master the psychosis with which the story of Orestes opens (his pursuit by the Furies) by replacing it with a technically more ominous one. From the point of view of the Furies, nothing changes from the beginning of the text to the end except that Athena has fictively instituted through them a new narrative, a pseudo-origin, a self-legitimation on the part of the gods. Athena's epilogue, in this sense, represents the founding and fictive legitimation of an interpretive order (Athens). The "tragedy" of the Eumenides, so to speak, is its happy ending, since it maps the installation of a patriarchal-mimetic-symbolic notion of history as the occlusion of a psychosis — which persists as an avoided remainder, however re-packaged. As a text, the *Eumenides* portrays an epochal moment of re-signifying, one that seems to conclude the end of one historical cycle and mark the beginning of another age. Yet in the above sense, Athena's judgment only presents a false retro-ending added on (like, say, the story of Isaac's rescue from sacrifice being rewritten over his actual execution), covering over a gap in the text's world represented by the Furies. The Furies occupy an unrepresentable order of language bound to the underworld or Hades, the site of inscription (as it is called in the text). They claim to speak on behalf of Clytemnestra's ghost, though their association with the murdered mother in a gendered narrative dominated by the patriarchal Zeus may also seem, in many ways, a fortuitous cover, as if the theme of gender itself were inadequate to give them a cause. From the beginning they seem to walk into a set-up of sorts, which is implicitly political: Athena, protecting her brother Apollo's patronage of Orestes and the nepotistic privileges of the gods, uses the occasion to extend the paternal laws of Zeus by exercising judgment in their name (thus legitimizing them after the fact). Athena outmaneuvers the Furies, in the process creating the more problematic psychosis of the symbolic order presented as a knowing ruse. Rather than "ending" the tragedy of the house of Atreus with a *deus ex machina*, the epilogue actually presents the genealogy of a false origin (here, supposedly, of Athens), a primal scene of re-inscription in which names are changed – the Furies are redubbed Eumenides and given a placating role in guarding the house. The text shows a decidedly Euripidean Aeschylus – one, that is, fully ironized – whose closing text of the trilogy reads more like the end of Wagner's *Rheingold*, with the corrupt gods' entry into Valhalla. Aeschylus marks that fiction by playing to the narcissism of the Athenians. (In the recent production by the *Théâtre du Soleil*, this division in the text itself is staged by separating three female Furies that are human from the remainder, the half-animal swarm, with the first accepting Athena's pay-off with exaggerated mock-happiness, allowing the multitude of untransformed Furies to remain unassimilated, placeless, and identified with non-verbal howling.) Figures of exteriority for whom nothing has changed since the opening, there remains a tension between the psychosis they represent and the historical resolution that pretends to recuperate them as the "Eumenides." The unincorporable Furies represent unsettled claims, and the history they stand to disrupt – and, at any point, interrupt as a fabricated narrative – remains tentative. In our own terms, the *pre-mimetic* role of the Furies within the mimetic regime that Athena establishes (and which Aeschylus clearly means to precede in the play itself) can be made parallel to the feet of the signifying order, the inscriptions of Hades, the legs of sense, sound, anagrams, letters, that appear effaced – as the lower order of signification, the slave-ciphers of textualization – managed by canonical interpretation yet ready to erupt, deterritorialize, or transvalue that fictional economy.

Index

Re Fuller e.g. of the Knot in rope

One's 'problem' — what it is keeps one involved w/ the quandary of one's own mind — is the knot.

And it slides across different ropes or texts = the knot stays the same but it shows itself differently, manifests itself differently w/ different texts —

e.g. John Clarke; Blanchot.

what would an attalope anamorphic

The argument here is very strong from a critical point of view, but it is as if every text by insisting upon its absolute difference (particularity of text) reduces all text to the same.

I want to say that the lines of thought that proceed still from the break-down of European Idealism (the trembling point to all post-Hegelian attempts, as Derrida) have reached a point where Deconstruction must by its own logic turn to construction — and that this is, properly, a turn from Theoretics to poetics.

That is the concept may not be our final, and that this turn involves profoundly in the development of new methodology and the reinstitution of the study of structure. The web of thinking that implicates Schelling, Hegel, Marx, Kierkegaard, Nietzsche and Freud was structural very poor. Freud is built structurally on an over oo to rl-